Other Avon Books by
John Bowers

STONEWALL JACKSON: PORTRAIT OF A SOLDIER

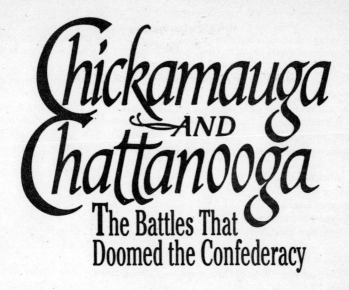

Chickamauga *and* Chattanooga

The Battles That Doomed the Confederacy

JOHN★BOWERS

AVON BOOKS ▲ NEW YORK

Excerpt from *Look Homeward, Angel*, by Thomas Wolfe, reprinted with the permission of Charles Scribner's Sons, an imprint of Macmillan Publishing Company. Copyright 1929 Charles Scribner's Sons; copyright renewed © 1957 Edward C. Aswell, as Administrator, C.T.A. of the Estate of Thomas Wolfe and/or Fred W. Wolfe.

Excerpt from "Chickamauga," by Thomas Wolfe, reprinted with the permission of HarperCollins Publishers, Inc.

Excerpt from *The Poetry of Robert Frost* edited by Edward Connery Lathem. Copyright 1916, © 1969 by Henry Holt and Company, Inc. Copyright 1944 by Robert Frost. Reprinted by permission of Henry Holt and Company, Inc.

All illustrations are reproduced by permission of the Library of Congress.

AVON BOOKS
A division of
The Hearst Corporation
1350 Avenue of the Americas
New York, New York 10019

Copyright © 1994 by John Bowers
Front cover drawing, "Battle of Chattanooga," by L. Prang, courtesy of the Library of Congress
Published by arrangement with HarperCollins Publishers, Inc.
Library of Congress Catalog Card Number: 93-38422
ISBN: 0-380-72509-6

The HarperCollins edition contains the following Library of Congress Cataloging in Publication Data:

Bowers, John, 1928–
   Chickamauga and Chattanooga : the battles that doomed the Confederacy / by John Bowers.
      p. cm.
   Includes bibliographical references and index.
   1. Chickamauga (Ga.), Battle of, 1863. 2. Chattanooga (Tenn.), Battle of, 1863.
I. Title.
E475.81.B77   1994
973.7'35—dc20   93-38422

First Avon Books Trade Printing: August 1995

AVON TRADEMARK REG. U.S. PAT. OFF. AND IN OTHER COUNTRIES, MARCA REGISTRADA, HECHO EN U.S.A.

Printed in the U.S.A.

OPM 10 9 8 7 6 5 4 3 2 1

To George and Edie Penty,
old friends who know how to read, laugh, and last . . .

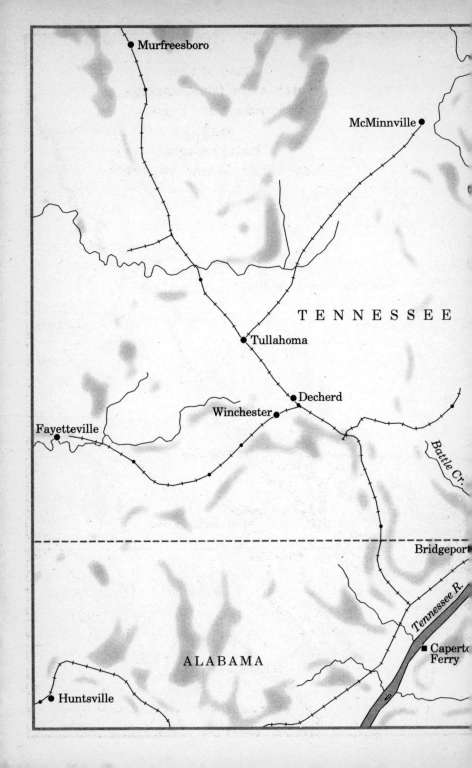

Murfreesboro

McMinnville

T E N N E S S E E

Tullahoma

Decherd

Winchester

Fayetteville

Battle Cr.

Bridgeport

Tennessee R.

Caperton
Ferry

A L A B A M A

Huntsville

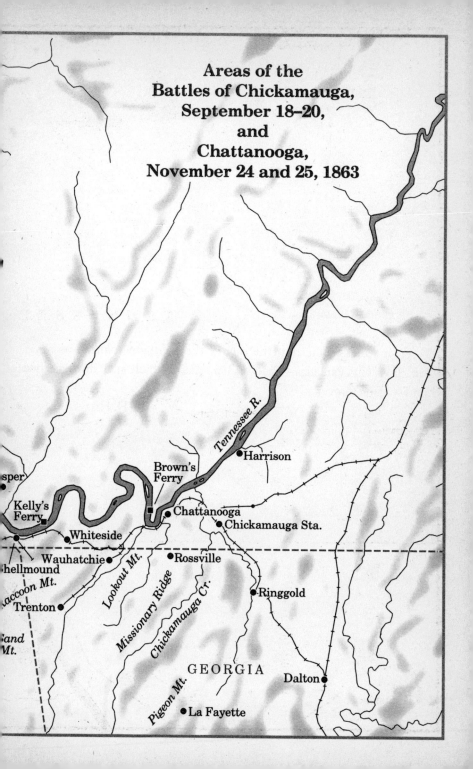

Areas of the
Battles of Chickamauga,
September 18–20,
and
Chattanooga,
November 24 and 25, 1863

Tennessee R.

Harrison

Brown's
Ferry

sper

Kelly's
Ferry

Chattanooga

Chickamauga Sta.

Whiteside

Wauhatchie

Rossville

hellmound

Raccoon Mt.

Trenton

Ringgold

Sand
Mt.

GEORGIA

Dalton

Pigeon Mt.

La Fayette

Lookout Mt.

Missionary Ridge

Chickamauga Cr.

... it seems to me that the *elan* of the Southern soldier was never seen after Chickamauga—that brilliant dash which had distinguished him was gone forever.

—D. H. HILL

Contents

A Prelude xi

1. "The Ugliest Man in the Corps" 1

2. "Just Before the Battle, Mother" 23

3. Your Turn to Curtsy, My Turn to Bow 47

4. The Big Bang 69

5. The Luck of the South 91

6. The Fatal Gap 113

7. The Granddaddy of All Elephants 139

8. Another Kind of War 165

9. The Beginning of the End 191

CONTENTS

10. "I Shall Take Those Guns for That!"   215

11. Fare Thee Well, Cause   235

Acknowledgments   241

Bibliography   245

Index   251

A Prelude

This book had its beginning when I was around eight years old, at a family reunion in the 1930s before the Tennessee Valley Authority had reached that part of eastern Tennessee where I grew up. The reunion was held on a farm scarcely a hundred miles from where the Battle of Chickamauga took place. In those days, many things were not all that different from the way they were in 1863. The farmhouse belonged to my Aunt Ann Spoone and her husband, Jim; my aunt was the daughter of William A. Bowers, who had fought at Chickamauga—my grandfather. My grandfather had died around thirty years before this reunion, but there were several present who could remember his tales of Chickamauga. Chickamauga hadn't gone into the archives, wasn't something you learned from words on paper or images on film. It was still a stupendous, awesome event in almost living memory—like an earthquake or cyclone of devastation and grandeur that had happened just down the road. When I heard the name pronounced, I knew, as only a child can, that it had been something momentous, that there hadn't been anything quite like it. In my relatives' dialect, "Chickamauga" didn't come out the way I've learned to say it today (Chik-a-*mo*-ga). It had more of a lilt to it, a drawing out of the final vowels. I try to recall how my father used to say it, but can't quite. My father drew it out to almost paragraph length, and he had learned to pronounce it from his father, who had been there. For all I know, the way Tennesseans used to say it, certainly how they said it when the battle was going on, may have gone the way of the Rebel Yell.

I'm fairly certain that our family reunion in the mid-1930s evoked life and attitudes and speech patterns that were close to those of the Civil War days. At the farmhouse, water came by pump, kerosene lamps glowed, stoves were iron and wood burning, and at night I went to sleep not on a Sealy Posturepedic but engulfed in a feather bed. There was no refrigerator. The Spoones had a dug-out cold cellar by the creek, like a small stone cave, where stacks of watermelons; pots of churned butter; crocks of milk; and barrels of apples, pears, and peaches lay. That farm had far from given up on the horse. If a T-Model Ford broke down on the dusty road in front, those on the farmhouse porch could be expected to yell, "Get a horse, get a horse!" A brace of horses pulled the plow for spring planting. They also pulled wagons that hauled hay, corn, and produce. The buggies and closed, curtained carriages on the property were still in decent shape and were sometimes used, and we children enjoyed jumping on them in games of make-believe. The Civil War was fought in a culture of the horse. We can hold letters from that era and touch one of its cannons, but we do not get to inhale the bouquet from that time—no sharp aroma from the boot polish, lamp wick, or hair pomade. Harnesses do not clink outside our door nor do hoof beats sound on the road. We are also removed—mercifully at times—from the raw uncensored emotions of that period. As I write about Chickamauga, that farm and its nineteenth-century way of life are never far from my mind. When I say Chickamauga, I mean Chattanooga, too, because the Battle of Chattanooga is part of the same fight for the "Gateway to the East." Braxton Bragg, commander of the Confederate Army of Tennessee, and George H. Thomas, commander of the Union Army of the Cumberland, as well as many other generals and common soldiers, were there throughout. William Tecumseh Sherman and Ulysses S. Grant arrived to settle matters in Chattanooga while Nathan Bedford Forrest and James Longstreet were departing—no small reshuffling of the deck, but still about the same recognizable deck.

Some people seem a little startled when I say that my grandfather fought at Chickamauga. After all, some of my friends' grandparents are still alive and kicking. Well, here's how it happened. My grandfather, William A. Bowers, was born in 1840; my father, T. R. Bowers, the youngest of twelve, was born in 1886; and I saw the light of day, the younger of two siblings, in 1928. Carrying on the tradition of late fatherhood, I welcomed one son into the world in 1976 and another in 1979. I don't exactly recommend that kind of scheduling, but it can be done. (At a recent Tennessee family reunion, on my mother's side, an elderly first cousin once removed told me that *his* paternal grandfather had been alive during George Washington's presidency; even I was startled by that.) The editor of this book also had a grandfather, John A. Wyeth, who fought at Chickamauga in an Alabama outfit under Joe Wheeler. John A. Wyeth later wrote an excellent biography of Nathan Bedford Forrest, which anyone who wants to come close to understanding Forrest must read. My grandfather fought in the cavalry under Forrest in the division of John Pegram.

Several years ago when I toured the Chickamauga battlefield, I was drawn to a dilapidated motel just outside the preserve of the battlefield that turned out to be on the very land where Forrest's men, my grandfather among them, had bivouacked before the battle. There I was encamped, too, beginning some hands-on research. Like more than one who's been touched by, or infected with, Civil War concerns, the motel's patron—a solemn fellow with smudged glasses—was becoming a little teched. He affirmed that Forrest had indeed camped on his land, but he said that the Battle of Chickamauga hadn't taken place where the federal markers over to the west said it had. "No, siree. No way. That battle didn't happen that way." He said the battle had taken place a few miles farther south or north, I forget which, and that the whole national park was in the wrong place.

"What about Snodgrass Hill where Thomas stood?"

"What about it?"

He wouldn't be pinned down with specifics. Rather, he began energetically blaming what he called misinformation about the battle on Yankees who had come down to make a buck on any land that turned up. It didn't matter if any fighting had occurred there. Not only had the Yankees beaten us with a numerically superior force, but now they had come back to lay out the wrong battle site and turn a profit. The motel's owner might have profited from some Yankee know-how himself. The water faucet in my room dripped; the bedsprings yelped at the least touch; and, worst of all, the lock to the room didn't work. "Just slam it shut good and hard," he said when I mentioned the door. "Who'd ever want to get in there anyhow?"

The owner's sense of geography might have been cockeyed, but his attitude was closer to the heat of the Civil War than that of many a tour guide or book-bound scholar. Although a large segment of East Tennessee favored the Union—Andrew Johnson came from Greenville—there has always been a hard core of those who thought separation from the Union was not the worst idea in the world and who weren't thrilled by Northern armies tramping over their land. My grandfather was a die-hard Democrat, as was my father, who died at age eighty-seven, still trying to find a Republican in the Appalachian Christian Village Retirement Home to mix it up with. The bent twig, though, does not always bend in the expected way. There was no question about my father's devotion to the Union, and he adored Yankees—to him they were smart and full of the milk of human kindness;

strange, but there it was. Till his dying day he hated farm life and (regretfully) never prized family land. He couldn't sell the land he inherited from my grandfather quickly enough. He was immune to the romance of horses (he'd had to stand too long as a boy behind a plow); he couldn't contemplate eating a cucumber because, according to him, hogs loved them and he didn't like to be reminded of once having had to slop hogs. He'd hated rising before dawn, laboring all day, reading by kerosene, and not having any entertainment except what you could think up on the farm. According to family lore, his "entertainment" as a child was being allowed—once a year, around Christmas—to pass down the long row of his older brothers and sisters and to kick each one in the shin. I never figured that one out, but there it was—told and retold.

And he seldom mentioned his father without bringing in the fact that he had fought at Chickamauga, much as some sons today proclaim their fathers' having fought in Normandy or at Iwo Jima.

One thing he never told me was that my grandfather went to prison as a result of serving in the Confederate army. I found that out in my research for this book. I looked up the daily report of my grandfather's company, which has been preserved by the state of Tennessee. There were no typewriters in those Confederate days. The script was in beautifully flowing calligraphy, and there he was listed: Private William A. Bowers, Fourth Tennessee Cavalry Battalion. Somewhere down in Georgia he turns up missing after Chickamauga, then—surprise!—he's in a federal penitentiary in Louisville, Kentucky, and there the record ends. Perhaps, like others, he had to take an oath of allegiance to the Union and then was permitted to return home. My generation was never told that he was captured and incarcerated. Why the secrecy? Possibly because families in the nineteenth century were horrified and closemouthed about two things: tuberculosis and being locked up. Braxton Bragg, from small Warrenton, North Carolina, never recovered from the fact that his mother had at one time been sentenced to jail.

Ironically enough, John A. Wyeth also ended up in a federal prison at Camp Morton, Indiana. But Wyeth's incarceration never evolved into a family secret because he wrote about his experience. The only ones who squirmed under the exposure were Northerners who didn't want to hear that federal prisons were in any way comparable to the infamous Confederate prison, Andersonville. In any case, Wyeth was a writer (he was also a distinguished doctor, the first president of the American Medical Association), and, as everybody knows, there are few family secrets where a writer is concerned.

What might my grandfather have thought in the midst of the fight—with his horse rearing, minié balls buzzing like bees, clamor and smoke engulfing him—to have been told that in the late twentieth century his grandson would be writing about it all? Private John A. Wyeth of Alabama? What if he'd been told, while he held ground around Lee & Gordon's Mills, that one of his grandsons would become a leading editor of Civil War material? What if my grandfather had taken a minié ball to the heart from one of Colonel Robert H. G. Minty's men? What if John A. Wyeth had inappropriately raised his firearm while being captured in the Sequatchie Valley? Well, for one thing, you would not be reading these lines now. There are a lot of "what if's" about Chickamauga.

Chickamauga AND Chattanooga

1

"The Ugliest Man in the Corps"

In 1863 the country was populated by slightly more than thirty-four million people and was referred to in the plural: "The United States *are*," not "The United States *is*." The singular usage would come later. The Civil War now raged. *Harper's Weekly*, in 1863, put it this way: "We are engaged in a war in which they will conquer us, or we shall conquer them. They are coming to the Lakes, or we are going to the Gulf. The victory on one side or the other will be radical and final. It will be a social as well as a military victory. It will be like the Normans in England."

It may be thought that the country stood still while such a momentous event was going on. It did not. A new society was taking shape—because of the war, and, in some cases, despite it. On May 5, 1863, Joe Coburn won the heavyweight boxing title by knocking out Mike McCoole in sixty-three rounds in Charleston,

Maryland. A new craze was sweeping the heartland—roller skating. James L. Plimpton had devised a four-wheel skate that allowed skaters to change direction by shifting weight from one side to the other. The craze started in New York and soon spread throughout the country; the Chicago Casino could accommodate 3,000 spectators and 1,000 skaters, and a San Francisco rink advertised 5,000 skates for rent. In Virginia City miners witnessed the triumphant performance of one Adah Isaacs Menken, who, at the close of her singing and vaudevillian act, was strapped to the back of a wild horse, in a flimsy gauze garment, and driven up a mountain trail to a wildly cheering audience who stood on chairs. In New York General Tom Thumb took as his bride Mercy Lavinia Warren Bump on February 10, 1863. It was the summer of the antidraft riots in New York that claimed 1,000 dead or wounded before Federal troops restored order. It was the year in which Edward Everett Hale wrote *The Man Without a Country*, and toward the close of the year, on November 19, 1863, Abraham Lincoln gave his Gettysburg Address. Stonewall Jackson died that year—on May 10—a few days after his victory at Chancellorsville. It was the year of Chickamauga, an Indian word that is said by some to mean "River of Death."

The soldier in gray who commanded the Army of Tennessee was tall, somber, and sickly thin—a man whose most prominent feature was a pair of majestic eyebrows that formed a straight bushy line beneath a wide forehead. You didn't know where one left off and the other began; it was as if he had but one long wide eyebrow. His beard and hair were flecked with gray, his grayish-green Scotch-Irish eyes often reflecting pain or rage, seldom anything in between. One look and you knew that here was a man who had seen trouble—someone who would deal it out, too. He might not be a boon companion, a good old boy, or a man with manners wrapped in magnolia and moonbeams, and although he was born in North Carolina, rather than Virginia or Louisiana, Braxton Bragg was as Southern as Robert E. Lee or Stonewall Jackson or Pierre G. T. Beauregard. He may have been crazy; he certainly was strange. He loved to write—letters, orders, memoranda—and always sought the final word, the final say. In another guise he could have been one of those crackpots who pen eccentric whining letters to the editor of a small daily, pointing out the errors of all save himself, latching on to some minor civic matter—a sewage ordinance or landfill—and worrying it like a dog with a bone. He had the unusual quality of being perpetually tenacious and perversely ineffectual. But he was not, in 1863, reduced to writing letters to the editor of a small-town paper. He wore the gold braid of a general. His Army of Tennessee was all that stood between the Federal Army of the Cumberland and its entrance through the gateway to the sea, at Chattanooga. At that moment, in the entire Confederacy, it had been left to Bragg to stave off the Federal advance and save the cause.

In January 1863, he had taken pen to hand and written a round-robin letter to all his generals. Sitting hunched over, cadaverous, at his campaign desk, busily dipping his steel stylus in black ink and then furiously scribbling, he ostensibly wanted to know what they thought of him. He asked for the generals' candid views of his capacity to command; also, by the way, he wanted them to admit that *they* had recommended retreating from Murfreesboro. The battle of Murfreesboro, or Stone's River, had taken place on New Year's Eve, 1862, and ended in a Confederate retreat on January 3, 1863. Even though Bragg's army was left in relative control of its position, the men had retreated—fallen back, tucked it in, withdrawn. In Bragg's mind it hadn't been his fault. His generals had been responsible. Back came their replies, with little time wasted, every one testy. The fiery young Irishman, Major General Patrick R. Cleburne, wrote: "[My brigade commanders] unite with me in personal regard for yourself, in a high appreciation of your patriotism and gallantry, and in a conviction of your great capacity for organization, but at the same time they see, with regret . . . that you do not possess the confidence of the army in other respects in that degree necessary to secure success." John Cabell Breckinridge, the former member of the U.S. House of Representatives and vice president of the United States, now a Rebel major general, wrote that his brigade commanders thought that Bragg did not have the confidence of the army whereby he was useful as its commander. "In this opinion I feel bound to state that I concur," he added. Sprightly Sam Watkins, a private in that army, wrote in his diary: "Not a single soldier in the whole army ever loved or respected him."

So much for the generals and enlisted men, so much for their opinions. If it came down to it, so much for every man, woman, and child in the Confederacy—even Mary Boykin Chesnut, from South Carolina, the astute observer of Southern mores during the war. In her polished diary Chesnut related with relish the possibly apocryphal story of how Bragg, in his retreat from Shiloh, had an enlisted man shot for killing a chicken. But Bragg was held in high esteem by the one man who counted: President Jefferson Davis of the Confederacy, a West Pointer and former U.S. secretary of war. Davis, the steely-eyed, gruff, and humorless Mississipian and an eminently fair and loyal administrator, thought highly of Bragg. He thought the world of Bragg, in fact. They had served together in the Mexican War, the brutal cauldron that had produced most of the fighting generals of the present conflagration. At the Battle of Buena Vista, on February 23, 1847, then Colonel Jefferson Davis found himself in near annihilation when Mexican General Santa Anna's enraged whooping soldiers bore down on his red-shirted Mississippi regiment, which, at that juncture in the seesawing battle, was all that stood between the enemy and the rear of the American army. Enter Bragg, in his one shining moment. It was a moment that turned him from a hard-luck case into a Goliath, for Vera Cruz was to Bragg what Manassas was to Stonewall Jackson—

an epiphany. Davis was calling on the Almighty when, amid the roar and billowing white of muzzle fire, Bragg and his battery moved up with merciless resolve. The Americans counterattacked, Bragg in the lead, Bragg so little concerned about his own hide that he was out front within canister range of the Mexicans. Bragg probably saved Davis's life that day in 1847; certainly he saved the day. Davis, who is said never to have forgotten a friend or to have forgiven a foe, took Bragg's measure that day and never changed his opinion.

So Bragg was standing watch as the might of Lincoln and the Union pressed toward the funnel of Chattanooga, toward its gateway to the sea and complete victory. With the prescience that marked his every move through the strife, Lincoln believed—and often told his doubting generals—that East Tennessee was the key, that whoever could control that mountainous piece of geography would strategically control the outcome of the conflict. From the start, the North had three main objectives: take the Rebel capital of Richmond and kill the secessionist spirit; control the Mississippi Valley and secure the western waterways; and, finally, seize East Tennessee and hold the Nashville–Atlanta corridor, the South's lifeline. East Tennessee was dearest to Lincoln's heart. For one thing, his family had traveled over it in frontier days.

After the defeat at Shiloh in West Tennessee on April 7, 1862, after the showdown at Perryville in Kentucky on October 8, 1862, and the subsequent Confederate retreat, after so much bickering among the leadership and capricious ill luck, after so much maneuvering and bloodshed, the Army of Tennessee, under Bragg, had fallen back in the usual cold rain on Murfreesboro, less than a hundred miles from Chattanooga. It was weather made for ducks. Uniforms were soaked through, this eve of 1863, as the last day of 1862 drew to a close. It had not been a particularly good season for the South, but the Confederacy was holding on and still had a chance at a settled peace.

On December 29, Bragg had moved boldly, but in his typically heedless fashion. He had all the confidence in the world. At first. He sent young General Joe Wheeler, age twenty-six, around the enemy's left flank to wreak havoc with his cavalry on the enemy's supply trains. Wheeler could always be counted on to fight—and win. (Fightin' Joe kept right on fighting through 127 battles in the Civil War and then fought in the Spanish-American War as a regenerated U.S. citizen.) The midnight raid was a mystifying cakewalk. Wheeler pulled off a brilliant coup, circling around the blue army in forty-eight hours. He tore apart 400 supply wagons, rounded up 600 prisoners, and captured enough arms to outfit a brigade. Youth and elan and romantic wild spirits continued to sustain the South and to keep the dream of victory alive. Bragg became fired up himself. Attack! He called Lieutenant General Leonidas Lafayette Polk and Lieutenant General William J. Hardee, his corps commanders, into his tent on the night of December 30 and mapped out an assault for the following morning, as if they were brilliant generals sitting down to concoct methods of choking the enemy to death. Bragg called for his army to assail the North's left flank at daylight. Strike 'em while their coffee was still hot! Polk objected.

Polk, a West Pointer and Episcopal bishop of Louisiana before the war, meaty faced and spiritually ambivalent, was a great naysayer. All his troops loved him, but not all his superiors did. Daybreak was fine, Polk said, but what about an assault on the Union right, which could be better outflanked? All right, all right, Bragg agreed petulantly, strike their right. They spent the rest of the night, getting little, if any, sleep, setting up positions. Polk placed his 13,633 effectives in two lines facing the foe, and Hardee, another West Pointer who had written the book (*Rifle and Light Infantry Tactics*) that the armies, North and South, considered the bible of strategy, took his two divisions (10,459 troops) and extended Polk's line westward toward a thoroughfare called Triune

Road. Batteries of artillery and brigades of cavalry stood at the ready. General Breckinridge placed his 7,698 troops on the Confederate right and east of Stone's River, as security and a reserve. All set! Looked terrific down there on a map.

Bragg called for a "right wheel." His army, all save Breckinridge's reserve, would pivot on Polk's extreme right and start to make a grand paradelike sweep, scooping up the blueclads like batter rimmed from a bowl. Bragg wrote out the order: "In making this movement, the general desires that your attack shall be vigorous and persistent. In so doing, keep up the touch of elbows to the right, in order that the line may be unbroken."

Bragg never learned a new tactic—or forgot one. At Shiloh and Perryville he had sent men forward with elbows touching, a maneuver of Napoleonic grandeur, and then had seen their neat lines torn asunder by rifle and artillery fire; he had witnessed rout and confusion and barbaric hell when men strode forward in close marching order and attacked on rough terrain. On the Plains of Abraham or at West Point, the smart, disciplined exercise might stir hearts and be suitable, but not at Stone's River, over an untamed thicket of cedars and briar patches. It hadn't worked at Shiloh or Perryville, but Bragg knew no other way. You put your pants on one way in the morning; you conceive of no other way of doing it. Here officers bellowed commands, and the men went forth like automatons, near trotting in close order, elbows rubbing, and wide eyed, suddenly to fall apart and lose each other in underbrush, vine, and tree—falling in gullies, banging into cedars, leveled by a low branch. The attack started when the light was dim, shortly after 6:00 A.M., and the Federals were caught for the briefest moment in panic and surprise. They themselves had planned an attack for later that day on the Confederates' right and now had to fall back on the defensive. You go to sleep thinking one thing; you wake in terror to another.

General Alexander McDowell McCook's men were rubbing sleep from their eyes when the Rebs came. As gray-suited cavalry charged, gray-clad infantrymen plodded and tripped and swarmed through the Union camp. McCook did the sensible thing: He sounded retreat. Confederate Hardee later wrote: "The enemy several times attempted to make a stand, but were each time forced back. Our troops were vigorously pressing forward." But true to form (and in keeping with Bragg's luck), the Confederate drive slowly and inexorably lost steam. By 7:00 A.M. the Federal army rose like a stunned giant and began to strike back. At the time, scrappy Pat Cleburne, leading his Confederate division forward, was the only one on the move; you had to drive a stake through Cleburne's heart to stop him. Two wild charges failed to move the Union back an inch over the broken terrain. Instead, booming enfilading artillery fire began raining down death on Cleburne's men. Hardee sent word to Bragg to order Major General Benjamin Franklin Cheatham to Cleburne's aid. Bragg scratched his head, dithered awhile, and then did so. It made no difference. There were three attacks and three repulsions—and at the center of the fighting there was a Sargasso of confusion, smoke, dust, blood, and noise. The artillery range between the two sides was no more than 200 yards. Within those 200 yards a better picture of hell has never been imagined. Around 1,700 Federals were killed, and five times as many were wounded or missing. The Confederates lost 1,294 dead, 7,945 wounded, and 1,027 missing. "Victories [can] only be gained by fearful sacrifices," Federal officer David S. Stanley, who fought there, wrote in his unpublished memoirs. "Our hospitals were mostly in big tents, and here the wounded did well, but when taken into private houses or churches the deaths from gangrene were very numerous."

It was mostly farm boy fighting farm boy now. On the Union side the young soldiers came mainly from small Midwestern farms, from homes and communities that were similar to those who fought on the other side. Some of these Northern youths could show a surprising hostility toward blacks, not so dissimilar to that shown by their opponents in gray. A number of them said "nigger." They were not firebrands of liberation. They weren't wading into the slaughter to free slaves and make democracy work. Any number of reasons, now misted over by time, made those farm boys from Indiana, Ohio, and Illinois slough through the Tennessee mud to disembowel the "Secess"—but seldom a noble one. There had been an insurrection, some criminal mischief by the Southerners, and they were coming to get them; the Northern boys were also in it to get away from home, to have some adventure, and to wear a uniform and shoot a gun. Maybe they'd find some girls. The two deadly enemies here were very much alike. They looked alike; they talked alike. They all knew about milking cows and the daily backbreaking farm chores. It was not a life held in high esteem or looked back upon with romantic affection. It was one to flee. (See *A Son of the Middle Border* by Hamlin Garland.)

In the battles of Virginia, it had been a different story. There a Southerner really had some people to hate, some real humdingers. There you had *Yankees*. There you had those *foreigners* from New York, babbling away in strange tongues—they weren't even Americans. And then you had those New Englanders who were so righteous and bloodless; all they wanted to do was to tell other people how to lead their lives and how smart they themselves were. *Yankees*, God damn them! Now in Tennessee, you had fellows fighting against you who might know how to slop a pig, but they wore better clothes than you, ate better rations, carried better arms—and, what was the most infuriating, they were walking right over your own God-given property.

Colonel Luther P. Bradley, U.S. Army, had this to say in a letter to his mother from a camp near Murfreesboro:

The Southerners are unquestionably a fighting people, and I have great respect for their soldierly qualities. They are well officered and far better drilled and disciplined than our army. They show great spirit and dash and perform their duties steadily and quickly. If there is any one thing in which they are inferior to us, it is in that stubborn quality which will make a beaten man fight, even when the chances are all against him. . . . The officers of the rebel army are generally intelligent and capable, and very much in earnest. They represent the wealth and power of the south and of course have everything at stake, but the rank and file of the southern army, I am satisfied, would willingly see the war end.

When these soldiers died in Tennessee, on the battlefield, it was difficult to tell them apart except by clothing and the type of arms they carried. After the first day's fighting at Stone's River, Stanley recalled the scene:

I rode over the ground where the first day's hottest battle occurred very early in the morning. The dead lay strewn upon the ground by the hundreds, the blue and the gray about equally mingled. Most men die on their backs. Frost had fallen the night before and the bearded men lay with their upturned whiskers whitened with hoar front, whilst the boys with clean fresh faces looked like the boys of the farmer's household not yet waked from the morning sleep. And there were so many of these boys! It seemed they formed one half of Death's harvest, strewn much like sheaves of wheat upon the ground.

Controversy about what had happened at Murfreesboro continued to swirl as the dust had, for controversy was never more than a hoofbeat behind Braxton Bragg. It followed, like an aide-de-camp, wherever he went. Some say Cheatham was slow in moving forward to aid Cleburne. If he had thrown himself into battle sooner, the outcome might have been a decisive Confederate victory. Critics of Bragg say Cheatham was there on time and pressing with full alacrity. Bragg himself later claimed that Hardee had told him that "Cheatham was drunk, and unfitted for duty during the heavy engagement on 31st December." Bragg went further, claiming that in discussing Cheatham's alleged booze-ridden mind of that day with Bishop Polk, Polk replied "that he regretted to say he had received the same information, and added that he had spoken or written to Genl Cheatham on the subject." If Cheatham had been loaded that morning, he probably was not alone. Private Sam Watkins, of "Co. Aytch," said that officers right and left were so drunk they couldn't tell Confederate from Federal units.

What man wouldn't have fortified himself with a drink if given the chance? Of the eighty-eight Rebel regiments, twenty-three had over 40 percent casualties. Forty percent of the infantry regimental commanders were killed or wounded; in some regiments every field officer was lost. Those who charged forth suffered the most casualties, whereas those who stayed in gullies where they fell stood a better chance. When the Northern troops counterattacked, they suffered, too. When the Sixteenth and Eighteenth U.S. Infantry regiments went on the offensive, they lost 436 out of 910 men. Men were mowed down when they charged across open fields—but they knew no better and could act no differently; they were merely following orders. By 10:00 A.M. Bragg's wheel of men hit the Union center head-on. Brigadier General James Ronald Chalmer's brigade of Mississippians loped across an open field, hopelessly doomed. No one could deny their courage. Half the Forty-fourth Mississippi Regiment was armed only with sticks—*sticks!*—and the Ninth Mississippi's rifles were too wet from a recent downpour to fire. Chalmer himself was wounded, and his brigade broke apart in all directions like a firecracker.

When the Mississippians went down, a brigade of Tennesseans stepped forward. The Tennesseans were fighting for their land. Some crazed Yankee from Indiana was eating *their* corn and stealing *their* pigs: No one was more inspired in the entire battle. They dashed themselves against the enemy's center, time after time. One regiment lost half its officers and 68 percent of its men, and another lost 42 percent of its officers and over half its men. But the Federals would not bend; they had come to fight, too. Meanwhile, Bragg, aching from head to toe from physical complaints, called upon his ragged mind once again for some quick intuitive commands, some feel for the general tenor of the campaign, some solutions to immediate problems. It was nearly more than a man could bear. He had thousands out on the battlefield whose lives depended upon what acumen he had left. Aides flew into his headquarters tent with intelligence reports: Several units out there, sir, without ammunition, some disoriented and disorganized, and everyone in the fray, every man jack, was either shot or exhausted. What is your command, General?

He called for the reserve—Breckinridge's troops—to help out Hardee's beleaguered corps in the heart of the battle. At 10:10 A.M. Breckinridge sent back a dispatch, informing Bragg that he had troubles of his own: "The enemy are undoubtedly advancing upon me. The Lebanon road is unprotected, and I have no troops to fill out my line to it." Bragg sent back word to advance on the enemy wherever he was, to advance on any enemy east of Stone's River. Just go out and meet him—and fight him. At the same time, General John Pegram sent word that his cavalry, which had charge of screening Breckinridge's right flank, was finding a strong infantry force crossing the river in his front. The Union seemed to be everywhere. Breckinridge, told to do *something*, dispatched a plea back that "he could be certain of nothing." Breckinridge did not move until 11:30. After high noon, at 12:50, he had progressed only half a mile.

Later, after the smoke cleared and the devastation became clear, Bragg pointed a quivering finger at Breckinridge and Pegram, saying that they were responsible—that it was all their doing—that their "misapprehensions" about a fantasy Union army bearing down on them had kept him from having three fine brigades in action when it counted most. Because of Breckinridge and Pegram's ineptness, the Union was able to halt Bragg's elbow-to-elbow attack and reestablish its lines. That was Bragg's story.

Whose fault was it? Did it matter, or were the battle ingredients so confusing and complex, so swift to change, that it was futile to try to place the blame? The fact was that when Breckinridge realized that he faced only an imaginary army—three hours after Bragg's first command—he found that Bragg had changed his mind once more and was directing him to cross the river and support Polk, not Hardee. Well, he made the most of it. When Breckinridge reached Polk's troops, Bragg ordered them to crush the Union center with "all the force he could collect" against an area called Round Forest. If Bragg had studied the map for a year, he could not have picked a worse spot. Troops were to be sent across an open field, already littered with their comrades' bodies, to strike at an enemy dug into tree-lined fortifications. Two brigades stomped through the field before Breckinridge got his chance. In an hour one brigade lost a third of its force, including all regimental commanders. The Thirteenth and Twentieth Consolidated Louisiana Infantry sent 620 men toward Round Forest. One hundred and eighty-seven came back.

Breckinridge could do little better, but he tried. He kept battering the enemy's breastwork until dark, until it was physically and emotionally impossible to try again. Close by, Hardee, without support, had refused to advance in late afternoon. "The enemy lay beyond the range of our guns, securely sheltered behind strong defense . . . It would have been folly, not valor, to assail them in this position. I gave the order . . . to bivouac for the night."

After a complete day of combat, both armies fell back on whatever position they held and collapsed. They were bone weary, crushed, and crippled. Few had any clear sense of why they had fought so hard and for such little result. Bragg sank in exhaustion without even inspecting his lines. He was only human. He did have the presence of mind, though, before crawling beneath his coarse campaign blanket, to send a wire to Richmond, saying that the Union had been driven "from every position except his extreme left." Covering himself, putting the best face on matters, assuming the posture of the victor before anyone could say otherwise—that has been the way of commanding generals since time immemorial.

No one slept easily that night. It was cold and rainy, and the screams of the wounded pierced the air. Generals Hardee and St. John Richardson Liddell got together and mulled matters over. Hardee was plain disgusted. Liddell thought that the Confederate line was now in an excellent position to attack the Union's rear and to drive the enemy back on its heels toward Murfreesboro. He thought about waking Bragg and presenting his case; the thought was none too pleasant. Liddell later wrote in his papers that he never forgave himself for not rousing the commanding general. "The truth is I ought to have gone . . . even if I had been arrested for it."

The next day, New Year's Day, 1863, Rebel skirmishers went cagily forward through the gray dawn mist. They probed and found scant resistance. Thus, they took Round Forest (or rather occupied it because the Federals had abandoned it), shortening their lines. All that bloodbath of the day before—the storming across an open field to murderous fire—had been for nothing. The Rebels merely walked in the next day and took it. But Bragg's problems were not over; they never were. By January 2, he could not determine whether these wily Federals were about to retreat. What were they up to, anyhow? Where were they going? Bragg sent the estimable Wheeler behind enemy lines to see what was happening with the Federals. Wheeler was not to come back, Bragg told him, until he could definitely "report whether any retrograde movement was being made." Bragg got the news, but not what he wanted to hear. The Federals were not retreating; rather, the fiendish swine had diabolically crossed Stone's River and had enfiladed poor Bishop Polk's lines on the sly. All right, Bragg would do what he could generally be counted on to do at first—*attack*!

Bragg called upon Breckinridge to drive the Union back across the wretched river. Fling 'em back! To aid in his work, Bragg gave Breckinridge 6,000 men, 10 Napoleon guns, and 2,000 cavalrymen under Brigadier Generals John Austin Wharton and Pegram. To divert attention, he ordered Polk to open an artillery barrage at midafternoon, and into this thunder and belching smoke, Breckinridge's division sallied forward at a quick step, bayonets fixed—told to deliver one volley and then charge with swinging, jutting bare steel. Once again across an open field, once again into the waiting, lip-smacking jaws of the enemy. Actually, this time the young Rebels moved "beautifully" and relatively unharmed across the open plain (according to Bragg's acting chief of staff), but when they reached the enemy's breastwork on a hill, all hell broke loose. The Union unleashed volley after volley, coupled with concentric shells from artillery. Somehow, some way the Rebels prevailed through the din and blinding smoke and dust and temporarily took the hill, only to have their left and right flanks thrown back in confusion and the usual disorder. The cavalry sat in their saddles, observing the melee, and did nothing. It was over before Breckinridge could determine where to strike, and for what benefit. As the acting chief of staff put it, "It was a terrible affair, altho short."

The combat lasted all of a horrific hour and a half. At the end, nothing had been accomplished. The armies stood where they had before. At the end, everyone on the Southern side blamed Bragg. He shouldn't have sent a bayonet charge across an open field against a fortified furious enemy. In the end, as usual, Bragg blamed others. He complained that Breckinridge hadn't conducted his attack properly and that the troops didn't fight as well as they should have. What did words matter now, though? The Confederate line was shaky, and its men were ground down. The weather was unmerciful: rain and cold for five straight days, with scant rest and no chance to regroup. In the middle of the night on January 3, Bragg was rousted out of bed and handed a note from Polk's divisional commanders, Cheatham and Jones Mitchell Withers. Cheatham was a politically appointed general from Tennessee, and though it was true that he drank too much, his men loved him; Withers was a Mexican War veteran who was esteemed by Bragg, but his health was deteriorating. The two men advised retreat. Immediately. Bragg read the note, rubbed his red-rimmed exhausted eyes, and sent his reply to Polk: "General, we shall maintain our position at every hazard."

The next day Bragg changed his mind. Stone's River was rising dangerously because of the rain; if it continued to do so, he might not be able to cross it and thus would be stranded. Captured documents told him that the Federals now numbered 70,000, and Wheeler's cavalry had spotted reinforcements arriving from Nashville to swell that number. He called in Polk and Hardee, and both advised a quick retreat. How much could they take? General Liddell, who had been expelled from West Point in 1833 for dueling, advised Bragg to stay put. He said that this was the decisive moment in the conflict. "Everything depends upon your success here," he later recalled telling Bragg. He wanted the army thrown between the Union forces and the reinforcements from Nashville— to cut the Union troops off from Nashville, and " . . . then I would fight them to the last. Give the order, General, and every man will obey you." In other words, he suggested that Bragg boldly and aggressively base the whole fate of the Confederacy on one roll of the dice. Stop them here, stop them forever. But Bragg, who could be bold at the start of a battle, again turned diffident at the end. No, no, retreat it must be. He'd lost 30 percent of his men, and those who were left were hardly able to pick up their guns. They must retreat. What would Stonewall and Lee have done? No telling. They did things differently in Virginia.

The Confederate troops retreated in a downpour. Fittingly. Heads bowed, homespun soaked, many ill, many more maimed, they departed Murfreesboro and the meandering Stone's River on January 3. They had to leave nearly 2,000 comrades behind who were too badly wounded to move; they had no other choice. The enemy, wherever it was, did not pursue. Supply trains wobbled over slippery rutted roads, the infantry slouched, and the cavalry rode to the side, prodding their foamy-mouthed steeds on with their crops. All tried to see ahead through the sheets of rain.

Bragg came down with a case of boils. Angry red welts with yellow tips broke out over his body—especially, in keeping with his luck, on his rear end. Riding on horseback was hell. An officer noted in his diary: "He is very thin; he stoops; and has a sickly, cadaverous, haggard appearance." He was a literal Job, hanging on when most sane men would have quit because a certain mulish stubbornness had been bred in his bones. Jefferson Davis was in Richmond. Bragg was going it alone.

Bragg had written, ". . . I shall retire without a regret if I find I have lost the good opinion of my generals, upon whom I have ever relied as a foundation of rock." After he asked for the generals' candid opinions and the replies came back, all candidly unfavorable, Bragg gave the matter some further thought. Couldn't they have seen what he was *really* asking for? Understanding? Knowing he was working against improbable odds? Love? Shouldn't they at least have sympathized with him and admitted some guilt at the fix they were all in? But no, they all concurred that Bragg, and only Bragg, was to blame. He turned further inward, and sourer. Back in Richmond, hearing of the round-robin letter and keeping abreast of the swelling dissatisfaction of the Army of Tennessee under Bragg—and being no fool—Jefferson Davis sent General Joseph Eggleston Johnston, whom, incidentally, he heartily disliked, to find out what was happening. Everyone liked Joe Johnston—save Jeff Davis. Dapper and trim, with a high prominent forehead and soft gray eyes, Johnston was the model whom many would-be patricians of the Cause emulated. He was an aristocrat, well read, tolerant, and as brave and fearless in combat as an Apache. A West Pointer and an immediate and lifelong friend of Robert E. Lee, thirteenth in a class of forty-six, Johnston left West Point in 1829 and soon found himself fighting against the Seminoles in Florida. He was wounded in that high patrician forehead, grazed by a bullet that left a lifetime mark. He went to Mexico to serve under Winfield (Old Fuss and Feathers) Scott and led troops into Molino del Rey and at Chapultepec—and was wounded five separate times. Scott, a generous and impish man, said, "Johnston is a great soldier, but he has an unfortunate knack for getting himself shot in nearly every engagement." Childless, devoted to his patrician wife—Mary Wood, niece of Virginia's famed Patrick Henry—Johnston traveled into frontier Tennessee to have a look at what was going on.

He didn't find an army that was unraveling; he found an army that was functioning, but only going through the motions. It rose at reveille and quieted after taps. The men weren't in tatters and were doing what soldiers had been doing since Caesar: Dealing greasy cards, horseplaying, griping, scribbling letters, cleaning their pieces, longing for liquor and women, and telling tall tales. The line officers were more or less enforcing discipline, staying a little ahead of their men in neatness and assurance. Nothing to get alarmed about. The reports of dire dissatisfaction had been obviously overstated. The deeper tremors could not be gauged at that level. Then he met Bragg, whose thin-wasted frame; nervous, abrupt ramblings; and endless tirades against any and all caused gentlemanly Joe Johnston to step back a little and his eyes to shine brighter. Alarm bells went off. What would happen if he saw to it that Bragg was sacked? He himself might be in danger of taking over. Joe Johnston was the master of retreat. He was too gentlemanly, certainly too cagey, to want to jump in and take over the Army of Tennessee. He listened to Bragg's generals—Cheatham, for example—declaring that they'd never fight alongside Bragg again. The generals were particularly incensed about Bragg's abandonment of Kentucky in October. Johnston made his report. If a change of command was necessary,

then it should come from outside the Army of Tennessee, but definitely Johnston should not be selected. Let him make that perfectly
clear. To suggest himself would be unseemly. He wouldn't touch the
job with a ten-foot pole. Bragg was saddled with it, so let Bragg
handle it. The Army of Tennessee didn't look too bad, though, and
therefore Bragg must be doing *something* right. Johnston had one
suggestion: The troops shouldn't be given so much fresh pork; sour
stomachs might be a source of the army's troubles.

Indeed, parasites in the stomach might have played a part in
Bragg's troubles. The piercing, leveling migraines could have been
seeded from the stomach, as could the loss of pep, weight, and
memory; the paranoia; and the erratic behavior. More than one in
the expedition to Mexico under Scott came down with a damaged
stomach. Stonewall Jackson, who also fought at Chapultepec, was
cursed evermore with intestinal ills. *Giardia lamblia* was undoubtedly in the water, amoebas strong enough to trot in the food. It was
Montezuma's (or Santa Anna's) everlasting revenge. Medical treatment in that era was hardly past the bloodletting stage, so cures
were not readily at hand. But stoically Bragg carried on—shuffling
constantly to a latrine ditch to relieve himself and blasting the can-
vas of his tent with noxious flatuses. Few liked to be around Bragg,
and perhaps there was more than one reason. Much speculation has
gone into the causes of Bragg's bizarre behavior, which could well
have been due, in large part, to having one of the worst stomachs in
the Confederacy. An army fights on its stomach; Bragg may not
have fought too well because of his. But there were other explanations, too.

Antebellum Warrenton, North Carolina, where Bragg grew up,
was quintessentially Southern, so Southern that it could almost
stand for the South, a paradigm—placid yet lively and often violent, charming yet rigorously divided by class and a certain artifi-
ciality, rich yet woefully poor. It was a wonderful place to live if you
had money and social distinction. It was hell if you had neither. It

was a puffed-up sort of place, a few miles from the Virginia border, sporting grand mansions, a racetrack, resorts, and a newspaper. Tobacco was the crop—slaves, who accounted for over half the population, were the harvesters. The Braggs were not loafers, gentle souls, or patricians. They were not landed gentry and to the manor born. They were industrious and out for the main chance. They were Americans to the core. Braxton's father, Thomas, came to Warrenton from the coastal region of North Carolina in 1800, earning his livelihood as a carpenter and later becoming a fairly successful contractor. He was a steady, bill-paying plodder, fierce in one way only: He demanded, by design and instruction, that his sons transcend their origins. They did with a vengeance. His oldest son, John, became a U.S. congressman, and Thomas Jr., the second oldest, went on to become governor of North Carolina and a U.S. senator. A father couldn't ask for more. During the war, Thomas Jr. served as attorney general for the Confederate States. There were other brothers of less distinction, and not much is known about them. The youngest son, William, was killed in the Civil War. Braxton, born on March 22, 1817, graduated from West Point in the famous Class of 1837 that included, among others, Fighting Joe Hooker; John C. Pemberton; and crusty Jubal A. Early, who remained a lifelong bachelor and who could swear like a mule skinner. Braxton's father had decided that a military career was the thing to propel his son upward, and had begun scheming toward that end when young Braxton was only ten. Braxton had just turned sixteen when he entered West Point. They say that Braxton was a superb horseman, about the only superlative ever used about him except that he was deemed "the ugliest man in the corps" while at West Point, a distinction that he took great pride in for some reason. There was no soft side to him—none—unlike Stonewall Jackson, who, despite a merciless side that called for slackers to be shot, was said at West Point to have a "womanly" side to him in tending a sick and weaker comrade.

Bragg was one Southern boy—perhaps the only recorded one—who never had a good word to say for his mother. Rather, it should be said, he never mentioned his mother, Margaret Crossland Bragg, in any of the thousands of letters he wrote. Not once. And not much is known about her except for one salient fact: She had gone to jail while pregnant with Braxton for killing a free black whom she believed to have committed the cardinal sin of impertinence. One account has Braxton being born in jail, but the best evidence is that, although his mother was jailed, she never stood trial for the murder and Braxton was born at home.

Quite a few Southerners of this period had hard beginnings, and Confederate generals were no exception. Lee's famous father, Light Horse Harry Lee, had become a broken, debt-ridden profligate by the time young Robert came along and was forced to flee to Barbados on a lifesaving sinecure when Robert had hardly graduated from crawling; the future commander of the Army of Northern Virginia cared for his invalid mother while growing up, lifting her in his arms from carriage to home as if she were a baby. Firebrand Stonewall Jackson, an orphan by the time he was seven, was raised by a rambunctious whiskey-drinking uncle on a farm in western Virginia—and so on. Young Braxton Bragg had risen each day in a snooty class-ridden town that never ceased to remind him, in all the myriad Mandarin ways the South is so capable of, that his people were plebeians, that his mother was an ex-jailbird, and that the lot were unfit associates for the more elevated and refined. Hate, envy, and malice can slip into one's bones very early in such an environment. Add to that a bad stomach and the worst luck in Christendom, and you have General Braxton Bragg, falling back toward Chattanooga with boils on his behind, in a driving rain. It was hardly the picture that the South had presented only a short time before: the grandiloquent Beauregard taking a Napoleonic stance in Charleston Bay as shells fell on Fort Sumter on an April night.

Bragg and his men had no illusions; those days had long passed. Now they well knew that they were retreating over their own land—and they were cunning and desperate enough to make their last grand stand on it. Where and how they would do so would be up to the "ugliest man in the corps."

2

★

"Just Before the Battle, Mother"

On the Union side there was no doubt that victory would eventually come. It was simply a matter of time, steady perseverance, and making sure that a fluke or mismanagement didn't ball up the works and produce a settled peace or modified victory and some kind of accommodation to the Rebels. Thanks to Ulysses S. Grant and his Union victory at Fort Donelson, Tennessee, in February 1862, where the small, narrow-eyed general told the Rebels they must surrender unconditionally or chance not breathing the next day, the term *unconditional surrender* entered the American lexicon. Now, in the final push through thorny frontier Tennessee, President Lincoln and Secretary of War Edwin McMasters Stanton thought they had finally found the man to impress their will on these miscreants in gray.

General William Starke Rosecrans ("Old Rosey" to his men)

and Braxton Bragg were similar in only one respect: Both had graduated fifth in their class at West Point—Bragg in 1837 and Rosecrans in 1838. There they parted company. Picture Rosecrans on a
horse: Back straight, reins up to chest level, head thrown back, an
unlit cigar clamped between his teeth, looking over the terrain,
peacock proud. He had a Roman look, down to his close-cropped,
slightly balding dark hair. He had a blade of a nose and bright hazel
eyes that bore through you. A fighter, a soldier's general, one of the
boys—Old Rosey. At the Battle of Corinth, Mississippi, on October
3–4, 1862, his devoted men took on the crazy Rebels in some hand-
to-hand combat, disregarding the Rebels' eerie godforsaken yelp as
they broke forward, and held firm. Old Rosey immediately rode
forth on his prancing horse and swept off his hat at the redoubt,
knowing instinctively how to capture a dramatic moment. He was a
showman. "Men, I have no choice but to stand bareheaded in the
presence of such bravery," he said. Three cheers for Old Rosey!

Picture him at Stone's River, where we have just seen Bragg in
action. Rosecrans stays up late the night before the battle. He's a
night owl, kinetic, hating to turn in, while there is any man jack
left to chat with. Anyone passing within a yard of the open tent
flaps is in danger of being hauled inside, more jawboning in order,
the hour growing later. Somehow, he is never the less for wear
despite his carefree attitude toward sleep. He seems incapable of
staying still. Some call it pep; others call it nervousness; in combat,
pressing forward, not flinching from the enemy, it's called bravery.
He reins his horse over the battlefield, seemingly oblivious to din,
shell, or shot, the ever-present stump of a cigar jutting from his
mouth. His chief of staff, Lieutenant Colonel Julius P. Garesche,
tries to keep up, his bay a few paces behind, always telling him,
"General . . . general . . . take care; think of your safety"—but to no
avail, of course. Rosecrans's black campaign hat is drawn firmly over
his forehead. Hell, he's got to keep moving; he's not sure what
would happen if he ever stopped. He likes to curse. He doesn't like

to put a damper on anything. Quite the contrary. Keep talking! You may go crazy otherwise. "This battle must be won! Hold your line there! This battle must be won!"

A cannonball whooshes by; then another. Suddenly, out of the hundreds of cannonballs unleashed that day, one takes the head right off Lieutenant Colonel Garesche, who is a few feet from his chief. Like Rosecrans, Garesche is a Roman Catholic, the only one on Rosecrans's immediate staff. They have much in common. He is brave and distinguished and highly competent. He has not been promoted as much as his ability warrants—a not-infrequent occurrence in the army—but lack of promotions will not matter any longer. He is a Cuban-born Frenchman, far from home. It all ends in a second—with no warning. The cannonball severs his head as neatly as would a guillotine blade. A spurt of bright crimson hits Rosecrans's deep blue general's tunic, but Rosencrans barely pauses. To pause, to feel pity, to acknowledge the horror is to lose. You must repress this scene—send it down to the bottom of your soul, along with all the thousands of others like it. The line must hold; the battle must be won. There are no second chances!

Rosecrans's conscious mind was ever active. He brooded and fretted over strategy and tactics. Federal historian Henry M. Cist, a newsman in peacetime, ever one to sniff out a telltale fact, called Rosecrans "the greatest strategist of the war." Cist had observed him the night before, and during, the Battle of Stone's River. The Ohio newsman Whitelaw Reid also rated Rosecrans at the head of a long list of Northern strategists. Eye-bulging, elbow-scratching Henry Wager Halleck might claim the dubious sobriquet "Old Brains," but Rosey was the Northern general, at the start of 1863, who was most esteemed for brain power where it counted: He knew how to plan and carry forth a campaign. Smoke seemed to rise from his cranium. He brought a Jesuit's careful but restless mind to campaign map and war council. Even the Rebels gave him his due. The *Atlanta Com-*

monwealth pronounced him, "A wily strategist." He was foxy, Old Rosey. He had been a roommate of Southerner James Longstreet at West Point, where Rosecrans was thought the most studious and Longstreet the most handsome in their respective classes. Rosey had been raised in a solid Methodist faith, in a household where John Wesley was the saint, but he converted to Catholicism later on. His intellect, not a sudden spiritual rebirth, had paved the way for his conversion, which came after long sessions of introspection. Emotion was swallowed; reason dictated. So it would ever be.

The Rosecrans family (their name means "wreath of roses" in German) had emigrated before the Revolution from Brandenburg and soon became well-known American patriots. Crandell Rosecrans, Old Rosey's father, fought under William Henry Harrison in the War of 1812. Rosecrans's maternal side included a great-grandfather, Stephen Hopkins of Scituate, Rhode Island, who had signed the Declaration of Independence with an aged but strong flourish. Rosey grew up in Delaware County, Ohio, where his father ran a country store and became moderately successful in various real estate and business enterprises. He had nothing to be ashamed of. He held his head high, confident in his lineage and assured of his future. If he was ever assailed by self-doubt, he never showed it. The need to prove himself never entered his psyche. The Black Dog of depression never took hold of him as it did of Lincoln; the bottle never overpowered him, as it did Grant. His nature was not excitable and frenzied and apt to race off like a Mustang, as was William Tecumseh Sherman's, and he was never in danger, as were more than a few generals—Stonewall Jackson, for example—of being classified from time to time as bonkers. He was steady, purposeful, and in firm possession of an analytical mind that knew its mission and lit after it.

After West Point, he went into the Corps of Engineers. Not long afterward he returned to West Point, where he designed and helped build some new barracks for the cadets. He served in Washington and found there a devoted champion in Jefferson Davis, secretary of war. He worked hard, but found the time for some good works, as men of upright character were expected to do in those days. Like Stonewall Jackson, he taught Sunday school for black slaves; every Sabbath morning in Washington, 700 dark faces gazed expectantly at Old Rosey, waiting for him to explain the mysterious ways in which the Lord performed His wonders. Old Rosey did not disappoint. He knew what was right and let the message go forth. Never question, never doubt.

Rosecrans missed the Mexican War, which had played such a strong role in molding the military character of Lee, Grant, Jackson, and Bragg. Like Sherman, Rosecrans missed serving under General Winfield Scott there. But aspects of his character were tested in other ways. Rosecrans resigned his army commission on April Fool's Day, 1854, believing he had learned all he could from the military and that he had done his duty and fulfilled his obligations after West Point. It was time to move on. He liked the new industrial spirit that was gaining a toehold in America, and put his army skills as a builder and an engineer to quick use. He traveled into West Virginia, discovered rich veins of coal, and saw the future. He formed a riverway company to haul coal to market and built a plant to explore ways of putting coal oil to use. He roved through the plant's laboratory, firing the Bunsen burners and heating the test tubes, trying to come up with an oil that would be safe and odorless and that would turn a profit and be practical to use. He was a go-getter, getting ahead. Restless, brilliant, alive in many fields. He came up with, among other inventions, a round lamp wick, a novel lamp chimney, and a new method of manufacturing soap.

Then something happened that was not in his plans, something totally unexpected. The Accident. He had been toiling in the laboratory for sixteen days straight when benzole gas in a misnamed "safety" lamp exploded. Glass flew, his clothing caught fire, and his flesh sizzled. He rolled on the floor, his clothes smoking, and then he fought calmly to save the plant—stamping out sparks here, burning oil there, and cursing from ingrained habit. Then, plant secured, fire extinguished, he numbly walked a mile and a half to his home and took to his bed, where he stayed for eighteen months. He pulled through—he willed himself to. His business partners, lacking his acumen, nearly let the company die, but it endured just as Rosecrans did. At nearly the same time as he rose to resume his duties, the war began, and he signed up. Soon he was colonel of the Twenty-third Ohio Volunteer Infantry, which included two future presidents, Rutherford B. Hayes and William McKinley.

Promoted in short order to brigadier general in the regular army, Rosecrans fought in West Virginia, Iuka, and then at Corinth. His civilian wounds still showed—a large scar across his broad forehead the most prominent, and one that is apparent in some photographs of him. Although a little erratic in his personal behavior—he kept odd hours, slept little—he ran a tight ship. There was scant litter around his bivouac; everything had a neat and clean appearance in his army. An anal-retentive's landscape. He saw to the care of his men, often to the annoyance of his officers. At Bowling Green some soldiers complained that they needed shoes, blankets, and canteens. "Go to your captain and demand what you need!" he yelled. "Go to him every day till you get it. Bore him for it! Bore him in his quarters! Bore him at mealtime! Bore him in bed! Bore him, bore him, bore him! Don't let him rest."

Some fellow officers didn't appreciate that type of solution. One officer, John Beatty, a brigade commander, had a personal run-in with Old Rosey. In camp, Beatty had become confused about an order, thinking it was intended for another brigade commander who was also named Beatty. Rosecrans had exploded, his oaths purple, his spittle flying. "Hell and damnation! Why didn't you mount your goddamn horse and come to headquarters to inquire?" The oaths rose, his white-hot fury expanding as Beatty, crimson faced, turned and walked away. Chief of Staff James A. Garfield witnessed Beatty's disgrace. In his diary that night, Beatty wrote, "For an instance I was tempted to strike him." Later, on a drill field, Rosecrans greeted him cheerfully—almost too cheerfully, as if to camouflage his previous rage, as if to say it might not have happened, as if to deny it. Some generals thought Rosecrans just a tad too excitable, with too short a fuse. *A commander like that could break.* He was known as a man who didn't turn down many drinks either. Major General Jacob Cox noticed that in battle, Rosecrans, his speech always hurried and rapid-fire, took on a stammer.

A *New York Herald* correspondent, W. F. G. Shanks, didn't like the way Old Rosey chitchatted pleasantly with the troops and then turned around and lambasted his officers—a trait that was demagogic in Shanks's eyes. But that was not the only trait that Shanks didn't like. Shanks, who thought that Rosecrans was a sad excuse for a general, was about the only contemporary observer who thought so. He claimed that Rosecrans failed as a strategist and a tactician, although he did admit that Rosecrans was tricky. "Tricky like an Indian," he wrote. Tricky or not, moody or not, Rosecrans's bubbling good humor always lay slightly below the surface and had a way of suddenly breaking free. He even chatted it up with prisoners. Once, according to an eyewitness, he was heard saying to a captured Rebel, "By George, old fellow, you fight well, but you can't whip this army!" (Only the expletive might not have been "By George" in this case—Old Rosey's more salty terminology laundered in the recounting.)

As Bragg's Army of Tennessee drew inexorably back through the countryside, Rosecrans's Army of the Cumberland kept probing, pressing, battling against them. As was standard with an offensive army, Rosecrans needed a supply base if he was not going to live off the land he was invading. Nashville, in middle Tennessee, was his supply base. He had to leave around 38,000 men to guard it, as well as rail lines, bridges, and field supply bases. The devilish Rebels were known to swoop down on rail lines and tear them up; they liked to make theatrical raids on depots and bases and then clear out in a storm of dust and whooping yells. This was their territory, and God alone knew what they might have up their sleeves. It was best to be cautious—to spend evenings by the campfire or over pow-wows in command tents, thinking about the right moves, getting prepared. Rosecrans was a thinker—there was none better in either army—and he wasn't a U.S. Grant, who flourished in action but became strangely remote when action ceased.

Rosecrans moved steadily down from Nashville with three corps commanders: Major Generals Thomas Leonidas Crittenden, George Henry Thomas, and Alexander McDowell McCook, all fine dedicated fighters. At Stone's River—that pivotal battle for Murfreesboro which we just glimpsed from the Southerners' side—Rosecrans put Thomas's and Crittenden's corps against the right flank of Bragg's army. Then McCook was ordered to set a line of campfires beyond his right, making believe that his line went out that far; next, he was to feint toward Bragg's left flank. Rosecrans wanted to paralyze Bragg into position, to have him dig in and commit his main forces there, after which, of course, he would sweep through Bragg's *right* flank with the redoubtable Virginian Thomas and Kentuckian Crittenden leading their corps. But who could anticipate Bragg, whose cantankerous and sour disposition made for unusual commands and responses? When McCook rattled his saber on Bragg's right, Bragg did not freeze into position as he was supposed to. Instead, the crazy son of a bitch attacked, in full force. What was more, he had the effrontery to attack before breakfast. Any man who would do that was certainly not civilized and no gentleman. He had no regard for a man's stomach or sensibilities. He was a heathen as well as a secessionist.

McCook's corps was half the size of the Rebels' and wasn't geared to take on such immediate awesome anger as the Rebels showed. The Federals were sitting down to a hot and hearty meal, belts loosened, full of good cheer, their coffee steaming, when the screeching Rebels charged forth like lunatics. God, what had they stirred up? Two of McCook's divisions tore apart, lost their bearings, and half the men went down. Battles can change a man's life, if not take it away from him in the twinkling of an eye. In the heat of battle a lifetime's way of thinking can shift and something well hidden inside a person can be revealed. Battles become searing moments—arenas of noise, dust, and death.

On getting word that his ruse was working a little too well, that his ploy might be turning into a catastrophe, Rosecrans initiated a frenzied reply. One officer remembered that Rosecrans's nose, usually scarlet, turned "pale" and that his beady eyes "blazed with sullen fire." The man, who had endured third-degree burns across his body, was tough and had a quick mind and—given time and adequate troops—could deal with an unexpected turn in a battle. But the unexpected was becoming all too common now—the unusual and bizarre and horrible beyond belief, the very norm. Rosecrans had been riding on a slight rise above the action while bullets and shells hissed and fell and exploded around him. One round of that fire had, as was mentioned, found his chief of staff, Garesche, who had been riding close by, ready as always to receive a command, offer a comment, or perform a function. Garesche's blood and brains had splattered across Rosecrans's face and shoulders, and Rosecrans hadn't had the time or presence of mind to clean himself off. One moment, Garesche, a person who chatted and coughed and relished a good cigar, had been there, and the next moment, his torso was headless. And Rosecrans had to put the sight out of his mind—how else could he lead an army and continue on? When some thought the general himself might be wounded, noting his red-splotched coat, he had told them, "Oh, no, that is the blood of poor Garesche!"

Brigadier General Philip ("Little Phil") Sheridan, caught in the melee, did not panic either and did not intend to give ground unless carried out feet first. Not so long before, Sheridan had been a misfit, someone you would not invite into your home if you valued your china. Born in New York and raised in Ohio, he had been suspended a year at West Point for assaulting a fellow cadet with his fists and a bayonet. Entering the army, he had almost immediately been threatened with a court-martial. He stirred things up, was a mixer, and was kept at a low rank and profile. Indeed, he entered the war as only a lieutenant. Best to keep him corralled as an administrator, and not let him out on the range to cause trouble. He was assigned for a while to purchasing horses, and then, unable to keep him still, the army at last gave him a command: colonel of the Second Michigan Cavalry regiment. His fortunes changed immediately, and he was soon a general. From lieutenant to general in nearly one fell swoop. The fierce wildness, which had been so unsettling in bivouac and parlor, was now appreciated in the field. "Square-shouldered, muscular, wiry to the last degree, and as nearly insensible to hardship and fatigue as is consistent with humanity. . ."—that was Phil Sheridan, as one of his staff officers described him. He was built like a street brawler, with bandy legs and a round cannonball head—and he sweated truculence.

Sheridan lost three brigade commanders that day, one a West Point classmate, but his troops held off three separate Rebel charges in the morning, and he played a large part in staving off a complete Federal debacle. The Rebels, who days before had been retreating over their soil, had turned in a fury. The battle seesawed, but was decided in the afternoon when the Rebels charged a clump of trees officially known as Round Forest but called "Hell's Half-Acre" by the men. Rosecrans placed artillery on some high ground and watched them come. A brigade of Mississippians came first, letting loose that ungodly high-pitched yell they had perfected at Shiloh that was enough to freeze a man's *cajones*. They trotted and high-stepped through a field of cotton. The Federals looked down and sent rounds from fifty guns on them. The noise was deafening, and the Rebels started to pluck cotton and stuff it in their ears. Still they charged. As they bore down on Round Forest, the Federal infantrymen, who had taken cover under the spread of cedars, suddenly let loose a torrent of musket fire. The Mississippians fell, and their places were soon taken by Tennesseans, who also yelled like banshees and fell. Finally, the Union troops braced as Bragg sent Breckinridge's four brigades against them. The attack was daring, courageous, and brilliantly executed—and it failed. It proved once again that anything Bragg might dream up was doomed to fail. The sun sank at 4:30 and mercifully stopped the slaughter. The musketry faded, replaced by moans and whimpering from across the length and breadth of the field. The Union had held.

During the night, Rosecrans moved his men from Round Forest, the small strip of land for which thousands had fallen, to straighten his line. And then he waited—for he knew not what. Everyone who was still moving was famished. General Crittenden had been preparing for bed, complaining of gut-wrenching hunger pains. His orderly had beamingly said, "Would a beefsteak serve your purposes, sir?" A beefsteak? Crittenden said he wouldn't mind that at all and fell on a slab of blackened steaming meat that his orderly pushed before him. The next morning Crittenden learned that he had eaten a hunk cut from a horse killed in the battle.

Throughout the next day bayonets gleamed and skirmishers roved, testing the flanks and the strength of their foes. But neither side was ready for another battle. The field stank from the carnage, and pickets spent more time burying corpses than firing shots. One last battle, though, was destined to be fought at Stone's River. The following day, Bragg sent Breckinridge's troops against some heights held by the blueclads. Breckinridge, who sported the black drooping mustache of a bandit, confided in a fellow general, "This attack is made against my judgment and by the special orders of General Bragg. Of course we all must try to do our duty and fight the best we can. But if it should result in disaster and I be among the slain . . .

tell the people that I believed this attack to be very unwise and tried to prevent it."

His men rushed the hill from which cannoneers and riflemen looked down, screeching and climbing in an excess of bravado. Halfway up, their number reduced in the heavy firing, they broke into a run as they sighted the crest. The Federals at the top lost heart and stampeded backward down a slope, the Rebels in hot pursuit. That was when Federal artillery, commanded by Captain John Mendehall, opened up from the side. Soon it was the Rebels who were stampeding back to where they had started. Someone observed that it was a double, simultaneous retreat. "It was difficult to say which was running away the more rapidly." And Breckinridge soon realized that 1,700 of his Kentucky men had fallen in just seventy minutes, which meant that one in every three men in the attack did not come back whole. "My poor orphans! My poor orphans!" he cried.

The Rebels retired, leaving behind all hope of taking Murfreesboro, and slunk back toward Tullahoma. There was no other word for it: A retreat. Yet many of Bragg's soldiers thought their side had won. Hadn't they mauled the Federal infantry and made them fall back in terror? It had been the safe and secure Federal artillery that had caused them misery. It had wreaked havoc, there was no getting by it, but, by God, where it counted—*on the field*—they had won. And what did dour, daffy Bragg choose to do? Retreat—just as he had at Perryville. Whip the Yankees and then fall back. "Why does he fight battles?" they asked. This was no way to win a war. Misery piled on misery. The usual icy rain fell, their stomachs growled. Bragg left them for a while. His everlasting bad luck and ill timing struck again. His wife had come down with malaria, and he took leave to nurse her. He was not missed by his men, who thought perhaps good old General Joe Johnston might step in and take command. Johnston had been inspecting the troops on orders from Richmond. But by the time Bragg came back to duty, Johnston himself fell ill, bothered once again by wounds he had suffered in Virginia.

Bad luck followed more bad luck. The town Bragg was holed up in, Tullahoma, got its name from the conjunction of two Greek words. *Tulla* meant "mud," and *homa* meant "more mud." But a Southern springtime eventually spread over Tennessee; the landscape exploded in a riot of color, and the earth turned sweet. It was the time of Easter and rebirth. Revivals and camp meetings took place, and many of the men found religion. A gaunt hirsute man, with a tortured expression, suddenly turned up in a line waiting to get baptized. It was Bragg, out front and ready to be saved. This act didn't make him beloved, and it didn't make him accepted as a merciful, charitable Christian. He might be sanctified in the blood of the lamb, but he was still the same, a man who brought down the spirits of all around him. Not everyone in the Army of Tennessee followed Bragg's example. Quite a few troopers whiled away the time by staging cockfights and rolling the three dice of chuck-a-luck.

After the battle with Bragg's army, Rosecrans became a more cautious, even hesitant warrior. He was given further cause for his newfound caution, too. In early March, he sent two infantry columns to probe the Confederates in their lair: Colonel John Coburn led one column and the redoubtable Phil Sheridan the other. The columns left separately and were ordered to unite at a place called Spring Hill and then move a dozen miles south against the town of Columbia. As they advanced, they were to forage and look about, testing the waters. Coburn moved out with scarcely 3,000 men and, before he could tie up with Sheridan, was met by troops under Mississippi Major General Earl Van Dorn. "Buck" Van Dorn, a West Pointer who had some failures in the war, was more than eager to prove himself. His height was rather diminutive, but his truculence more than made up for it. He was a risk taker, full of life, who in May of that year would be struck down by a bullet, not from the enemy in blue, but from the gun of a Tennessee doctor who became enraged when he found out that Van Dorn was having an affair with his wife and shot him dead. Now, in beautiful Tennessee weather, Van Dorn struck Coburn straight on, while Nathan Bedford Forrest descended by flank and rear. Coburn became stunned and was soon taken prisoner, along with 1,221 of his men. His cavalry, artillery, and some infantrymen made a narrow escape. Van Dorn wasn't satisfied with the spoils and pressed toward Sheridan, who, fortunately for him, had heard the booming cannons, determined he was outnumbered, and took off the other way.

Rosecrans dithered. Who was *out there?* How many? He had time to think, and that was bad. He was not in any hurry to commit himself, for he had come within a hairsbreadth of disaster at Stone's River and had survived with something that resembled a victory, so why move out until he was good and ready? What was the hurry? June rolled around, six months after Stone's River, and still Rosecrans dithered. He came down with "the slows," that dread condition which Lincoln had once applied to General George B. McClellan. The North had the reverse of the South's overriding problem. It suffered, at times, from too much and too many. The Northern commanders requested, and were often granted, extra troops and additional supplies, at a time when the South was scampering to fill ever-increasing shortages. A seasoned Union officer had been brought up short by a strange sight at the Murfreesboro depot: 40,000 cases of hard bread stacked up straight, flanked by overflowing quantities of flour, salt, pork, vinegar, and molasses. He couldn't get over the wealth of his army in this one lone tableau. In Tennessee, Rosecrans had asked for, and received, 18,450 horses and 14,067 mules. He ended up with about one animal for every two men in his army. He asked for more men and got them, too— 87,800 effectives by mid-June, compared with Bragg's total of 41,680. Still he could not shake off "the slows." Of course, he had his reasons for being cautious. One was the tricky terrain of mountainous East Tennessee. It was not Ohio, certainly not Kansas. He wired Washington, "The country is full of natural passes and fortifications, and demands superior forces to advance with any success."

Fighting was going on at Vicksburg, and Grant was hard pressed, when Lincoln wearily dipped his pen in ink and wrote: "I would not push you to any rashness, but I am very anxious that you do your utmost, short of rashness, to keep Bragg from getting off to help Johnston against Grant." Rosecrans turned haughty, à la McClellan, and replied briefly: "Dispatch received. I will attend to it." "Old Brains" Halleck, now Lincoln's general in chief, scratched his elbows in Washington and then demanded by wire that Rosecrans get rolling. Rosecrans let the capital know that he was nearly ready—but didn't define "nearly." Rosecrans kept planning, thinking, conferring—and on June 24 moved most of his forces, 65,137 men, ten divisions, against Bragg, leaving 22,500 behind to defend his supply train. Everyone was carefully briefed, the smallest detail looked at, nothing left to chance. Rosecrans told Washington neither the exact direction he was taking nor what he planned to do. Who knew who might intercept his message? He moved out well before first light. Major General Gordon Granger—tough as nails, regular army, and itching for a fight—swung his corps to the right and pressed forward in a clink of metal and braying horses. He was told to build an array of campfires at night to make the Rebs think that the main attack was here and that the number of Federal troops was larger. Crittenden moved his men to the left with equal instructions for a feint. The formidable Thomas, who commanded the largest number of men, pounded straight ahead with McCook's corps following. Rosecrans planned to use the wild country of Tennessee to screen a flanking movement whereby he hoped to trap Bragg.

It was not meant to be. Bragg's ill luck perversely came to his aid. It began to rain once again, as if from a storm cloud that hung perpetually over Bragg's head—and not rain this time, but a flood.

An almost biblical downpour descended, sinking caisson wheels deep in the ground, blinding troops moving out into the open. Rosecrans later labeled it "one of the most extraordinary rains ever known in Tennessee at that period of the year." After a while the blueclad troops simply ignored it as best they could, letting it soak them, letting the water squirt out of their shoes.

On the other end of the field Bragg hunkered down in his tent in abject misery. His staff officers didn't like him and didn't want to serve under him, and they kept letting him know it. Richmond had steadily taken men from him to send to needy Lieutenant General John Clifford Pemberton at Vicksburg. His wife had nearly died. His deadly boils kept him from sitting squarely in the saddle. He writhed in agony and felt near a nervous collapse, but he wouldn't fall or give up. It wasn't in his Calvinist character. On June 25 Bragg counterattacked at a place called Liberty Gap, which had fallen to McCook. He failed to drive the Federals back, but he sank down for the present and held his ground. The following evening, after thinking about taking the offensive and after having the usual contretemps with his subordinate Bishop Polk about the matter, he learned that a Federal column under Thomas was heading his way. The column was led by a strange sight: soldiers on horseback, unleashing rapid-fire rifles. This was not saber-slashing cavalry; it was infantry astride horses. This brigade was under the command of Colonel John T. Wilder, a former industrialist from Indiana, who had been humiliated by Bragg the preceding September in Kentucky. Wilder had been forced to surrender 4,000 men and ten guns to Bragg and he was seeking revenge. One thing you could always say about the Yankees: They learned. They had a foot in the New Age. Wilder put seven-shot Spencer carbines in his men's hands, and they became the first outfit in the West to hold such mobile deadly firepower. While the Rebels were swabbing musket bores as if they were at Valley Forge, the Yankees were harnessing modern technology to give them an edge.

Wilder and his men knew how to get things done. Presented with a problem, they could work out a solution. When Wilder heard about the Spencers, nothing would do but he must have them. There was no money? No problem. He signed a personal note through bankers in his hometown of Greensburg for the purchase, and then his men agreed to have their pay reduced to cover the costs. The Indiana brigade was 2,000 strong, and, although infantrymen, they mounted horses and moved out with blood in their eyes. They would make a big difference in the war; you will hear from them again. For the moment they presented one good reason for Bragg to leave Tullahoma in a hurry.

Grumpily, Bragg mounted his horse, and his troops—thousands of them—moved out in the inevitable rain, slouching through the mire once more. They had escaped Rosecrans's trap, but that was the extent of their success. Bragg jiggled and squirmed in the saddle and finally could take it no more; his butt was in full rebellion. He transferred to a railroad car for the rest of the trip to Chattanooga and left the care of his army in the hands of his lieutenants. He didn't get to recline long. The Federals were on the move, and this time they needed no prodding from Stanton and company in Washington. Rosecrans sensed that now was the time to strike, to grasp those despicable graybacks in a pincer and squeeze them for all they were worth. It's strange how lethargic armies may be for a period— watchful, indecisive, inert—and then, suddenly, move forth in an inexhaustible rush. Rosecrans moved. He divided his great Army of the Cumberland, sending his main force south of Chattanooga, just over the Tennessee border: Thomas's XIV Corps forded creeks by pontoons, cut through Stevens Gap, and pressed toward the Confederates' vital rail line to Atlanta. McCook's XX Corps tramped a dozen miles south of him through Winston Gap. Above Thomas, Crittenden's XXI Corps skirted the north face of Lookout and moved directly on the prized target—Chattanooga—from the rear.

Rosecrans was sly, though. While this main force moved

through the green summer foliage of this pristine mountainous terrain, he sent three infantry brigades in all their finery *north* of Chattanooga, as if he planned to attack the city from there. It appeared all too reasonable. Union Major General Ambrose E. Burnside was not too many miles north, slam-banging his way into Knoxville. The Southerners would all too likely believe that Burnside and Rosecrans were going to tie up together and then descend on Chattanooga. Logic said an assault on Chattanooga would come from the north. Rosecrans did the opposite. He instructed his phantom force to the north to playact. Every cool mountain evening these Federals lit multiple bonfires as if Hannibal and his elephants would soon descend on Chattanooga. They sawed the ends off planks and threw the scraps into the Tennessee, as if a great flotilla was being constructed, the better to float downstream to Chattanooga—all to the accompaniment of soldiers thump-thump-thumping on empty barrels as if engaged in desperate, hearty construction. These ominous tom-toms sounded throughout the day and night without letup. A battery was hauled up on Stringer's Ridge, an unprotected promontory that looked down on the city, and some shells were quickly launched. A few fell in the streets, and two scored direct hits on steamboats that were tied up at the city's wharf. All signs pointed *north*. They were coming! Bragg stirred himself. He moved a Rebel brigade from a bridgehead fifty miles downstream to meet the challenge and left the Tennessee River all but unprotected south of the city. Within hours, an endless blue army crossed: Thomas over pontoons where a railroad bridge had been burned, McCook twelve miles below, and Crittenden ten miles above. No one gave them any resistance. The Federals crossed the Tennessee to the south while the Rebels looked north.

There was a need now for speed and self-confidence. Rosecrans, his blade of a nose raised, rode in a middle column, standing in the stirrups, goading his lieutenants on—time was of the essence! But what vistas unfolded before them on their way. On view before the boys from Ohio, Illinois, and Indiana were mountains and valleys and suddenly, from atop a breathtaking precipice, a long, snaking stream below—untrammeled and unmarked, an Indian kind of territory. A soldier from Illinois described it thus: "Far beyond mortal vision extended one vast panorama of mountains, forests, and rivers." They came to Lookout Mountain and began to pass through Stevens Gap when forward scouts sent the word back: The Rebels were abandoning Chattanooga. Bragg was retreating once again! This time he hadn't even fought; no shot had been fired. As Crittenden's loyal blue Kentuckians came within sight of the sleepy town on a bend in the Tennessee River on September 8, Bragg was halfway through removing his ragged gray troops from it. The Rebels slipped southward through Rossville Gap, using Missionary Ridge as a screen, and got out before Rosecrans got in.

Surely Rosecrans could feel proud of himself. He'd outthought Bragg and the Rebels once again. Now pathetic Rebel deserters began laying down their arms before Federal pickets, ready to sing their tales of woe. And what a sad sight these gray scarecrows made! According to them, it was all over for Bragg; his troops were near complete demoralization and were slouching toward Atlanta. If Rosecrans wanted to end their misery, he should act quickly. He shouldn't rest on his laurels. It made sense, the ever more confident Rosecrans thought. Here was a living example of the rebellion in its final stage. Give these men fresh clothes and hot food! Charge!

What Rosecrans did not know in his euphoria, in this moment of bloodless victory, was that these deserters had been planted by Bragg himself. Bragg had chosen those who could dissemble, those who could look you in the eye and tell a downright lie. He chose those who could make you believe they were babblers and the vanquished while all along they were sucking you into a trap. Bragg was not yet defeated. A man who had been berated as incompetent by his lieutenants, whose stomach churned bilious gas, a man with boils covering his butt, had a lot of hate in his heart. He did not have a kindly patrician side to him, as Lee had. He planned to get the Yankees on terrain of his own choosing and then close his hands around their throats and choke them for all they were worth.

Bragg wanted to do it his way and did not fancy fighting in mountainous terrain. The government in Richmond, which was primed to supply him additional troops, had sought to have him move across the Cumberland Plateau and attack Rosecrans. Although these extra troops eventually came his way, Bragg did not want to move out against an army ensconced in any mountain. He wanted to make a surprise attack on a field, not up a precipice. "It is easy to defend a mountainous country," he said, "but mountains hide your foe from you, while they are full of gaps through which he can pounce upon you at any time. A mountain is like the wall of a house full of rat holes. The rat lies hidden at his hole, ready to pop out when no one is watching. Who can tell what is hidden behind that wall?"

Bragg made this sly observation to General Daniel Harvey Hill (known as Harvey), a fellow North Carolinian, who had recently joined Bragg's army; Hill was dark and humorless and didn't accommodate fools easily. Flying enemy shells might dislodge him from a field chair and send him rolling on the ground; he merely got up, straightened the chair, sat down again, and went about his business. He was no-nonsense; he was the brother-in-law and the best friend of Stonewall Jackson, who had lost his life that past May at Chancellorsville.

Hill came from the Army of Northern Virginia, where the commanding force was of a more steady yet daring nature. Lee was beloved by his lieutenants and men. Hill had served in Bragg's sterling battery in Mexico a dozen years before and had expected to find the same calm and brave commander when he reported for duty. He found instead a gloomy and jittery specimen, someone who had aged greatly since they had last met. Not only was Bragg fighting Rosecrans, Hill soon learned, he was also fighting his subordinates, men, and the whole world—save his wife and Jefferson Davis. Here was not planned warfare; here was chaos in the making. And while Bragg brooded and lashed out, showing occasional signs of acute peasant cunning—as in the case of the bogus deserters he sent to Rosecrans—his Army of Tennessee grew like Topsy. From late August into early September, his army grew from two to four corps, each with two divisions, to become 55,000 effectives, including cavalry. The cream of the Southern fighting force was now in despondent Bragg's hands.

Bragg halted his troops after two dozen miles, planting his left flank at La Fayette and his right at a place called Lee & Gordon's Mills, where the road from Rossville crossed Chickamauga Creek. Now he prepared to lure Thomas—who, like Hill, had served in his battery in Mexico—into a cul-de-sac known as McLemore's Cove. The Rebel cavalry under Wheeler and Forrest were to impede the advance of McCook and Crittenden's columns while steady old Thomas brought his column into the killing field. Bragg gave an order of attack on the evening of September 9 immediately upon learning that Thomas's lead division was entering the cove in late afternoon, seemingly set to bivouac by sundown on the banks of Chickamauga Creek.

It had the appearance of an order, but soon took on the earmarks of the usual Bragg operation: simple and direct but subject to being botched up by human error. Patrick R. Cleburne's division in Hill's corps was to seal the outlet at Pigeon Mountain; Thomas C. Hindman's division in Polk's corps would move from Lee & Gordon's Mills to put a stopper on the mouth of the cul-de-sac. It seemed simple. Bragg would then have Thomas's corps in a bag, with no escape possible, and he could put it through a meat grinder. Hindman duly set out an hour after midnight on September 10 and pulled up at dawn, four miles short of the enemy. So far, so good. Perfect, in fact. He waited for a signal from Cleburne, to tell Hindman that he was in position. No signal came. The sun rose to a full blazing height. Then came word from Hill. Cleburne was sick in bed and, furthermore, he, Hill, deemed the attack unwise. Next a messenger galloped up with word from Bragg: *Attack* now. Critten-den's Federal corps was coming through Rossville Gap from Chat-tanooga and would soon be at his rear. What was wrong? *Attack!* Hindman fretted all that night, paralyzed as to what to do. The next day Major General Simon Bolivar Buckner arrived to support him. Cleburne had been roused from his sickbed and was through Dug Gap. At last Hindman put his troops in the attack mode and moved toward the kill. When he came across the late-arriving Cle-burne that afternoon in McLemore's Cove, they found, alas, not Thomas, but birds in the trees and the wind whipping over bare grass. Stolid George Thomas had smelled a rat and had withdrawn to the safe side of Missionary Ridge.

Bragg fumed. He screeched, he exploded. A golden opportunity lost, all because of wishy-washy Hindman and dour, insubordinate Hill. But maybe something could be saved out of luring the Yankees into his arms. Crittenden had occupied Lee & Gordon's Mills after Polk had withdrawn to La Fayette at his approach. Now Bragg directed the good Bishop Polk to take his united corps, together with Major General William Henry Walker's, and attack the vul-nerable Crittenden. The order of attack was given for September 13. Polk protested. He claimed that Crittenden had his whole corps dug in. No matter, Bragg countered, Polk had four divisions to Crit-tenden's three—besides, he would send Buckner into the fray if needed. The premise was simple, and time was running out. Must he explain it once again? The Federals had divided their force into three separate columns. One column—Crittenden's—was now iso-lated at Lee & Gordon's Mills. Polk was ordered to attack. On the morning of September 13 Bragg rode on the field at nine o'clock and found ... Polk sitting down to a hearty breakfast. Bragg beat his chest, turned his eyes to heaven, and asked what sin he might have committed to have deserved such as this. Attack—for the love of God, *attack*! Bragg set up Polk, Walker, and Buckner into file and sent them forward, to find . . . that Crittenden, like Thomas, had smelled a rat and had hightailed it to behind the safety of Missionary Ridge. Bragg sank into himself and ordered his whole army to take position at La Fayette.

Now there was a stalemate for three days. If Bragg fumed and sulked and cried over lost chances, blaming his subordinates (with much justification) for his misery, Rosecrans fretted over reports that Bragg was being reinforced by troops from the Army of Northern Virginia. Longstreet, he was informed, was heading his way over the rails. Rosecrans, who only days before had been so optimistic and certain of being able to crush the rebellion once and for all, now feared being cut off and isolated in this wild frontier country and slaughtered like the Cherokees who had lived there so recently. The masses of blue and gray troops were separated now by a matter of yards, not miles. Only a ridge separated them. Both suffered alarms and excursions. There was much crowing and pecking, like game birds, set to claw each other in mortal combat. And within days, it would come. In fact, in the woody terrain by Chickamauga Creek, the most horrendous and bloodiest battle of the war was destined to be fought. None suspected its magnitude, but it was as inevitable as the first shot fired upon Fort Sumter a little over two years before.

3

★

Your Turn to Curtsy, My Turn to Bow

For a while there was the usual jockeying for position. There was feinting and subterfuge, intelligence work and cables to headquarters, in addition to a war of nerves. For a while, just before the storm broke, the relationship between the two armies was almost cozy. The two enemies near the banks of the Chickamauga were separated at times by only a loud hoot. A few of these western soldiers, on both sides, got so close that they could call out familiarly to each other. As was pointed out, these weren't foreigners who were facing one another; on both sides, these were mainly farm boys who were away from home for the first time. Corps Commander Harvey Hill, fresh from Virginia, observed and noted to one of his brigadiers, "When two armies confront each other in the East, they get to work very soon. Here you look at one another for days and weeks at a time." The brigadier replied, "Oh, we out here have to crow and peck straws awhile before we use our spurs." The brigadier knew a thing or two about cockfighting, a prized sport and perennial source of metaphor in East Tennessee.

While their troops crowed and pecked, the two commanders, William Starke Rosecrans and Braxton Bragg, drew plans and looked to the heavens trying to figure out exactly what to do. Fight they would—but where and for what immediate purpose? Simply put, Bragg wanted to slip around Rosecrans's left flank and cut him off from Chattanooga. He had gotten that bee in his bonnet and would not let it alone. Rosecrans did not want his troops to be cut off. He had just recovered from thinking that he had Bragg's tattered troops in full retreat toward Atlanta, and now the two sides stood cheek by jowl, separated by some foliage near Chickamauga Creek. While Rosecrans had pursued a supposedly retreating Bragg, he had divided his corps. Now he saw that he desperately needed to bring his great army together, to make it into as straight a line as possible. The retreating Bragg suddenly was in the position to go on the offensive. The trouble, the everlasting trouble of waging war at Chickamauga, was that the commanders not only didn't know where the enemy stood, they frequently didn't know where their own men were. The mountains and foliage hid troops from view. Communication often broke down.

By the time the sun sank on September 17, Rosecrans had his corps under Generals Gordon Granger, Thomas Crittenden, George Thomas, and Alexander McCook within six miles of each other up and down the course of the Chickamauga, just east of Missionary Ridge. Why the Chickamauga? Well, why Bull Run? Both were small, meandering streams. The Chickamauga looks like a child's scrawl on a map, darting up and down in haphazard fashion. It's hard to tell at times whether it's flowing north or south. But it is deceptively deep—ten feet in places—and its banks are steep and rocky. Bridges and fords were vital in the movement of troops across it, now that Chickamauga was shaping up to become one of the most important battles of the war.

Cherokees had, but a short time before, lined its banks with tepee villages and had contracted smallpox in devastating numbers, brought to them by the pioneering white settlers. The Chickamauga had never exactly been good news. No one would pick the Chickamauga—or Bun Run, for that matter—for grandeur or inspiring vistas. No one would choose it for a scenic boat ride. But war chose it, as war did the Shiloh meeting house at Pittsburg Landing and the McLean house at Appomattox. War, like a tornado, chooses what is in its path, and it seldom picks what looks good on a picture postcard.

The battleground-to-be, between Chickamauga Creek and Missionary Ridge, was hardly a picture of bucolic splendor either. True, there were small farms that cropped up every so often, but mostly it was an expanse of dark forest, with here and there a small reprieve of glades and clearings, near the site of rough log cabins. No matter where one stood it seemed that the heavens had disappeared and, even on the sunniest day, only the faintest light broke through the heavy branches of oak, hickory, and pine. Near the rough cabins the underbrush had been gnawed clean by farm pigs and livestock. Elsewhere it was thick and dense—like jungle growth. It all beckoned like the jaws of hell.

On September 17 Bragg spread his troops out along the east bank of the Chickamauga, locking them into position before nightfall. He planted his left flank at Glass's Mill, a mile south of what would become one of the landmarks of the upcoming battle—Lee and Gordon's Mills. He put his right near Reed's Bridge—also destined for fame—five miles north. The Federals lay in wait on the western side of the Chickamauga.

Lieutenant General Leonidas Polk immediately gave the commander his opinion of what they should do. They should quickly march on Rossville Gap, which was north and a few miles from Chattanooga. If they were quick and brutal, they just might be able to seal off the Federals from Chattanooga, cut off their supply route, and make them flounder. No, Bragg had another idea. In fact, it was another version of his idée fixe, the "swinging gate" maneuver. He wrote out the order in the small hours of the morning. Polk was to feint across from Lee and Gordon's Mills, as if he was ready to charge, thereby holding Crittenden and his men in place. This feint would allow Buckner and Walker's Rebel corps time to cross the fords and bridges below. These Rebel forces would then sweep up the Chickamauga toward Lee and Gordon's Mills, at which point Polk would cross, and all would unite to force the Federals southward into McLemore's Cove. Then the swinging gate would swing shut and the bluecoats would be summarily slaughtered. Rebel cavalry would ring the corps, and Hill would hold fast at Glass's Mill to the south, primed to strike at any Federal reinforcements from Thomas's corps who might come to the rescue, shepherding them through the gate and into the meat grinder.

Bragg wrote out his order in a fury, already on the qui vive for snafus, already seething that some miscreant, something, might ball up the works and doom him once again. He was angry before one shot had been fired, before he had even flung down the final period in his order. "The above movements will be executed with the utmost promptness, vigor and persistence," he wrote at the close of the order.

The first strike was set for the far right at Reed's Bridge—at sunrise.

Bragg had some reason for good cheer. General James Longstreet was on the way—"Old Pete," Robert E. Lee's right-hand man and "The Old War Horse." He was coming by rail. In one of the South's most imaginative and tricky gambits, Longstreet was hauling two entire divisions by train down from northeast Virginia. Troops had been moved by rail since the beginning of the war—Joe Johnston rushed into First Manassas with billows of engine steam trailing behind him—but nothing came near what Longstreet had in mind in terms of the number of miles traveled, the number of troops, and the tangled connections that were required.

Longstreet first moved his ponderous, sturdy frame inside the tent of the Commander of the Army of Northern Virginia to say farewell. He had a complex relationship with Lee. He had advised Lee against Pickett's Charge at Gettysburg and lived to see the fiasco that followed. He stood before a man who had served at times as a father figure, a competitor, a comrade-in-arms, and a thorn in his side. Lee was loved by all—all save those he tried to shoot, and Longstreet. By this time in September 1863, fumbling, boyish, ringlet-haired George E. Pickett might also be one of those who were not exactly enamored with Ma'sa Bob. Pickett had seen his men scythed down in the ill-fated charge that bore his name—and he blamed Lee. Now psychically battered—the term *shell-shocked* was not then coined—Pickett, brooding and fast losing his youth, was left behind with his division in Virginia while Longstreet got ready for the train ride south. Longstreet was a Southern fighter. He might be slow, he might be methodical—but eventually he could be counted upon to fight hard and never to tire. He had the temerity to take on Stonewall Jackson as to who was the better tactician, and after the war, after the guns had been silenced and sweet peace reigned and no one was looking for trouble, he took on the cause he had so bravely served and became a Republican. A Republican! He was smart—no one doubted his intelligence—and he kept, in the tradition of the frontier Scotch-Irish stock from which he sprang, his feelings to himself. Tight lipped and inscrutable—"Here's your five and I'll raise you five." He might even have had a sense of humor. Some years before, in the Mexican War, while passing time in bivouac, Longstreet staged Othello for the troops. He dressed up a young and pretty Ulysses S. Grant for the part of Desdemona, and accounts say that Grant did a credible job in the role. Longstreet: smart, tough—and always looking for the main chance.

Not long before the Battle of Chickamauga, Longstreet had lost his wife and three young children to a fever, which passed through his home and killed them while he was away at battle. This enormous loss nearly destroyed him, but he endured. He was never sunny again. He fought at Gettysburg, and he carried on. Now the time had come to bid Lee adieu.

Lee, stung by the disaster of Gettysburg in July, already suffering from the foreshadowings of the heart trouble that would kill him within the decade, gave his usual advice in the gentlemanly way he always assumed: "Now, General, you must beat those people out in the West."

Lee said this as Longstreet was preparing to mount his horse for the ride to the train. Longstreet had seen a lot of deaths, since he had been in the thick of the fighting from the start, and doubts were in his mind. He said to Lee: "If I live. But I would not give a single man of my command for a fruitless victory." Was he reminding Lee of Gettysburg? With this remark, he went off to Chickamauga.

Major Frederick W. Sims worked out the necessary tricky logistics to move the troops by train. In every war a supreme expert seems to emerge—Jackson's mapmaker, Jedediah Hotchkiss, was one—who is often as crucial to the outcome as the most deadly sharpshooter or astute commander. These experts, like the inventor of the rapid-fire Spencer repeater, take a brief twirl on stage and then sink into history's oblivion. The problems facing Sims would have stayed most "experts." The condition and efficiency of Confederate railroads were not exemplary. Only a Southerner could perhaps understand the system and make it work. The first plan was for Longstreet to move along rail lines beside the Rapidan River in Virginia to Chattanooga, passing through Lynchburg, Bristol, and Knoxville and on to battle at Chattanooga. A 550-mile trip. It was an extremely ambitious plan, for this route involved lines owned by different, privately owned companies. Only four months before, the Confederates had served notice that the lines were in governmental hands, but the decree had not been tested. Private ownership has a way of wanting to remain private, war or no war. And it was not one rail line to Chattanooga, but six—a patchwork of short lines, running from town to town, often without junctions or any means of tying up. The trip was a nightmare, and it had to be accomplished immediately. Blueprints were drawn and then came a surprise—Burnside had taken Knoxville on September 2 and the Union was ensconced there, so no gray troops could, of course, pass through.

Back to the drawing board. Sims hardly paused. He quickly drew a plan for the troops to be routed, not through East Tennessee, but roundabout—through the Carolinas to Augusta, Georgia; and then north to Atlanta; and finally, to Catoosa Station, a hop, skip, and a jump from the two armies verging on battle near Chattanooga. Distance: 965 miles, twice the original number. Sims made the telegraph lines hum. A typical one to a railroad agent in North Carolina read, "We want to move about 18,000 troops through N.Ca. in five days. Had you not better be at Weldon [N.C.] to Superintend it? The first train will probably be at Weldon Wednesday morning. Answer immediately."

Gauges differed on the lines, schedules were uncoordinated as a matter of Southern regional pride, equipment varied, and rates were not the same. It was difficult in the best of times for a Southerner to take a train trip of any length without losing his mind. Now, equipment was wearing out, and there were no replacement parts because no one could manufacture any, and there were no trained mechanics around to change parts in any case; the mechanics were off fighting somewhere else. Sims kept working. It would be done!

By September 8 the troops began moving, and for them it was a lark. Fighting was still far off; now they could lie back and let others figure out how to get them where they were going. They climbed aboard an array of cars—passenger, baggage, mail, coal, box, platform. Horses were shoved and pulled up ramps and into boxcars. A clatter of freshly shod hooves sounded, the smell of hay and lather and manure in the air, nineteenth-century aromas. Guns and caissons came creaking and groaning aboard flatcars. Some artillery pieces took the space of two flatcars, and men squeezed together in open spaces, making room for ammunition and rations. *All 'board!* These holiday-minded veterans of the Army of Northern Virginia waved good-bye.

Lee was not with them. Confederate President Jefferson Davis had wanted him at Chickamauga, a convenient and courteous way of removing Bragg as commander for what looked like the decisive battle of the war, but Lee would have none of it. Lee's heart was first and forevermore in Virginia. Virginia brought him into the war, and he would leave the war in Virginia. Virginia was his country. Something went out of him after Stonewall Jackson died at Chancellorsville, something died after he sat on his horse Traveller by the swollen Potomac, rain beating down, and watched his men retreat from Gettysburg. He wished Longstreet well, he wished his soldiers well, but, no, he was staying at home. Not so another fighter— Brigadier General John Bell Hood, a Kentuckian turned Texan, who found himself stranded in Virginia, nursing a recent war wound. Hood's left arm had been shattered at Gettysburg in front of Little Round Top, and most sensible men would have retired from warfare after that. The general had turned over command of his troops to Brigadier General E. McIver Law, but he was far from out of it. As the troop train carrying his men reached Richmond, a strange, ghostly, but certainly welcome figure stood by the tracks, calling to be hoisted aboard. God damn it, Hood was going to fight, arm or not! First his horse went up, then him. No one was going to leave him out. He could not bear to have his troops commanded by someone else at such a critical juncture in the war. *I'm coming, boys!*

And what a ride these Southerners had, who were off to battle. The ancient wobbly cars and engines snaked through pristine countryside in late glorious summer, going about ten miles an hour, the rails groaning and complaining, the honeysuckle wafting. At every depot a crowd gathered, lifting food and offering affection. Longstreet's chief of staff, Gilbert Moxley Sorrel, later wrote, "Kisses and tokens of love and admiration for these war worn heroes were ungrudgingly passed around." It was exhilarating and eerie—like a dream. Men passed through towns where they had been recruited and where their kinfolk pressed near to clasp them briefly and then say farewell. Mary Boykin Chesnut, the prescient witness of the war, was at Kingsville, South Carolina, to watch endless trains pass by:

God bless the gallant fellows; not one man intoxicated, not one rude word did I hear. It was a strange sight. What seemed miles of platform cars, and soldiers rolled in their blankets lying in rows with their heads all covered, fast asleep. In their gray blankets packed in regular order, they looked like swathed mummies. One man nearby was writing on his knee. He used his cap for a desk, and he was seated on a rail. I watched him, wondering to whom that letter was to go. To his home, no doubt. Sore hearts for him there!

A feeling of awful depression laid hold of me. All these fine fellows to kill or be killed, but why? A word took to beating about my head like an old song, "The Unreturning Brave." When a knot of boyish, laughing young creatures passed, a queer feeling of sympathy shook me. Ah, I know how your homefolks feel. Poor children!

Mrs. Chesnut viewed the passing troops of an evening. Other moments were not so tame. As men left one train to board another, they sometimes strayed; mischief sometimes called. In Wilmington some of Hood's Texans mixed it up immediately with the town's constabularies, who for the moment took the place of Yankees as people to fight. The constables, though, for the most part, were old-sters past the age of combat. The soldiers had come upon liquor in a low section called Paddy's Hollow and—like soldiers before and since—they got drunk and raised hell. They had to be wrestled back aboard the caravan. And off they went—beating out sidewalls to have better views, climbing on top of boxcars for the air and exhila-ration.

These men were just recovering from the savagery of Little Round Top and Devil's Den, and anything would do for relief. Days before, when they were encamped along the Rapidan River in Vir-ginia, a religious revival spirit had passed through the corps, as was usual during the Civil War. A member of an Alabama brigade wrote of twice-daily church meetings, usually followed by some being sub-merged in the river in Christian baptism. They went from hell-and-brimstone religion to hell-fire-and-damnation drinking and cursing and trying your luck at chuck-a-luck. Extremes. Half the war was fought with budding modern weaponry and technique, and half was fought with bygone Napoleonic maneuvers of flanking and close-armed assaults. And half the force that left Virginia, meandering by rail through the countryside, would not arrive in time to fire a shot at Chickamauga. Half of the convoy arrived in time; half did not. What difference would it have made if Burnside had not taken Knoxville, and the Confederates could have used the shorter, more direct route and got the whole corps to Chickamauga in time? The question joins a host of others: What if Stonewall Jackson had lived? What if John Wilkes Booth hadn't been born?

Back in Virginia Major Sims was busily telegraphing agents along the road not taken, the direct route. The troops wouldn't be coming through after all. Forget those 20,000 people we said were heading your way. Strangely, everyone seemed to know about this mass movement except those who would be affected most, those they were fighting against. It was not until September 13 that Gen-eral Henry W. Halleck in Washington learned that the railroad south of Richmond was extremely busy. On September 14, General George Gordon Meade cabled him that Longstreet and his corps had mysteriously disappeared from the face of the earth. They were no longer at his front in Virginia. Old Brains slowly but surely began putting two and two together—but too late. The North did nothing whatsoever to stop the Southern transfer. Also, Bushrod Johnson's division, together with General John Cabell Breckinridge's crack troops, had been slyly withdrawn from Mississippi and brought to Chickamauga to fight. Bragg was getting help faster than he knew what to do with it.

The North might let matters slide at times, might appear somewhat inured to harsh events, but muscle and technical know-how were on its side. The North had the men and the technology. When Union Secretary of War Edwin M. Stanton and his council of war got the message of what firepower Bragg had come by and what havoc he was causing, the North threw its might that way. Reliable General William Tecumseh Sherman was called from Mississippi with his crack divisions of the Army of the Tennessee. General "Fighting Joe" Hooker was awakened from a catatonic state after his mauling at Chancellorsville by Jackson and put in charge of two corps, the XI and XII, that would be speeded to Chattanooga by the means the Rebels had used—train. Again and again the North answered the South: If you think *that's* something, look at this! They'd show these Rebels how men could really be moved.

Rolling stock in the North was far superior to the rather lackadaisical notion the South had of proper rail lines; yet the road to Bridgeport, Alabama, which the Federals held, was not without its problems. Hooker's men had to change cars four times, and the usual administrative foul-ups ensued. No army travels without them. The combat material was not front loaded, so the guns, ammunition, and assorted firepower did not leave the trains first for action. Railroad baggage handlers had mixed the tents, mess chests, clothing, and what-not together with the weapons, so it took days to sort things out after they finally arrived. A lesson was learned: Never leave military hardware in the hands of railroad baggage men. And the North was no better able than their counterparts in moderating the holiday spirit and curbing the intake of liquor. General Oliver Otis Howard, a fierce and evangelical teetotaler, was commanding Hooker's XI Corps. Howard had his head out the window watching green summer foliage pass by, on the way to battle, when he saw men tumbling from boxcars. The train had to be halted and the men lifted back aboard. Howard later observed: "For some reason the soldier's thirst for whiskey (which is perhaps greater with them than other men) seemed to be increased by the unusual excitement of the move." He ordered that "all liquor shops should be closed during the passage of the troops," but the festive air could not be quelled entirely.

Townspeople they passed rushed food and lifted open arms up to them—much the way the Confederate country folk had done to the other side. In the place of fried chicken and sweet potato pie came staples from another cuisine. A Wisconsin infantryman remembered, "Our mouths were crammed with cakes, pies, cookies, meat, eggs, and fruit, which the loyal Ohio people brought us without money or price." And what a caravan headed for battle! There were two army corps totaling 25,000 Union soldiers and 3,000 horses and mules. *Three thousand* snorting, braying, kicking animals on the way. There were ten batteries of artillery and 100 freight cars of assorted baggage. All on the way to mayhem. The Rebels did see them coming and broke tracks in spots, but Yankee know-how quickly came to the fore, and the breaks were quickly repaired. Onward! The journey covered 1,157 miles; the first train arrived five days after it started, and the final one arrived in 11½ days. Here was more than a match for Bragg. The problem was that all of them arrived just after the battle at Chickamauga. But there was still plenty of fighting to go around before it was all over.

* * *

On the morning of September 18, Bushrod Johnson, late of Ohio and now a Confederate general, moved to take the pivotal Reed's Bridge and secure a crossing to the west bank of the Chickamauga for his division. The time had arrived. Coming from the other side was the Federal First Brigade, Second Cavalry Division, under Colonel Robert H. G. Minty. Here is Minty's crisp few words of what happened:

The Rebel line advanced and I was steadily driven back across the ridge.

My only means of crossing the creek was Reed's Bridge, a narrow, frail structure, which was planked with loose boards and fence rails, and a bad ford about 300 yards higher up. I masked my artillery behind some shrubs near the ford, leaving one battalion of the Fourth Regulars to support it, and ordered the remainder of that regiment to cross the bridge, holding the Seventh Pennsylvania and Fourth Michigan in line to cover the movement. Before the first squadron had time to cross, the head of the rebel column, moving at the double-quick as steadily as if at drill, came through the gap not 500 yards from the bridge. The artillery opening on them from an unexpected quarter evidently took them by surprise and immediately checked their advance, causing them to again deploy . . .

Bragg's plan remained constant through the day: Cross Chickamauga Creek and get secured; then swing from the right (north) and envelop the hapless men in blue. Again, it was a fine idea and could have worked. That is, if the Federals had done what they were supposed to, which was to stay in place and stand still for an assault. But Rosecrans, shielded by the rough foliage, moved his left flank two miles to the north, so that Bragg's force did not have the *position* to enfilade. Throughout the night of September 17, the sound of rustling bushes, braying horses, curses, and snapping tree branches filled the air. A chorus came from both sides. No one could see through the dark; no one's vision could penetrate the flora. No one knew where anyone was. Nerves were taut, and sweet deliberation was absent.

After the sun burned off the night's chill on September 18, one of the first sights in evidence, ready to impress his will and get things going, was a strange upright figure, theatrically outfitted in a white linen duster, a sword and pistol strapped at his waist. He was a cavalry officer but dismounted, leading his gray-clad men on at 7:30 A.M. against the ubiquitous Minty at Pea Vine Creek, about a mile east of Reed's Bridge. He was the first Confederate in the battle that became known as Chickamauga, firing away, itching to fight. He was the kind of general Lincoln had been seeking since Bull Run—a fighter. As it happened, he was on the enemy's side. His name: Nathan Bedford Forrest. Forrest had been molded, like Lincoln, on the frontier. Like Stonewall Jackson, with whom he had much in common, he had lost his father at an early age and had lived a hardscrabble life at first. Unlike Jackson, though, he found religion not in his formidable years, but while he was on his last legs, the fight finally out of him. He was called many things—"Wizard of the Saddle" and "Master of the Bowie Knife and the Card Table"—but the main ingredient in his makeup was that he was a son of the West. His first home was a log cabin in West Tennessee, his surroundings a barnyard; small, cleared acreage; and a pack of dogs. The eldest son of a large family, he took charge as a boy when his father died. He had almost no formal schooling—he couldn't be bothered. He took to guns and games. But, most important—like Lincoln and numerous others of superior talent—he wanted out. Away from hog feeding at daybreak. Away from crops that failed and nothing to look forward to but the next plowing. He wanted to attain that *other* world, where perhaps wealth and status might sweeten one's path through life. He left the frontier, but the frontier never left him. He continued to take care of his family, started one of his own, and became one of the most successful slave traders in Memphis. In time, he also became a rich Delta planter—all before he was forty. He became a sharp dresser and something of a dandy. He was six feet two, cut a fine figure, was dark haired, and had clear gray eyes that bore through you. Picture the mythological riverboat gambler, and there you have Nathan Bedford Forrest.

Violence was never far from him at any time, whether he was rich or poor. He faced confrontations in village squares, at open doors, and on horseback. It seemed he couldn't go a day without pulling his knife or drawing his gun. He possessed one of the shortest fuses in the South, the land of the hair trigger; Forrest had a temper that knew no bounds. He would not tolerate an affront or insult, and he was extremely lucky. A bullet might strike him—and some did—but one wasn't made that could kill him. He possessed, in spades, what made civilized folk elsewhere turn in revulsion and horror from the South at that time: a raw naked racism, a dependence on violence, and the inability to restrain himself and do otherwise. Forrest would have had trouble taking tea with Ralph Waldo Emerson.

Although Forrest never graced the plains of West Point, as most of the generals of the Civil War had, he lived as much as any of them by its motto: Duty, Honor, and Country. He lived to do right by the standards of the culture he sprang from. He enlisted as a private in the Confederate army and before the war ended was a lieutenant general. Lee called him the best general in the whole shebang, and his tactics were often similar to those used by Lee's favorite general, Stonewall Jackson: Strike boldly and quickly and where the enemy least expects it. Have superior forces when you do, too. Forrest believed in hitting an enemy on both flanks and then charging the center. His own pithy aphorism for military success was "Get there first with the most," which has been bowdlerized to the backwoods vernacular of "Git there the furstest with the mostest."

Again and again it was that inestimable quality of being a *fighter* that distinguished Forrest. He was not crazy. Even though his tactics were daring, they weren't harebrained or unsound. He would not have led Pickett's Charge. He fought to win. He had twenty-nine horses shot from under him. When one animal was hit, Forrest plugged the spurting blood from an artery with his finger and rode on. When he found a new mount, he withdrew his finger, and his former warhorse fell dead. He himself was shot near the spine at Shiloh, lifted right up out of the saddle, but he was back in action in weeks. He fought the Yankees, and he occasionally fought those on his own side. An affront was an affront. In June, before Chickamauga, Forrest had one of his worst violent encounters. A Lieutenant Gould under Forrest's command got in a heated argument with the general. Gould was being transferred and believed he was being accused of cowardice; he did not like the feeling of being humiliated. When he and Forrest met in the Masonic Building in Columbia, Tennessee, Forrest thought Gould was reaching for a gun. Forrest drew a knife, opening it with his teeth, and went at the lieutenant. Gould was trying to remove his revolver and in doing so caught Forrest with a bullet in his side. Forrest grabbed Gould's shooting hand, raised it, and then drove his knife between Gould's ribs. Gould ran, and Forrest was taken to a doctor who said, in haste, that his wound might be fatal. Enraged that he would not have revenge, Forrest flung off the doctor, rolled off the table, and raced to find Gould, picking up pistols en route. He found Gould stretched out on another doctor's table. Everybody back! Forrest yelled. "Get out of my way. I am fatally wounded and will kill the man who has wounded me."

Gould was then the one to flee an examining table and tried to hobble toward safety. Forrest found him in some high weeds, where he used his foot to turn him over and then walked away. He had satisfied the affront. After tempers quieted and it was determined that the bullet Forrest had taken had lodged in a muscle, not in his intestines, the climate changed. By then, Gould was stretched out in a bed, fading toward eternity. Southern-style sentimentality, which has few equals, then changed the scenario. Now that he knew he was going to live, Forrest called for all attention to be paid Gould. He declared that the lieutenant was brave and wished he could have him back in his army. One report has Gould calling for the general to come to his deathbed, where he took Forrest's hand and said he was thankful that he was the one to die and that Forrest was spared to serve his country. He asked Forrest for forgiveness, which was readily given. This deathbed scene may border on the apocryphal, but scenes of violence and reconciliation are dear to the hearts of Southerners.

Now Forrest stood in the smoke and din of the skirmish with Minty near Reed's Bridge at Chickamauga on September 18. His back was hurting from yet another bullet wound he had received that summer. But cross the Chickamauga he must, and cross it he would.

At noon, while the late September sun beat down overhead, Minty still clung to Reed's Bridge. Off in the distance, through a stretch that contained no trees, he saw a long expanse of Confederate regimental colors flapping in the breeze. They spread to the north of him, where farther on, toward Dyer's Ford, a huge dust cloud swirled upward, never a sign of good cheer to an opposing army. An enemy was on the way, a very big enemy. It looked as if the weight of the Confederacy was about to fall on him. As if Forrest's mad dashing cavalry was not enough to contend with, here came the whole South. Minty commanded but a brigade. He sent a courier galloping by horse to Colonel John T. Wilder for aid. The stalwart Wilder dispatched some mounted troops and a section of Captain Eli Lilly's artillery. Lilly had been a druggist, and his medicines would one day line the bathroom cabinets of most Americans. Today, his medicine was steel. Take it in large quantities and then lie down. But Lilly's fuselages were not enough to hold off the wave of Southerners who pushed Minty back, step by step, until he finally broke in midafternoon. The onslaught had gained such momentum that Minty was not able to destroy the tactically important bridge behind him. He could only pull up a few boards in his haste. But he bravely delayed the Rebels as best he could and for as long as he could. Bushrod Johnson began taking his 3,600-strong division across Reed's bridge at 4:30 P.M., by then too late to battle the Federals and hope to encircle them. Minty had served his country well.

Down below, at Alexander's Bridge, Forrest was now in the heat of battle and trying to get across the bridge. General William Henry Talbot Walker needed it for his corps of two divisions to reach the west bank of the Chickamauga. Actually, a scant force faced them, and on paper it seemed no contest. If will and daring and wild banshee cries could have won, the bridge would have fallen easily. The Federals had will and daring; what's more, they had advanced firepower. Four guns of Lilly's perfectly placed Eighteenth Indiana battery let loose. Whack, whack, *whack*! They rained down with pinpoint accuracy on the Confederates 600 to 1,200 yards away. Wilder's men simultaneously raised Spencer repeating carbines to their shoulders, aimed, and plucked off advancing gray-clad soldiers. It was like shooting ducks in a gallery—and fast. Forrest's chief of artillery, twenty-year-old Captain John Watson Morton, whose birthday was the next day, tried to reciprocate. He took his guns on a bluff overlooking the bridge and blazed away. While he was occupied, a mule ate a new uniform he had packed for his birthday celebration, his servant ran off with his food rations, and his three horses were killed or wounded. By the time he got across Alexander's Bridge, he possessed only the weather-faded, grime-ridden uniform on his back.

Forrest charged here and there, leading his men on, when his beautiful mount—a gift from the good people of Rome, Georgia— was shot right out from under him. He stepped aside and kept up the fire. By 5:00 P.M., Wilder had done all he could. With but part of a brigade and four guns of Lilly's battery, he had been able to hold off a whole corps and keep it from crossing the Chickamauga. Wilder was among the new breed who had roots in the past but who spelled the future. Born in the Catskills of New York, he came to Columbus, Ohio, to work in an iron foundry, and—like Rosecrans—found his niche as an inventor. He became an expert in hydraulics and thought up a new kind of turbine wheel. He liked to tinker and make new things work, and he had deep ties to the country's beginnings. His great-grandfather had lost a leg at Bunker Hill. His grandfather had shouldered arms at Saratoga and Stony Point. His father had fought in 1812 and had still not quieted down; at age sixty-nine he had written Wilder in Tennessee, asking permission to come down and fight—permission that was delicately refused. Now Wilder took his limited force, including Lilly's battery, and made his way in the darkening light to the Viniard farm on the all-important La Fayette road, miraculously losing only a few horses.

The dash of Forrest and the brute force of Johnson and Walker were more than offset by something so simple (and revolutionary) as the rifle. Bragg still hadn't given up the idea of a fixed bayonet charge, whereas Wilder and some others in the North knew that a rifle with range and accuracy (and rapid fire à la the Spencer) could take out a wheat field of bayonet chargers, armed with smooth-bore muzzle-loaders, no matter how brave. The Northerners responded to new technology; they sensed what awaited the country down the road. The South always had trouble giving up an old idea, and always would. Others often had to force them.

Wilder and Minty had done their job, and light had already gone by the time Walker led his troops across the bridge to the far side of Chickamauga and melted into the woods.

Few rested that night. Rosecrans, alarmed as well he should have been, began moving his left farther north toward Chattanooga. Thomas left McLemore's Cove and marched doggedly north. Through the bone-chilling night his men plowed forward,

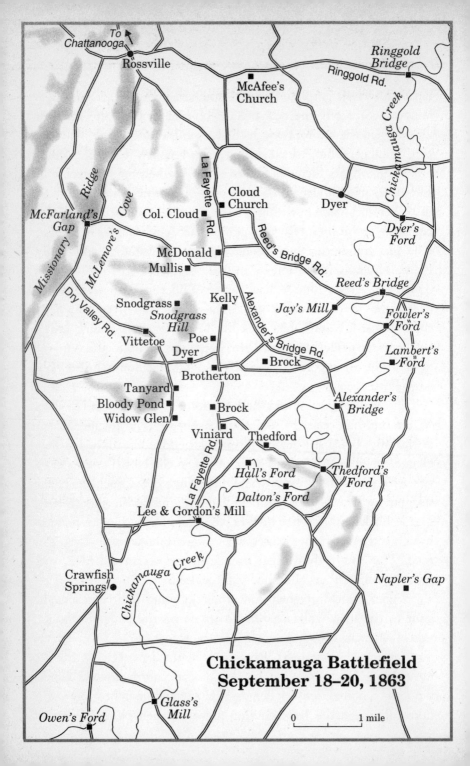

**Chickamauga Battlefield
September 18–20, 1863**

0   1 mile

through Crawfish Springs and Pond Spring and around Crittenden's rear, to well above Lee and Gordon's Mills. Rosecrans chose Thomas because Thomas was the best. If anyone could hold a position through thick and thin, it was the husky Virginian who now wore blue. Old Pap, as his men affectionately called him, sat four-square on his horse and brought his troops through the night. They burned fences along the side of the road for light, and an eerie series of fires marked their path. They broke occasionally to warm themselves, for these mountains of southern Tennessee and northern Georgia could reach a cold in late summer that could cause a man to shiver all over. They took water at Crawfish Springs, gulping in the cool limestone spring water, little knowing that it would be the last available water they would have through what awaited them tomorrow. The smart ones filled canteens.

The sun was up, burning off the mist, when Thomas reached the Kelly House with Brigadier General Absalom Baird's division. He was within a stone's throw of the La Fayette Road. Brigadier General John Milton Brannan's division of his corps took a position on his left, the northernmost position of Rosecrans's army, and the closest to Chattanooga. Somewhere in front of them, so close they could almost smell them, and certainly occasionally could see them and their campfires, were the Rebels. Leaders on both sides waited to see what they would do to each other.

4

★

The Big Bang

A little less than a year earlier, on December 13, 1862, the Federal army had tried to storm Fredericksburg, a civilized town with mahogany-burnished spinets in parlors and art and bookcases adorning the walls, while the Confederates under General Robert E. Lee stood on a promontory of the Old Dominion town and blasted them to Kingdom Come. Lee then made his famous statement to Major General James Longstreet: "It is well that war is so terrible, or we should grow too fond of it." His side stood, the other side came forward into hell; it was Napoleonic in its horrific grandeur. At Gettysburg, the tables were in certain ways reversed. Lee flung himself forward, and Brigadier General George Gordon Meade stood. George E. Pickett's men had charged across an open field, thousands of boys in butternut gray, in the late sunshine of a July day in Pennsylvania, and been scythed down—again a

Napoleonic landscape. It was army facing army. Both battles had been "up there," "up East"—amid solid farms, clean and cozy inns, order and cultured life. Chickamauga was frontier. It was "down there," "out West"—amid bush and bramble and the recent presence of Indian tent life. Maps were few and of little use. It was like fighting in a dark uncharted jungle—thousands and thousands of troops, groping to get their hands around each other's throats.

It started so simply that cool crisp morning of September 19. Steady George H. Thomas was tired; he had marched his men through the night, up the La Fayette Road, and had just encamped by a log cabin known as the Kelly House. Not only was he physically tired, but his nerves—if his calm, steady nature could be said to have any—were jagged. Where were those infernal Rebels? Where were they hiding, and when would they spring? He got his motor running with scalding coffee, but didn't say much, as was his custom, and watched the sun rise. Old Pap knew his Southerners. He was, of course, one of them. Although he wore the blue of a Federal officer, he was from Southampton, Virginia—the Deep South. He kept to his steady, slow pace and little could throw him. In fact, nothing had yet been thought up that could throw him. His own sisters had disowned him for forsaking his mother state, but he carried on, even though their grand, sweeping dismissal ceased only with their deaths. (They returned his Christmas cards, destroyed his portraits, and would not speak his name.) Northern generals, such as Ulysses S. Grant, distrusted him fundamentally because he was so decidedly, aristocratically, of the Southern gentry. He shrugged. Thomas—like Lee and Stonewall Jackson and James E. B. Stuart— was a West Pointer from the South, but when the call came, he chose to stay with the North. Why? Some said he did so because he had married a Northerner. Perhaps. The reasons why anyone does anything, particularly during moments of great import, are often shrouded in mystery, but a good place to look for clues (as Freudians are only too glad to remind us) is in one's early life when the twig is being bent. Thomas was fifteen in Southampton County, Virginia, when Nat Turner, the firebrand slave, staged his bloody rebellion. Few revolts have equaled it. On the hot night of August 21, 1831, a wild, marauding band of blacks wove through the countryside of Virginia. They struck at random, raping, plundering, ripping apart the landscape. They were mad, delirious with power, and drunk on the havoc they could wield. Rebellion!

Young Thomas was called to the saddle to ride to neighboring farms and warn the incredulous that they were in peril. (His own family barely escaped with their lives.) Thomas never forgot what chaos could do, what unleashed unbridled passions could cause—no matter the justification of the anger and hate: flaming farmhouses, massacred bodies, littered ground. From then on, Thomas was a conservative, never developing into what the South seemed to produce in abundance—the go-for-broke cavalier. He wore a simple uniform in the field, never a fancy one with embroidery or sash. He was quiet, taciturn—and unyielding. He became the prototype of what Americans love to see represented in legend: the quiet, unassuming hero who will not back down, a Gary Cooper or Jimmy Stewart. Only Thomas did not fit the lean and rangy look of such a hero. He was moon faced and bulky in girth; he looked as if he had served more time at the dining table than in the saddle. But he was there at the first deceptive shot of Chickamauga, and he would be heard from throughout—and, most important, at the critical end.

Thomas sent two brigades under John Brannan to crush a lone Rebel brigade reported to have crossed the Chickamauga over Reed's Bridge. Crush them before they could get situated and cause trouble. Do it now, too, right after sunup before breakfast is digested. Brannan's large force marched off to skirmish, sabers clanking, guns bouncing. It should be manageable. Then they met Nathan Bedford Forrest. Forrest and his men were mounted, pressing forward, as was their wont, when, suddenly, through the foliage and the rising greenish haze, they encountered men in blue. "Dismount! Open fire!"

The Confederates blazed away in a torrent of fire, and the Federals reacted with instinctive care—as if they'd somehow disturbed a hornet's nest. Skirmishers backpedaled and called for reinforcements. Infantry trotted forward, battle flags rising, bugles blasting, curses resounding. They came at each other, both having conveniently found a small open space among the timber that allowed them a few hundred yards to see and murder each other. It was at Jay's Mill, a frontier sawmill, that Forrest made his stand. He had some Yankees in his sights, and he went to work. His men swung from their steeds and became instant infantry, one knee on the ground, rifles raised. Light artillery boomed. Oh, how glad they were to meet the enemy! Here were Yankees on their soil, on the border between Tennessee and Georgia. It was rugged frontier South, and no one from Ohio or some such place should have the effrontery to bring rifle and cannon down here and try to tell them what to do. Hate went both ways, and its intensity was awesome. And the Yankees thought: "The goddamn Rebels were just that— Rebels, people who were breaking the law and who did not know right from wrong. Dumb crazy sons of bitches." It's hard now to contemplate the degree of hate—but hate they did; they hated each other enough to kill and mutilate without remorse. Forrest stood in the middle of it all, on the second day of Chickamauga, at Jay's Mill, in a white linen duster that came below his knees, firing away through the dust. He was not a man who took prisoners.

The action kept building. Overwhelmed, Forrest moved back a mite, but only a mite. Confederate General William Henry Talbot Walker, who was forking in his breakfast when he heard the cascading gunfire, rose and called for General States Rights Gist to take his division and rush to the battle. He couldn't see where it was, but he could sure hear it—and it was coming nearer, like rolling thunder.

We do not know what pain Gist's given name—States Rights—ever caused him, if any, but it certainly never left him timid about living up to it. He was handsome and courtly and had come up through the ranks of the South Carolina militia. He had graduated from Harvard Law School a short time before the war, and it might be imagined how his name was received in hallowed Harvard Yard. Ralph Waldo Emerson, the transcendental sage of Harvard, once observed, "The young Southerner comes here a spoiled child with graceful manners, excellent self-command, very good to be spoiled more, but good for nothing else, a mere parader. He has conversed so much with rifles, horses and dogs that he has become himself a rifle, a horse and a dog, and in civil, educated company, where anything human is going forward, he is dumb and unhappy, like an Indian in a church." Gist didn't shy away from fighting, another trait Emerson noted in young Southerners, and he was near Barnard E. Bee when that general fell at First Manassas. (Bee was the general who had given Thomas J. Jackson the nickname "Stonewall" during the battle.) Gist had taken over Bee's brigade at Manassas and fought to a victory, the South's first. Now he rode into the early morning fight at Chickamauga and flung Brannan back.

The stakes were then raised. Upon hearing that Brannan had run into more than he could handle, Thomas committed Brigadier General Absalom Baird's division to the fray. It was developing rapidly into much more than the suppression of a lone brigade, which Thomas had originally supposed the operation to be. In fact, after Gist's men had broken pell-mell from between the trees, firing on the run, one of Brannan's reeling brigade commanders had sent back a rather light-hearted message, considering the circumstances, asking *which* brigade among the many he was supposed to take out. After Baird joined the Union forces, the battle seesawed until Confederate Walker, breakfast long forgotten, sent Brigadier General St. John Liddell's division to aid Gist. Thus, commanders sent thousands of troops against one another, not in any coherent tactical way, but as bodies trying to push back and annihilate other bodies. Colonel John T. Wilder later wrote, "There was no generalship in it. It was a soldier's fight purely, wherein the only question involved was the question of endurance. The two armies came together like two wild beasts, and each fought as long as it could stand up in a knock-down and drag-out encounter. If there had been any high order of generalship displayed, the disasters to both armies might have been less." Crimson fire and acrid smoke overlay the gloomy woods. The sound, as one Southerner reported, was "one solid, unbroken wave . . . as if all the fires of earth and hell had been turned loose in one mighty effort to destroy each other." The inevitable slackers, those frozen into place, were hidden by foliage and hardly noticed in later accounts—or possibly there were too few to notice. It was as if they had all read the history books in advance and knew that here, at Chickamauga, the really decisive, win-all battle of the Civil War had commenced. All the regional hate over the decades was now unleashed. Every man seemed infected. When a Tennessee private was told to pick up the colors that had fallen in his outfit, he refused, and for this reason: "There's so much good shooting around here I haven't a minute's time to waste fooling with that thing." Woodland animals scattered and were tossed about. A frightened owl took to the sky only to be devoured by crows. "Moses, what a country!" a Tennessean said, gaping. "The very birds are fighting!"

And in the eye of the storm, once again, a tall gaunt specter in a linen duster, sword and pistol buckled outside: Bedford Forrest, who was busy shouting commands and directing fire with his hands. A brigadier's adjutant came galloping up, sweat popping: "Compliments from General Ector, sir. He has directed me to say that he is uneasy about his right flank!"

The Master of the Card Table rolled his eyes and said, "Tell General Ector that he need not bother about his right flank. I'll take care of it."

The aide galloped away—amid shots, flying dirt, and acrid smoke. Forrest resumed fire, his mind returning to the blueclad soldiers who loomed from out of the haze and peered from between trees. He sauntered over to a battery of horse artillery, the better to aim their fire, when here came the hoofbeats again. The brigadier's aide reigned up and leaned down. "Compliments from General Ector, sir. He wishes you to know that he is now uneasy about his left flank." Forrest's eyes widened and his jaw tightened; he could hardly speak. Then he exploded. "Tell General Ector that by God I am here, and will take care of his left flank as well as his right!"

Forrest was ready to take them all on. The din was almost enough to knock them over by itself, and the smoke was suffocating. Thousands of men were locked together amid bramble and branch, firing at almost point-blank range at each other. Forrest held. The Confederate adjutant, C. B. Kilgore, who after the war became a U.S. congressman and district judge, reported Forrest's reassuring words back to Ector. Forrest, irritated or not, did indeed secure Ector's right and left. Unfortunately for Ector, the Federals then pounded his front and drove him back. He was no Forrest.

Meanwhile, the commander of the Army of the Cumberland, General William Starke Rosecrans, was leading his entourage up from Crawfish Springs to join the action. But where was it? Up narrow Dry Valley Road, where they rode, the vista was bare. Off to the right *somewhere*, like a raging self-contained beast, a living ball of fury, the battle of Chickamauga raged within the woods. *Somewhere there in the woods.* Old Rosey and his troop saw signs of its unholy dimensions as trees shattered, fire streaked above, and smoke swirled. To peek in might possibly never allow one another sight on earth. Old Rosey and his staff were like patrons at a restaurant where a calamitous fight is going on out of sight in the kitchen; it is better not venture past the swinging doors too precipitously or a chef's cleaver may greet you. The dark primeval woods of Chickamauga held a mystery, but it was best not to mosey too near; it would be better to get your bearings first.

Rosecrans made a fine figure in the saddle once again—black britches, a snow-white vest, and a plain blue coat. Cheeks flushed, black hair gleaming outside his black campaign hat, he held his back ramrod straight and trotted forward with all the confidence in the world. Near him rode the Assistant Secretary of War, Charles Dana. Dana, a wordsmith first, a governmental functionary second, had been, not long before, managing editor of the influential *New York Tribune*, Horace Greeley's paper. Dana had stirred Northern blood with his series called "Forward to Richmond," which had been a bugle call for the untried Federal army to smash through to the Confederate capital posthaste and to end the rebellion. Of course, the editorials led not to Richmond but to disastrous Bull Run (or Manassas, in the Southern lingo), but Secretary of War Edwin M. Stanton liked Dana's spunk and brought him to Washington after Greeley, sick with the knowledge of Bull Run's casualties and ultimate defeat, fired Dana. Dana had been around. He was another ex-farm boy, whom the country seemed to be producing in droves, and, like many others, he wanted much more than what hardscrabble farm life provided. He learned Latin and Greek, went to Harvard, and spent some time in the company of the transcendentalists at Brook Farm. Dana reported back to Stanton on the state of the Army of the Cumberland; in fact, despite his high status, he was more or less an undercover agent for Stanton—a spy within Rosecrans's fold.

Dana was not the only one leaking privileged information. Brigadier General James A. Garfield, Rosecrans's recently appointed chief of staff, could also be included in this number. Garfield had replaced the ill-starred Julius P. Garesche, who had been killed while at Rosecrans's side at Stone's River. Garfield, of course, later attained higher office, and then was promptly shot himself. Like others we have met, he was of a humble background—a carpenter and Campbellite preacher before becoming a college professor. (Rosecrans feared that Garfield might break into sermons, but none came.) Without braid or pomp, Garfield might well have passed as an ordinary workman. He was of a formidable boxlike build, the forerunner of a bodybuilder. He had large hands that he proffered at the least opportunity. "Vote early, vote right," was how his hand-shake struck one observer. Behind Rosecrans's back, he was sending confidential messages about Rosecrans and the Army of the Cumberland to the artful Secretary of the Treasury and soon-to-be Chief Justice of the Supreme Court, Salmon P. Chase, in Washington. One shudders to think what Stonewall Jackson would have done to someone of that ilk in his inner circle if he had caught him, although it's hard to think of such a person being on his staff. Grant would have skinned Garfield like a rabbit and left him out to dry. Rosecrans optimistically went about his business.

He drew his staff into a log structure on a slight rise, a few miles southwest of where Forrest was locked in desperate conflict with the blueclads of Thomas's army. The battle must have been nearby, for the floor was shaking as the staff trooped in. It was the dwelling of a Mrs. Glenn, the widow of a Confederate soldier killed in action, and she was currently in residence. The dapper Rosecrans paced the small cramped front parlor as china rattled and the scent of gunpowder wafted in. Widow Glenn welcomed the conquerors as best she could. Southern hospitality was bred in her bones, and it didn't matter that guns popped and shells banged. The battle out there seemed to be reaching some unearthly crescendo. Rosecrans began advising Mrs. Glenn to take flight, to get out of there—as one would warn someone in the path of a hurricane. But first, *where was it?* "Now, Madam, if you could kindly please tell us where you *think* that . . . *noise* is coming from." A cannon had just given its report.

"Well, sir," she replied, "hit might be nigh out about Reed's Bridge. I figure that's a mile fornest John Kelly's house. You know whar that is, don't you?"

It could have been in Kalamazoo for all Rosecrans knew. He paced, he called for a map, he pointed here and there for Widow Glenn to make a choice. *Bam, bam, bammmm!* Dust and plaster fell from the ceiling. An engineer with a compass and pencil stood by to mark an exact position on the map—a map, incidentally, that bore no resemblance to the terrain it was designed to represent. Mrs. Glenn had no idea what was required of her or what the world was coming to. She could be of no help.

Rosecrans quietly eased her on her way to behind the lines and safety. Her slave John, presented to her by her father when her husband left for war in 1861, put her in a wagon and drove to a safe haven by Horseshoe Ridge behind Lookout Mountain. Later the battle would reach there, and she was quickly transported to her father's home farther away. By then her home would be blown away.

At the moment Widow Glenn's front parlor was a command post, officers rushing in and out, the sound of shouting, creaking leather and clanging metal mixing with the explosions outside— since no one was quite sure what was happening, least of all the supreme commander. Even in the woods where guns blazed there was no sure knowledge. It was mob against mob. At the Glenn house more than directives were going out. Dana began connecting telegraph lines to send secret reports to Stanton. Everyone was busy.

Here was not Napoleon in a cocked hat, astride a steed, surveying the sweep of flank against flank on the plains of Austerlitz. Here was a dapper Rosecrans in a stuffy cabin parlor, not certain what size beast was being unleashed in a maniacal rage in the woods outside. As if in a hallucination, a freshly caught Confederate was brought before him: a slightly built boy with a Virginia accent. The boy had been captured by an officer of Wilder's brigade, who thought the catch so important that Rosecrans, the commander of the Army of the Cumberland, should interrogate him. "We've caught ourselves a Virginian, sir," the officer said. "This boy is from Longstreet's Corps. Longstreet's here now and this boy is proof."

Rosecrans ceased pacing and fumbling with his useless map. Now he had something to do. "You lie, little boy," he screamed. "This is a damnable trick! How dare you tell us Longstreet's here when he's not!" The boy who was hardly of an age to shave had only been on the field an hour or so. Now he was talking to the commanding general of the opposing army. What kind of mess had he got himself into? He stuttered and turned beet red and tried to get his tongue to work. He was more frightened here than back where the rifles had been cracking. He had never seen anyone as mad as the man before him. He kept trying to speak as he was led away.

Rosecrans looked around and beamed after a while, the picture of confidence and authority. Bragg or whoever should know better than to try to pull a stunt like that on Old Rosey. He'd show 'em! A reporter who had invaded the command post noted that the commander's eyes sparkled and that he became of good cheer, perhaps a little too much so—the gaiety as extreme as his anger had been, as if he might be going a little bit around the bend. Rosecrans asked if another prisoner might be corralled, and soon a rangy Texan stood before him, a Captain Rice of the First Texas. Rosecrans took Rice away from prying eyes, outside the parlor to a tree trunk some thirty yards away. The commanding general grabbed a stick and began to whittle. Whittle, whittle, whittle. Then he talked, as he continued to whittle. He went at it energetically. "Captain, I'm curious as to where your lines are. Just point, please, off to those woods as to where they might be."

"General," Captain Rice said, "it has cost me a great deal of trouble to find your lines; if you take the same amount of trouble, you will find ours."

Captain Rice sat easily on the stump, finding it a pleasant diversion to converse with the Northern commander. But, scratching his cheek, he couldn't remember what division or corps he belonged to. He couldn't say where he had come from or where he was going when caught. But Texans have pride, and Rice didn't want the Northerner to think he was connected with anything that was small potatoes. He intimated that some powerful forces had arrived to aid the Confederates and that he was part of them.

Rosecrans's whittling slowed. "How many men would you say you've got? Just estimate, if you will, please."

"About forty-five thousand," the captain said, without pause, without blinking an eye.

"You're with Longstreet, aren't you?"

"Oh, no, sir! General Bragg is in command."

"Captain," Rosecrans said, snapping his pocketknife shut, "you don't seem to know much, for a man whose appearance seems to indicate so much intelligence."

"Well, General," the captain said, "if you are not satisfied with my information, I will volunteer some. We are going to whip you most tremendously in this fight."

The thunderous sphere of battle had been confined heretofore to the area where Thomas and Forrest had been slugging it out, on the Federal left and the Confederate right, west of Reed's Bridge and the Chickamauga. Now the action spilled down to the center, where the troops facing each other went on for four miles. They were all jockeying for position, and they had all come to fight—young and old, skilled and unskilled, the frightened and the cold-blooded.

Major General Alexander P. Stewart, a forty-two-year-old narrow-eyed man in gray who sat bolt upright in the saddle, a West Pointer, was leading his division north toward the thunder. It was around 2:30, and the light was slowly dimming. Stewart was fast marching up to see what he could do. Old Straight, as he was called—as much for his posture as for his demands for straight lines when a teacher of mathematics in peacetime—sniffed the woodsy air and narrowed his eyes. Not long before, on such a September day, he would have stood before a blackboard, chalk in hand, disciplining students and screeching out equations and logarithms on the board. The sharp air, a hint of fall, heralded the start of the school year. Now he was set on finding fellow human beings who were somewhere there in the woods to his left and blasting them to the hereafter. His neat problem-solving mind told him it might be better not to fling his division right into the exploding knot of fire a mile or so north of him. Why not just peel off in the woods where no one stirred and see what might result? No telling what he might find. As it turned out, he struck right into the middle of the Federal line.

Brigadier General Horatio P. Van Cleve did not expect what came flying out of the woods at him. His troops were then nervously listening to richocheting shells and booming cannons a slight way north. They were nervous and exhausted from two long night marches. Van Cleve, at fifty-five the oldest brigadier on the Northern side, had graduated from West Point in 1831 and had been out of uniform for twenty-five years. All at once, seemingly out of nowhere, the woods exploded in wild Rebel screeches, and Stewart's men were upon him—firing, racing forth, and whooping above the gunfire. It was enough to give a man a heart attack. Stewart was a Tennessean who was leading other Tennesseans against the invader. Kill 'em, boys! Shots and screams rent the air as the soldiers in blue fell back, stunned, overwhelmed, and near panic. Stewart's Tennesseans drove the blueclads back across La Fayette Road, the all-important conduit to Chattanooga. La Fayette Road was the main dividing line between the armies: Whoever crossed it was on the way to victory; whoever fell back from it tasted ashes and defeat. Stewart threw his arm forward, urging his men on while the surprise held. Don't let 'em escape! All at once, through the haze of gunsmoke, the Widow Glenn's house rose before them on a slight rise. What was this? Officers and horses and a general busy air of importance engulfed it. The rolling mass of

Rebels kept rolling forward, seemingly invincible, and Stewart had the Union's command post in his sights, when some fresh Federal divisions entered the fray. They came to the battle as the Tennesseans had—in the confusion, more by chance than by design. The divisions of Major General James S. Negley and Major General Joseph J. Reynolds had been marching north themselves, on the way to help Thomas in his fighting, when they came upon Old Straight. For only the briefest moment, then, did Stewart get to savor the Widow Glenn's house in his sights. To top it off, Brannan's division appeared after hearing the terrible racket, and now it was three divisions to one against Stewart.

Negley and Reynolds had done a smart right face while Brannan's men rushed in from above. Stewart had to backpedal in a hurry. Tennesseans by nature do not favor backpedaling, and it was with a heavy heart—the grand Federal command post before them, Rosecrans probably peeking out the window—that they fell back into the dark woods from which they had just emerged a few minutes before like savages. They were not whooping now. Securing themselves behind trees and shrouded by shadows, they stopped the Federal charge. The Yankees might have trouble shaking them out of the woods, but they were weary beyond telling and could not imagine charging again. The Rebels held their ground, firing in a dissolute manner, as the September 19 sun lowered just a trifle more.

Then came Hood from Kentucky, who led a band of Texans. He had been champing at the bit on the left of Stewart, just across the Chickamauga and west of Alexander's Bridge with his division. He had no orders to attack—who knew exactly where anyone was fighting anyhow?—but he knew that where a racket was there was action. On his own, asking no one's permission, he put the divisions of boyish-looking E. McIvor Law on one side of him and the redoubtable Bushrod Johnson on the other and got set to charge into the cauldron—wherever it was, whatever it was. Hood reined his steed with his one arm and gave the command to charge into the woods and fight whoever they found. It was four in the afternoon, and they couldn't wait to get at the Yankees once again, these hardened veterans of the unholy fighting in Virginia and at Gettysburg. It might seem, in a more gentle time, that they would have seen enough blood and splintered limbs and disemboweled bodies to last a lifetime—but this view would leave out the unreasoning hatred they had for those in blue. No devil, no tyrant, no idea was ever so viscerally scorned as a *Yankee*. Pluck every limb from Hood (and that would eventually almost be the case) and he would still keep, as they say in Texas, "a-comin."

If anybody liked to fight (or talk about it) more than Tennesseans, it was Texans. Hood's Texans soon met up with those bone-weary Tennesseans who were standing their ground in the woods against the blue line. Some were lying down, panting, exhausted from their charge and hasty retreat, bug-eyed from what they had seen of what men at arms could do to one another. Their supine position was a merry sight for the Texans, one of whom called out, "Rise up, Tennesseans, and see the Texans go in!" These Texans practically skipped into action as the beaten-down Tennesseans watched the gray backs of their comrades disappear into swirling gunsmoke. The Texans screamed, periodically raised their muskets to get off a round, and drove headlong into a lone Federal division about a mile south of where Old Straight had struck.

The blue division they met was under the command of Brigadier General Jefferson C. Davis, who had something of the severeness of his more prominent namesake on the other side. He had shot a fellow officer, Major General William Nelson, in cold blood at point-blank range when he fancied he had been rudely treated by Nelson. It was earlier in the war, in a busy bustling hotel lobby in Louisville, that Davis had heated words with Nelson. Nelson, who weighed 300 pounds, had a mean temper himself, and after he called Davis "an insolent puppy" (and Davis had thrown a dirty wadded-up calling card in his face), had laid the back of a large red hand across Davis's firm and jutting jaw. Davis had immediately borrowed a pistol from a fellow guest in the hotel and then accosted Nelson in a deserted second-story hallway. Nelson, who played more by the rules than did Davis, never had a chance. He was shot clean through his massive body from eight feet away. Somehow a team was able to heft Nelson's bulk onto a hotel bed, whereupon the mortally wounded man called for a preacher to baptize him. He then said: "I have been basely murdered." In less than an hour he left this world. Davis was never tried for murder; was half-heartedly reprimanded, if that; and was soon back on the field, killing all and sundry. As Lincoln would testify, fighting generals were prized and in short supply in the North then.

Now Davis stood at the center of the Federal line where Hood's men were directing their attention. His blueclad division soon found itself outflanked; heavy pressure was being exerted at its center and heart. Davis fought in his sleepy-eyed deadly manner, but numbers counted here, not willpower. He was being outgunned and pushed back. So once again that day the Confederates had broken through, had crossed the La Fayette Road, and were on their way to glory. Once again Rosecrans was puffing on a cigar, looking out the parlor window at Widow Glenn's—and here the sons of bitches came again! Smoke, shells—*boom, boom, boom*—and the Rebels were two steps from his front yard. If Bragg had known that the Federal center had collapsed, he could have thrown his whole might there and crushed Rosecrans for good. But he was nowhere near. Bragg was hunkered down in a deep dark glade several miles away—not for safety but because he had no idea where the action was or where to go to find out. He might as well have been in Charleston and communicating by telegraph. He knew nothing and did nothing; the battle continued to rage like an animal of its own accord.

Hood was coming close, close enough almost to sniff the aroma of Rosecrans's cigar, when suddenly, miraculously, a pair of Federal divisions appeared as if in a vision. They charged into the Rebels, firearms popping and drowning the Rebels' strange screeching. Wood's division of Thomas Crittenden's corps led the counterattack, rushing in from Lee and Gordon's Mills, followed quickly by Philip Sheridan's troops, who came up from Crawfish Springs. Together they forced Hood to consider whether a further stay in the open field was prudent, whether it might not be wise to back into the safety of the dark woods from whence they had sprung. Only moments before they were tearing up a thin blue line before them; now they were the ones scattering back. Wilder's men had jumped in the fight, too, leveling their mystifying rapid-fire carbines on them. And banty-rooster Sheridan, never happier than when he was astride a steed, saber out and raised, pressed his men to slaughter these revolutionaries who dared advance their tawdry cause against the might of the United States of America.

Hood's Texans, the wind knocked out of them, ended up as the Tennesseans had before them. Nothing had changed—save lives lost and bodies mangled. It could have been otherwise. Two other Rebel divisions were in the area—Simon Bolivar Buckner's and Thomas C. Hindman's—but they had no orders to come to Hood's aid. In fact, they had no idea who was slam-banging whom in those forbidding dark woods. They listened, they suspected a grand spectacle going on, but made no move. They had no orders. It was best not to fall into a trap. Let whoever was in there handle it themselves. They could perhaps have turned the tide and broken through the center and straight through Rosecrans's heart. But they tarried, and Hood, with no overall commander on the scene, had to go it on his own.

Bragg was not still, though; it wasn't in his nature. At his dark glade headquarters, he kept worrying about his right where the battle had started and where he thought it was more or less confined. He was also fretting that someone who should be fighting wasn't.

Someone somewhere was asleep or drunk. As his spirits sank, his exasperation rose. What was General Daniel H. Hill doing? This wasn't Virginia anymore! Impulsively, Bragg called for Irishman Patrick Cleburne to take his feisty division from Hill's corps and go fight on the right. It wouldn't hurt. Cleburne, a native of the Emerald Isle, who was practically born with a pistol in his hand, didn't have to be asked twice. He led his men, their rifles raised, across the bone-chilling Chickamauga, where the water sometimes rose to a man's nose. On the west bank they shook off the water like dogs, turned right, and started north. They heard the furious banging of Hood's assault but—again—no orders to strike at the middle. They had been ordered north, and they were going north. They were soldiers. Hood had no idea aid was so near, and he did not try to stay his men from retreat. He had ended up like Old Straight Stewart and was thrown back into the gloaming. His men staggered right past the Tennesseans, whose spirits at last rose at the sight of these whipped Texans. They hadn't forgotten the jibes thrown their way and the bravado with which their fellow countrymen had gone in. "Rise up, Tennesseans," one called, "and see the Texans come out!" Even Hood decided to call it a day, for the sun was sinking. "Just hold 'em off, boys. We'll get 'em tomorrow."

Cleburne's men weren't stopped by the conventions and caprices of the sun, though. They hadn't been really in the fight, and they continued moving toward the northern perimeter of the battle, planning to give Old Pap Thomas's army as good a surprise as possible. Cleburne himself was not conventional. Like Forrest, he was not a West Pointer. He came by his tactical knowledge on his own, an autodidact, and his truculence as well. At first glance he seemed an unlikely candidate to be leading a large body of men to fight in some dark woods near the Tennessee–Georgia border. Born in County Cork on March 17, 1828, of Protestant forebears, he studied at Trinity College in Dublin, hoping to become a doctor. But he failed his examinations and joined a British infantry regiment in a pique because he was at a loss for anything better to do, gaining the rank of corporal and serving three years. At twenty-one he was still undecided about his future. He went to America, taking along some family members for company. (One of his brothers later fought for the North.) Pat Cleburne eventually landed in Arkansas and gradually made a name for himself, in the American success-story tradition, rising from a drugstore clerk to a prominent attorney. He became a large landowner and was outspoken about the evils of slavery. He took part in Arkansas politics and helped organize an outfit out of Helena, Arkansas, when war was declared. Soon he introduced British foot soldiering, which he had learned many years before, into the Confederacy. He was a spectacular drillmaster, rolling his r's to the utter delight of his troops. He carried a heavy brogue to his death. "All right, me lads, For-r-re-ward Mar-r-rch." The recruits from the hills of Arkansas had never heard such language and were charmed. He was an emotional Irishman who took the cause of the Confederacy as much to heart as any Mississippi plantation blueblood or Charleston squire, even though he viewed slavery with distaste. He shouted to his troops before the battle of Tupelo: "If this cause which is so dear to my heart is doomed to fail, I pray heaven may let me fall with it, while my face is turned to the enemy and my arm battling for that which I know to be right." He first commanded a regiment; then a brigade; and now, at Chickamauga, a division, and always his troops called themselves "Old Pat's boys." At this point in the war he was showing his scars: an ugly scar around his mouth where he had been wounded at Richmond, Kentucky, a wobbling gait because of a leg wound at Perryville.

On the other side, at its northern rim, Old Pap Thomas went about his duties with his usual laid-back efficiency. He knew they were coming. Something in the wind, some quietness in the air he couldn't explain, made him strain his eyes and cock his ear. At the far left he placed the divisions of Generals Absalom Baird and

Richard A. Johnson, on the rim, the outer perimeter, telling them that he expected an attack there before the day was out. Down from them the divisions of John McCauley Palmer, Joseph J. Reynolds, and Brannan spread, ready to come to their aid if needed. The sun sank slowly, inch by inch, behind Missionary Ridge, and throughout the ranks an exhaling of breath could almost be heard. Not today, Nellie. They weren't coming. Old Pap was too cautious, but thank God for him. The blueclads began leaning against trees, squatting, gossiping, roughhousing, the way relaxed armies have always done. Darkness was creeping over the land. Just then, as they became more concerned with the chilly air than the Rebels, five thousand yelping racing Confederates came at them out of the woods. The noise itself knocked them back. A fearsome explosion of musketry shook the firmament. Three Rebel brigades were lined up, elbow to elbow, in a one-mile line. They meant business. One Alabamian remembered its awesomeness to his dying day. "It seemed," he recalled, "as if all the fires on earth and hell had been turned loose." The big bang lodged so firmly in his mind that every time he had a head cold thereafter, all the booming cannons and yells boomeranged once again through his cerebrum right down his sinuses.

The battle became hallucinatory, another world. Men on both sides felt the urgent need to fire so intently that they often left their iron ramrods in the gun barrels and fired away, sending the irreplaceable tools forward. Later the trees of the battlefield were dotted with these bent ramrods as if by the remains of an arrow attack. The battle was fast becoming uncontrollable. The laggards could now fall back in the darkness without fear of a reprimand. The men sometimes, unhappily, kept firing and striking their own comrades in front. Confederate artillery, which had the chance now to level the surprised Yankees, shot too high in the fading light and took out high timber instead of soldiers. Their main effect was to bring tree limbs and trunks down on their enemy. A pale quarter moon shone now, and a mountain mist was mixing with the gunpowder and dust. In the confusion a Pennsylvania regiment rushed over a crest and opened fire on the first body of troops it found; unfortunately, it was a Hoosier outfit, and it took time, with much screaming and couriers rushing back and forth, to straighten things out and push on. The Northerners weren't about to be thrown into full retreat. No, sir, not by these dimwitted savages who came bursting out of the woods like hyenas. They fixed their lines as best they could in the dimness and met the Southerners, rifle for rifle. Before long, there was hardly any separation between the enemies. They formed one great maelstrom of fighting humanity. When there was no room to fire, they went at each other with gun butts and bayonets. If all else failed, they threw their hands around each other's throats. Blue and gray uniforms ceased to identify the fighters—any figure was a likely enemy. Brigadier General Preston Smith was moving his Confederate brigade forward to support another command that was falling back when he ran across some troops at a halt. "Get out of our way! Clear this ground!" They turned and shot him dead. They were Yankees.

A Union bugler, William J. Carson, was not content simply to sound Forward, Rally, and To the Colors. He couldn't restrain himself and finally flung his bugle away to fly into action with both a sword and a musket. He won a Medal of Honor that day. Earlier that day, Bob Stout, of the First Tennessee, had not been so lucky. He had become so certain he would not last through the battle that he had refused rations and asked that some keepsakes be sent home to his family. For a while he didn't receive as much as a nick in the bloody fighting. While he was reclining during a lull in some incoming cannonade, a buddy called over: "Bob, you weren't killed as you expected." Right then a shot sounded from the other side. A minié ball disemboweled Stout, and his premonition proved true.

The Union held. Pat Cleburne may have wanted to fight more, but he couldn't see who to fight. After an hour of freelance dueling in the dark, he called it quits. His men simply settled down on the ground where they were and prepared for what rest they could manage amid the cries of the mangled and the dying. Thomas had been pushed back about a mile in a few places, but that was all. His men settled in for the night, too. A bone-chilling night air covered them, and they shivered under whatever rag or blanket they could throw over themselves. It had been one hell of a fight this September 19, but not much had been decided. Tomorrow was another day.

5

The Luck of the South

MORNING: SEPTEMBER 20, 1863

Armies seldom fight where those responsible for the fight itself—the political decision makers—have ensconced themselves and call for a fight. Soldiers have found themselves on tiny burned-out atolls in the Pacific, in desolate snowy retreat from Moscow, and sunk in muddy trenches at Ypres. War is capricious in determining its whereabouts. Who would have picked wooded, vine-clogged land that was but a few years from Cherokee dominance to play host to perhaps the most brutal and strategically important battle of the Civil War? Someone from an Indiana farm or small Kentucky town now found himself under a cold quarter moon in a wooded no-man's-land with no idea what God or his superiors intended. Modern studies have shown that the more intelligent a soldier, the harder he fights. These soldiers, blue and gray, sure must have been smart.

Many of General Patrick Cleburne's men were still wet from crossing the Chickamauga. Their bodies shook and their teeth chattered, but they could not light fires. They were too close to the enemy, and a spark in the night might send an immediate volley their way. They were cold and thirsty. There is one constant in every battle—thirst; all chroniclers of that frightful hazard mention the urgent need for water. From Thermopylae to Ia Drang, there has been an unbroken record of pathetic whimperings for water on the battlefield, and not just the wounded and dying, but from all soldiers. The Confederates had crossed the Chickamauga and drunk its muddied waters. The Federals brought up 1,000 canteens full of spring water from Crawfish Springs. The delivery was made at midnight. Others made it down to a fetid pond in back of the Widow Glenn's, locally known as "the Sink" but soon to be baptized "Bloody Pond." The pond didn't get the name because of any fighting done there, but because men who had dragged themselves to its banks from the fighting often bled into it and turned its clay borders a dark red. A captain in Colonel John T. Wilder's brigade had been badly wounded in the fight that day and had lain down where he was hit. In the night his wound froze to the ground, and he had to be carefully chopped loose the next morning. The wounded moaned through the night and here and there a scavenger picked the pockets of the fallen—friend or foe. Most did not sleep at all this night. Who could, except those beyond exhaustion. The Rebels listened through the night to Federal axes plunking into wood where fortifications were going up. It was not an enjoyable sound for a man on the other side to hear. All knew that the battle would resume the next morning and that many of them would die.

Lieutenant General James Longstreet—big, gruff, and bearded—had detrained that afternoon at Catoosa a few miles south of the battle. No one from Braxton Bragg's staff was there to meet and guide him in. He fumed: What sort of outfit was this? Furthermore, he was without a horse and had to wait two hours for the next train with horses aboard. One thing in his favor was that he never tired, even after the long trek from Virginia; anyhow, fighting, something that he had great familiarity with, was near at hand, and he must find it. With two members of his staff, he plunged into the woods to find Bragg. The quarter moon broke through the branches now and then, but mostly he was swallowed in darkness. Ahead he heard the report of shots and an occasional cannonade. Vision was reduced to looming shadows and an occasional glimpse of the road that was to take them to Confederate headquarters. Every now and then they stumbled off the road, into briar and bramble and low limbs. All at once, some shadows moved and muffled voices sounded. Longstreet did not wait to be challenged. He reined in and called out, "What regiment is this?"

A number was bellowed out proudly. Longstreet kept his horse reined in. He knew all too well that Yankees gave numbers to their regiments whereas Southern ones went by their commanders' names. Lieutenant General Longstreet, fresh to Chickamauga, had just stumbled on a Federal outpost. But no one ever accused Longstreet of being dumb—or not wily. "Let us ride down a little way to find a better crossing," he sang out in a casual voice.

He and his aides wheeled and headed for the cover of some large trees and then regained the main road and galloped off to find Bragg. They found Bragg at around eleven o'clock, asleep in his ambulance, snoring above the distant gunfire and done for the day. One can only wonder at the pleasure Longstreet felt to wake the man who had sent no escort to meet him at Catoosa and who now was sawing logs while Longstreet's belly was empty and yearning for supper. Bragg unwound his scrawny frame, rubbed his eyes, and then explained in his cranky, nervous way what the plan was for daybreak tomorrow. Glad to see you, Longstreet. The army was to be divided into two wings, one under Bishop Leonidas Polk on the ever-important right, and the other under Longstreet, who would take charge of the left. There were plenty of good men here now to give it to the Yankees. Under Polk would be Daniel H. Hill's corps of John Cabell Breckinridge and Cleburne's divisions, plus divisions of Benjamin F. Cheatham, William H. T. Walker, St. John R. Liddell, and States Rights Gist. Next would follow Nathan Bedford Forrest, who would be under Bragg's personal command. Longstreet would have the rest to form a sturdy and deadly left: the divisions of Alexander P. Stewart and William Preston in Simon Bolivar Buckner's corps, along with the divisions of Bushrod Johnson and Thomas C. Hindman; John Bell Hood's corps was there, too, with the divisions of E. McIver Law and Joseph Brevard Kershaw. Little Joe Wheeler's cavalry was in place on the left to ward off the Federal cavalry. In effect, here was an army that was stretched out for over four miles. Polk, at the north end, would begin the battle, and the other troops would follow, right down the line. Polk would begin turning the blueclads at the north end (the enemy's left) at first light and would force them finally into the not-forgotten McLemore's Cove. Turn their flank and move them back in a swinging-door fashion—the same battle plan as always. It couldn't be more simple. Once again, the attack starts on the right and then moves right down the line. There is no room for misunderstanding and confusion. Simple.

Longstreet wouldn't have minded an offer of at least some coffee, if a hot meal was too much to expect. Maybe a jovial word or two would have helped, but he had come to the wrong command for that. At one time, before he lost his wife and three young children, Longstreet had been a sunny man himself. He just wanted to perform his tasks now, keep on a dogged path, and guard himself from emotion. He warmed himself at the campfire and then he rode through the woods during the darkest part of the night to return to his troops. It was all plain and simple, yes, but let us not forget one thing: Braxton Bragg was in charge.

Over at the Widow Glenn's, in the glow of lamplight, the Federal commander called a council of war at eleven o'clock. William Starke Rosecrans was known as a man who liked to burn the midnight oil; in fact, he flourished as the hour lengthened and the talk waxed philosophical. Brigadier General James A. Garfield, his chief of staff now, and U.S. president-to-be eighteen years hence, opened the council by unfolding a map that more or less pinpointed the positions of the two armies. The armies faced each, hardly a hairbreadth apart, that much was clear. What to do in the morning was the next item of business. Officers and orderlies moved about in the cramped space, tobacco smoke rose, and chairs creaked. Alexander M. McCook and Thomas L. Crittenden, two corps commanders, did their best to offer some insight, but their effort was more dutiful than inspired. The council was something they had to endure, rather than enjoy, at this point. McCook was once described by a fellow officer as having a grin that led to the "suspicion that he is either still very green or deficient in the upper story." Crittenden had been pegged early on as a man who was handy with the bottle, a good drinker, and someone who, drunk or sober, knew how to toot his own horn. McCook, age thirty-two, was a West Pointer and a captain in the regular army when the war started. He had taught tactics at West Point that had led others to believe he could put into practice what he had taught. They were wrong. This night McCook and Crittenden were somewhat chagrined because two of their divisions had taken such a mauling on George H. Thomas's left flank that afternoon. The wild screech of the Southerners still rang in their ears. They leaned forward, good natured, soldiers through and through.

Lieutenant General Thomas, the third corps commander present, sensibly nodded off when the palaver became too heavy. Take sleep where you find it—he had done the same thing at a Stone's River council. But he kept some antenna working, for when Rosecrans pointed a tactical question at him, he opened his eyes, spoke one sentence—"I would strengthen the left"—then fell back asleep. When Rosecrans asked where the men would come from, Thomas slept on.

Rosecrans was not going to retreat—he made that clear; retreat was not an option. But he couldn't be sure what the Southerners' intentions were. Maybe *they* would back off and go farther into Georgia. It was up to Bragg. For his part, Rosecrans wanted his ten-division line of battle squeezed closer together. Gordon Granger's three-brigade reserve force should guard Rossville Gap (which was an escape valve back to Chattanooga if it came to it), but it could come forward if an emergency arose. Thomas would stand in place with his five divisions, and McCook would move his two up against Negley's one, right against Thomas. Crittenden would solidify the center or be ready to move on the qui vive wherever needed. The memory was still fresh of the screaming Rebels charging to within an axe handle of Widow Glenn's parlor where the Federals now comfortably sat. Defense was the overriding concern now, and it could be accomplished if the divisions stayed relatively close together, kept full contact, and were set to counterpunch. Did everyone agree? Thomas slept, and the others nodded.

Trusty Garfield was called upon to put all the details in writing, and then the plan was read out loud in final form, so everyone, excluding Thomas, heard it presented formally one more time. All right, so much for business. Fresh cigars came out, and steaming coffee appeared. Old Rosey was no Bragg. He knew how to be a host; he did not cotton to being alone at any time. Now at midnight, on the eve of the bloodiest of bloody battles, McCook was tapped to provide a little divertissement—a song. McCook had the generous round figure of an opera singer, and he belted out a favorite number of the time—"The Hebrew Maiden's Lament." Of German origin, the song told the story of a Jewish girl who was torn between her faith and her love for a *goy*. She held true to her faith in the last stanza and bid the forlorn gentile adieu. *Ah thou seest not the bitter, bitter tears I shed for thee!* McCook belted out.

Rosecrans's war council and social hour broke up at two in the morning. Somewhat refreshed by his nap during the proceedings, Thomas left to take stock of his position and to hear the thoughts of his subordinates. There would be no time for anyone to sleep until that task was done. Absalom Baird had some gnawing doubts that he would be able to extend his line to Reed's Bridge as he'd been instructed to do. He thought that his line would be stretched a little too thin—for fresh in his mind, hardly cooled from a few hours before, was the unholy sight of Cleburne's banshees erupting out of the woods at twilight. The line should be strong enough to restrain such maniacs, or the whole Federal force would be sunk. Thomas agreed—in the moonlight, a couple of hours before sunup—and he immediately sent a runner galloping to Rosecrans to ask that Negley, who'd come in the nick of time to shore up the center that afternoon, should be instructed to resume march and to aid Thomas's position on the left. Sleep? No, no, not quite yet. Rosecrans was still lively in the lamplit parlor at Widow Glenn's, and he sent word back that the request was approved. It wasn't too difficult to get ebullient Old Rosey to agree to most anything—a nightcap warming his esophagus, the floor of the parlor creaking from the many boots, in the heart of the night. Negley would move at first light.

After receiving word from Rosecrans and checking on his last outpost, Thomas took to his bed, which turned out to be the soft earth beneath a spreading oak. He rested his square-bearded face against a slightly protruding root, using it as a pillow, and drifted off as spotty gunfire echoed through the woods. He had hardly closed his eyes when a fierce red sun rose on that Sunday, September 20, the air still smoky from yesterday's fighting. Thomas came awake with a start, the first thought on his mind the last one he had before drifting off. Negley: Where was he? The sun increased in redness and rose an hour above the landline, and still no Negley. There came an upright figure in a gold-braided blue jacket, though, his steed prancing and being reined in from time to time. It was Rosecrans, going among the troops, an act he was comfortable with. He sung out the words: "Fight today as well as you did yesterday, and we shall whip them!" He was optimistic and full of good cheer, with a wave and a smile to all, but his face was puffy and haggard looking and hardly went with his words. "I did not like the way he looked," a soldier later recalled. At the Widow Glenn's, Garfield had risen to the blood-red sun and said, "This will indeed be a day of blood."

That day Bragg awoke expecting that the thunder of battle would soon erupt from his right, where Bishop Polk's troops had been given the task of starting the fireworks. Polk would charge, and then right down the line, the others would follow suit. It was all very military, rather unimaginative, and hardly subject to misunderstanding. Before daybreak Bragg rolled from his camp bed, dressed by moonlight, mounted his horse, and waited for light to break, surrounded by his staff. Perhaps in his heart of hearts he expected a foul-up, perhaps deep down in the murky wilderness of his soul he sought it—disaster: It happened frequently enough. But, then, it would have been miraculous if timetables had literally been held to in this gigantic evolving battle. Two vast armies, each larger by far than the combined populations of Chattanooga and Atlanta, faced each other in deep primitive woods not far from a creek bank. It would have been unusual for everything to have gone off like clockwork, to have proceeded as the commanders on either side had wished. Yet there are tolerable limits to what any man can stomach.

Bragg dispatched an aide to find out what the hell was holding up Polk. Are we going to fight or not? Bragg was hearing not the sound of gunfire from beyond, but sawing and hammering as the Yankees across the way were putting the finishing touches to the breastworks they had started the night before. What kind of warfare was this anyhow? The aide galloped off over dewy ground and early morning haze. He reined in his horse at a farmhouse three miles from the Confederate line of troops, three miles from Polk's corps. On the farmhouse's upper-story gallery, in the pleasant early-morning sunshine, he found the bishop. Polk was in a relaxed state, feet up, reading a newspaper, waiting for his hot breakfast to be served. A handsome man with a full head of wavy graying hair and strong Roman features, he always seemed on the verge of giving a benediction or asking that the fried chicken be passed. Bragg's aide wasted no time telling him that his commander wished for him to make an attack promptly and with his full force. As instructed. Then the aide remounted and galloped back to his dyspeptic commander with the news of Polk with his feet up, the newspaper out, and his lips smacking in anticipation of a rasher of bacon and fried eggs. Bragg cursed, startling those around him. The commander had been baptized not long before and had manfully held his barracks oaths in check through some harrowing times. Now he let fly: *Goddamsonofabitch!* The bishop could drive a man to drink or murder. Bragg himself now rode off to find Polk and do to him he knew not what.

But Bragg did not find Polk. Instead, he found an empty chair on the farmhouse balcony and the breakfast dishes cleared. The good bishop had departed for the front lines, leaving these words behind: "Do tell General Bragg that my heart is overflowing with anxiety for the attack. Overflowing with anxiety, sir."

Another screeching curse issued forth from the commander—but he hadn't heard the whole story. Now he learned for the first time that the night before, moody dissatisfied Hill had not been able to find either headquarters or Polk, his superior. Here was a corps commander who couldn't find squat and who was still in a pet over being in what he perceived to be an inferior position. (Why, asked Hill, wasn't he a wing commander? He had been given a corps, and *he was a lieutenant general of the Confederate army!*) Polk in his majesty had sent a lowly courier in the night to find Hill and inform him of the battle plans for that dawn. That was it, just a low-ranking courier, riding off to tell Hill to start fighting at dawn. But though the courier had searched and searched through the dark woods, he did not find Hill. He had wearily reported back to hapless Polk in the early morning while the bishop was digging into his famous breakfast. That was when Polk wiped his mouth, left his few words for Bragg, and took off for the front. He sent a message ahead for Breckinridge and Cleburne to start the battle.

Bragg got there first. Perhaps his anger made him whip his horse more—or he knew a shortcut—but, in any event, he rode ahead of the pack to where Hill had planted his corps' flag, halfway between Breckinridge's and Cleburne's divisions. At last, the elusive Hill— and Yankees a few hundred yards in front. Bragg found Confederate troops, though, not in battle formation but just sitting down to breakfast, as if this were a regular Sunday morning before church. With cold fury, he asked sad-eyed Hill why he hadn't attacked at dawn. With great satisfaction, from one who believes himself terribly wronged and bossed by yahoos to boot, Hill replied that he knew nothing about any dawn battle. At dawn? You don't say. As he later wrote in his account of events at Chickamauga, "I was hearing then for the first time that such an order had been issued and had not known whether we were to be the assailants or the assailed." Bragg would have chewed a rug if one had been handy. His stomach could not take much more. To top it off, here came Bishop Polk riding up. Soon both Polk and Bragg were entreating Hill to get cracking. To the south, Old Pete Longstreet was trotting his horse up and down his lines waiting for the battle to begin, waiting to hear the shots that would send his troops into battle. All he heard was the random fire of pickets. Farther along, Hill kept delaying. He slowly lined up his troops and saw to it that ammunition was carefully packed, that flags were unfurled, and that cannon were properly lined up. The sun rose higher. At nine-thirty, he nodded to the Kentuckian Breckinridge, whose division moved out to battle. Fifteen minutes later, he nodded to Cleburne, whose division followed suit. The fight began.

Many men, of widely varying backgrounds and points of view, stood in that dense woodland. Confederate Private Sam R. Watkins had awakened to watch the sun rise "clear and beautiful." The sun had that look about it that Southerners know well—a Sabbath-day look. But no one was dressing for church. "The battlefield was in a rough and broken country, with trees and undergrowth, that ever since the creation had never been disturbed by the ax of civilized man. It looked wild, weird, uncivilized."

On the other side stood a junior officer in the Ninth Indiana, Ambrose Bierce. He had been born in a log cabin in Ohio where his dirt-poor father had poured more money into books than into bridles and a plow and thus had paved the way for his talented son's march into American letters. Bierce witnessed the savagery of Chickamauga firsthand, as opposed to Stephen Crane, who was not born when the fighting at Chancellorsville, which he so brilliantly evoked, took place. Bierce never wrote the equal of *The Red Badge of Courage*, but his work shines with authenticity the way more lauded and popular works of the Civil War do not. Bierce was there.

In his short story "Chickamauga," the gore of battle has seldom been made as plain and graphic. A child who is a deaf-mute wanders from his nearby farmhouse onto the battlefield, and the sound-less scene is described through his eyes. He observes the broken and maimed who wander away from the carnage, but he is not certain about what he is witnessing:

He moved among them freely, going from one to another and peering into their faces with childish curiosity. All their faces were singularly white and many were streaked and gouted with red. Something in this— something, too, perhaps, in their grotesque attitudes and movements—

reminded him of the painted clown whom he had seen last summer in the circus, and he laughed as he watched them. But on and ever on they crept, these maimed and bleeding men, as heedless as he of the dramatic contrast between his laughter and their own ghastly gravity. . . . He now approached one of these crawling figures from behind and with an agile movement mounted it astride. The man sank upon his breast, recovered, flung the small boy fiercely to the ground as an unbroken colt might have done, then turned upon him a face that lacked a lower jaw—from the upper teeth to the throat was a great red gap fringed with hanging shreds of flesh and splinters of bone. The unnatural prominence of nose, the absence of chin, the fierce eyes, gave this man the appearance of a great bird of prey crimsoned in throat and breast by the blood of its quarry. . . . And so the clumsy multitude dragged itself slowly, and painfully along in hideous pantomime—moved forward down the slope like a swarm of great black beetles, with never a sound of going—in silence profound, absolute.

The very name—*Chickamauga*—captures it: the River of Death. Add to it the lonesome primitive woods and two huge armies unleashed at one another's throats. Thomas Wolfe, from the hills of North Carolina, was another author who fell under the spell of the battle. He took down the words of his great-uncle who had fought there and fictionalized it in a story called, like Bierce's, "Chickamauga":

We seed some big fights in the war. And we was in some bloody battles. But the biggest fight we fought was Chickamauga. The bloodiest fight I ever seed was Chickamauga. Thar was big battles in the war, but thar never was a fight before, that'll never be a fight again, like Chickamauga. I'm goin' to tell you how hit was at Chickamauga. . . .

The Battle of Chickamauga was fought in a cedar thicket. That cedar thicket, from what I knowed of hit was about three miles long and one mile wide. We fought fer two days all up and down that thicket and to and fro across hit. When the fight started that cedar thicket was so thick and dense you could a-took a butcher knife and drove hit in that anywheres and hit would a-stuck. And when that fight was over that cedar thicket had been so destroyed by shot and shell you could a-looked in thar anywheres with your naked eye and seed a black snake run a hundred yards away. If you'd a-looked at that cedar thicket the day after that fight was over you'd a-wondered how a hummin' bird the size of your thumbnail could a-flown through thar without bein' torn into pieces by the fire. And yet more than half of us who went into that thicket came out of hit alive and told the tale. You wouldn't have thought that hit was possible. But I was thar and seed hit, and hit was.

Colonel George Humphreys of the Eighty-eighth Indiana stood in the eye of the storm, facing the Southern attack. He was a Scotsman who had been born in the same house as the poet Robert Burns. The blueclad Humphreys was a Scot through and through, carrying his truculent temperament with him when he immigrated to this shore. He had joined the Union cause with alacrity when Bragg and Edmund Kirby Smith had invaded Kentucky and threatened to go farther. Humphreys wasn't about to let some harebrained Southerners take away his Scottish right—his right to self-determination. He didn't like the idea of being invaded. (Strangely enough, quite a few Scots in the South didn't like the idea of Northerners invading *them*.)

Humphreys's Eighty-eighth Indiana was a pivotal part of Brigadier General John Beatty's brigade on the far left of the Federal line, left of the breastworks that might slow the Rebels. Breckinridge's Southerners hit the Federal left in full fury where fortifications did not impede them. They hit with a bang. Down from them Brigadier General Benjamin Hardin Helm, of the South, brother-in-law of President Abraham Lincoln, of the North, threw his men against those breastworks, which contained everything the Federals had been able to cut down and pile up the night before—logs, brush, and tree trunks with sharpened ends pointing toward the enemy.

From the report of Brigadier General Charles Cruft, Army of the Cumberland: "By daylight of the morning of 20th, the various regiments of the brigade had constructed rough log breastworks along the front. There were but few tools in the hands of the men, but they worked cheerfully and industriously with what they had, and availed themselves of every device to provide some protection."

Helm—tall, slender, and dark, with an unmistakable aristocratic tilt to his head—carried himself well. From an old and distinguished Kentucky family—his father was governor of the state in the 1850s, his grandfather a U.S. congressman—he was deeply, immutably tied to the Cavalier South, a grave mistake, as it turned out. He was a West Pointer (entering at age sixteen), a Harvard man, and a lawyer. He came from Bardstown, where bourbon whiskey was cooked up. He might well have considered himself equal to his brother-in-law Lincoln—he had married Emily Todd, Mary Todd Lincoln's younger half sister, in 1856—and he certainly didn't kowtow to the ex-rail splitter. He voted against him for president and refused Lincoln's offer of a commission in the Federal army after Fort Sumter. Despite their political differences, the two brothers-in-law got along extremely well, but war was war. Lincoln tried to present Helm with a commission to be paymaster, a non-fighting post. Helm conferred with Robert E. Lee and Jefferson Davis and then recruited men for a Kentucky outfit, going off to war forever tied to the gray.

Helm fought extremely well at Chickamauga—right up to the end. His time in the fighting was short, only an hour or so, and furious. He sent most of his force against the breastworks while a regiment on his right, the Sixth Kentucky, and the Fourth Kentucky skirmishers, went for an exposed Federal flank on the right under Federal Brigadier General Beatty. Beatty's force included the Fifteenth Kentucky Federal regiment—and so here once again was Southerner against Southerner. The Fourth Confederate Kentucky was under Colonel Joseph P. Nuckols and the Fifteenth Federal

Kentucky was commanded by Colonel Marion C. Taylor: two gentlemen from the Bluegrass State who were trying to kill each other.

In the Sabbath sun, now clouded by wispy smoke and flying dirt, Kentuckian fought Kentuckian. They spoke the same language, had the same twang—and they couldn't have hated each other more. President Lincoln's favorite brother-in-law was struck in his right side by a Kentucky bullet. He slid from his horse to the ground, and everybody who saw him knew one thing: He was going to die. He fell into Federal hands, and later, after the Sabbath sun had set and one of the war's bloodiest days had passed, the cavalier Helm died. Upon hearing the news, Lincoln was more moved by this Confederate death than by any other in the war. That was the kind of war it was; that was the kind of man he was. Lincoln had been charmed by the lanky, drawling Helm when Helm had visited him in Springfield. He could get off a good one around him (always a requirement with Lincoln for companionship), and Helm was not only family but someone with whom he could talk law. He was Youth, he was Family, he was the Best and Brightest of the South, a South of which Lincoln was so much a part. The crowning item perhaps was that Lincoln fondly remembered lifting Emily Todd Helm when she was a child in Lexington. Now she was a widow. "I never saw Mr. Lincoln more moved than when he heard of the death of his young brother-in-law," someone in the White House said, having observed the president a short time after he got the news. "I saw how grief stricken he was so I closed the door and left him."

At Chickamauga it was the woods, always the dark beguiling woods. Who knew what was going on when you could not see either the enemy or your own troops? Who was who and what was happening? From Sam Watkins: ". . . our nerves strung to their utmost tension, listening to the roar of battle in our immediate front, to hear it rage and then get dimmer until it seems to die out entirely; then all at once it breaks out again, and you think now in a very few minutes you will be ordered into action, and then all at once we go double-quicking to another portion of the field, the battle raging back from the position we had left."

The action flew pell-mell, back and forth, on the Confederate right and the Federal left. The battle was a cauldron that beckoned to the mad and fearless—the believers. Confederate Brigadier General Daniel W. Adams drove against the outer northern rim of the Federal defense—the space clear of breastwork. Here comes Adams! He was born hotheaded in Kentucky, and age and near-mortal wounds had neither slowed him nor sweetened his disposition. He lost an eye at Shiloh and took a round of hot lead at Stone's River, and still he kept coming! He and his brother William (also a brigadier general) came from Kentucky, like Helm, and both had the distinction of unceasing, unmitigated hostility to the press— military men ahead of their time. Back home, Daniel had fought a duel with an editor and shot him dead. Brother William suffered a reverse fate when an editor shot him dead after the war on a street in Jackson, Mississippi—the sword mightier in his hand than the editorial pen. Now, at Chickamauga, the band of an Alabama regiment struck up martial music (something to put fire in your gut and a way to lose reason), and Daniel Adams charged once more into the furnace, and once more with the same result: He was shot right out of the saddle. Unlike other times, though, he was captured and carted away.

The Rebels followed the plan, and they didn't follow the plan. Bragg, who had cooked up the ingenious plan to strike in a series of attacks right down the line, was stalled at the top, the Confederate right. The weakest point in the Federal line was on the outermost northern rim, but, although Hill—gloomy, smart, and tart tongued— might have sensed that the Union's vulnerability lay there, he didn't have the will to say, to hell with it and Bragg, and to rush his troops there to clobber the enemy. The plan was the plan! Brigadier General Lucius E. Polk hurled himself and his men against the middle bulge of the breastwork in mid-morning. A fine nephew of the bishop, Leonidas Polk, Lucius was a sturdy piece of aristocratic Southern manhood. He went in with dash and daring, knowing he was right and expecting to prevail. Prevail he did—at first, and spectacularly. "I never witnessed a more enthusiastic charge, and it carried everything before it," Captain William Cairnes, of his staff, who charged beside him, later said. "It carried everything before it." First they hit a blue skirmish line—serious, deadpan Federals, who promptly popped some rounds at them and then were beaten back. Still in a full rush, Polk's gray brigade met a log barricade, the famed Federal breastwork, and began leaping across it and pushing it aside. By God, they were coming. Look out!

"Go back and tell the old general [Bishop Polk was fifty-seven, his nephew, thirty]," Lucius said, in fine fettle, to Captain Cairnes, "that we have passed two lines of breastworks; that we have got them on the jump, and I am sure of carrying the main line."

Like everyone—or perhaps better than most at this particular moment—Lucius Polk was seeing a piece of the battle at Chicka-mauga. He couldn't see the main sweep. Who could? But he believed he was about to defeat the Army of the Cumberland. Cairnes tore his horse through branch and bramble and found the bishop in a glade conferring with Major General Cheatham. When he heard the good news from his nephew, he turned to Cheatham, the Tennessean, and said: "General, move your division and attack at once." There was a roar from that direction that must mean a breakthrough. Cheatham had five brigades at the ready—over 5,000 men—and he was ready, as always, to fight. "Forward, boys, and give them hell!" the Tennessean screamed. The bishop could slaughter in the spirit of the Old Testament, but he could not curse. "Do as General Cheatham says, boys!" Off these troops went, to decimate the Yankees.

What no one in the glade knew—what no one could know who wasn't there on the spot—was that Lucius Polk's brigade had met a further line of blue that would not bend. No dash, no charge, no amount of lead and steel could turn it. No Episcopalian with impeccable manners and a well of self-confidence could make it otherwise. The line held. Cheatham's broad mass, expecting a roadway into scurrying blueclads, found instead that the breastworks were not only still operating, but were operating in full deadly acceleration. Farther down, the hot-tempered Cleburne threw his two remaining brigades against the Federal breastworks. It was impossible to keep him out of the action. Lucius Polk, somewhere out of sight in the woods, now committed his entire division to the fight. His welcome turned out to be much hotter than when he had gone in. From the breastworks now came a bright glow with an orange center, a steady unremitting rain of firepower. It was the welcome of a glowing cauldron, the pit of an iron furnace. Anyone who dared poke his head in front of it went down.

The Rebels fired into the breastworks' wood, not dimming the glow at all, and soon they were running low on bullets. Colonel Robert Q. Mills, of the Sixth Texas, sent word to his brigade commander, James Deshler, of this dangerous state of affairs, and brave Deshler moved personally to check the ammunition supply down from him, putting himself for a moment in the open. He declined to send a staff member. Confederate Brigadier General James Deshler—West Point, class of 1854; son of Pennsylvanians who had moved to Alabama; a man who had seen a lot of action, from being seriously wounded at Cheat Mountain through the Seven Days' Campaign to save Richmond—had awakened on September 20, this Sunday, expecting to fight the Yankees once again and to do once again what he could to push them back to their homeland. Out in the open, before those Chickamauga breastworks, he took a shell in the chest. The shell literally took the heart right out of him, and he died on the spot. Colonel Mills, who had notified the general about the shortage of ammunition, went on to become a U.S. senator after the war.

Finally, at around 10:45 A.M., the entire right wing of the Confederate army was committed to breaking through the Federal left under Thomas. Bragg would have much to complain about later—and would, of course, do so—but he couldn't say that the Southerners didn't throw themselves into the fight once they were committed. It might have been hard to wake them up, but now that the sun had fully risen, they charged. Somewhere in the fight, as always, could be seen a tall handsome man in the saddle, in his white linen duster, his sword and pistol strapped to his side. When his cavalrymen went in with Breckinridge's division, they dismounted and advanced like seasoned infantrymen—kneel, fire, advance! Like a crack drill team. Hill, usually unimpressed with most mortals, caught sight of these undaunted fighting men. "What infantry is that?"

"Oh, that's Forrest's cavalry."

When Forrest himself rode up, the usually stern and abrasive Hill swept off his hat. "General Forrest," Hill said, "I wish to congratulate you and those brave men moving across that field like veteran infantry upon their magnificent behavior. In Virginia I made myself extremely unpopular with the cavalry because I said that so far I had not seen a dead man with spurs on. No one could speak disparagingly of such troops as yours."

Forrest was not a man of grandiloquent words. He was not, in today's lingo, a politically correct person. He was no cavalier; he was no Lee. He was simply Forrest. He once remarked, "I ain't no graduate of West Point, and never rubbed my back up against any college." He claimed that all his tactics, his successes, his generalship came from campaigning, learning on the job. In accepting the compliment from a corps commander, Hill, he simply waved his hand, wheeled his horse, and went back to business.

Try they all did to do in Thomas. No one can fault them. After the smoke lifted, ready answers flew as to why the Federal left held and Bragg's swinging-door assault failed: They all got started too late, Polk was reading his Sunday paper, Hill stayed petulant; they didn't attack en masse behind Breckinridge when his brigades happened to have made penetration through the breastworks, and so on. Later, of course, one and all imagined how Stonewall would have done it. He would have done it, they said, the way he did it at Chancellorsville. The only trouble was that he was taken from this earth as a result of Chancellorsville. No, the Southern troops didn't follow one consistent plan that morning, nor was there high invention and a grasping for advantage (à la Stonewall) when opportunity arose. An example: The reserve corps, under Major General Walker, came to Hill for assignment that morning. Instead of throwing the corps against Thomas's far left flank, as Bragg wanted, facing it down La Fayette Road, Hill sent it to relieve Breckinridge and Cleburne after they had battered themselves to a standstill against the breastworks.

It was as if they had slugged themselves out. Leading a fresh brigade was Colonel Peyton H. Colquitt, who brought in some eager Georgia and South Carolina troops. How they charged! Not long before, Colquitt had arrived at the Rome railway station with his men, hearing the sounds of battle in the distance. He hurried forward, leaving all his baggage behind. Only rifles and ammunition were needed! He was afraid he was going to miss the battle! They found the fight, or what they took to be the fight, soon enough and plunged into the dark woods. Colquitt did not even send skirmishers in front. There was no time—and Breckinridge must be in front of him somewhere. Colquitt's inspirational charge went past everything, Confederate and Federal alike. He might have ended in Chattanooga except that he suddenly took stock and saw that all around him—to the east, south, and west—there were Federals. He had plunged into the heart of the enemy. Good enough, he'd just fight where he stood. While he was groping forward, trying to determine his position, a lead ball struck him, and he fell dead. Somehow his men fought their way back to the Confederate lines, and their daring pell-mell charge took a savage toll on their number.

Major General George H. Thomas, U.S.A., "The Rock of Chickamauga."

Braxton Bragg as a Brigadier General early in the war.

Lieutenant General James
Longstreet, C.S.A.

Major General William Starke Rosecrans, U.S.A.

Lieutenant General
Leonidas Polk,
C.S.A.

Major General Philip Henry Sheridan, U.S.A., early in the war.

Major General Joseph
Wheeler, C.S.A.

Major General Joseph
Hooker, U.S.A.

Lieutenant General Nathan
Bedford Forrest, C.S.A.
(He was a Brigadier during the
Battle of Chickamauga.)

Brigadier General
Thomas J. Wood, U.S.A.

"The First Gun at Chickamauga." Confederate artillery opening fire upon Union cavalry, who had begun destruction of Reed's Bridge, September 18, 1863. Drawn by Alfred R. Waud.

Battle of Chickamauga. Wash drawing by Alfred R. Waud.

Longstreet's soldiers debarking from the trains below Ring-gold, September 18, 1863. They hastened from here into the Battle of Chickamauga, which was already raging. Drawing by Alfred R. Waud.

Steedman's charge at Snodgrass Hill, Battle of Chickamauga, September 19 and 20, 1863. Pencil drawing by Alfred R. Waud.

Battle of Chattanooga. Lithograph by Prang.

The Twenty-fourth South Carolina lost 169 out of fewer than 400 men. The South was losing a lot of men that morning.

On the Federal side, they just went about the business of winning the war. That morning Thomas took what he had and made the best use of it. He later estimated that the Confederate attacks lasted about two hours (or an eternity for those in it) and that it was composed of "assault after assault with fresh troops" until they were spent. It was as if the Federal mind-set might be depicted as a thoughtful, pipe-smoking, clear-eyed resolute fellow. No need to get hysterical, boys, let's just do our duty. Major General John M. Palmer's division happened to be established that morning in an area that was strangely devoid of foliage; it was clear in front of him. Palmer always believed that if the Rebels had come at him early—come at him, in fact, the way Bragg ordered Polk to do—then all the blue troops would have been forced to race back to Chattanooga—to take their pipes, their mustache brushes, and their serious miens and fly away. By the time the wild-charging Rebels did get their steam up, the surprise was lost, and the Federals could lay down a field of fire that swept the horizon. Yet the Rebels kept coming—as they had at Gettysburg—as if they had lost their minds. And the Confederates got close. Palmer witnessed some get within thirty yards of the breastworks. And all for nothing.

Perhaps, just perhaps, in the back of the Northern mind was the assurance that "we're going to win. Maybe not this battle, maybe not today or the day after tomorrow, but, finally, we're going to win. Steady as she goes!" Somewhere in the dark recesses of the Southern mind may have been the thought: "Oh, Lord, it's lost. It's always been lost. We're going down. But we're going to create holy hell because damned if we know why or how—or, finally, *when*."

A Southerner's deeply held feelings, often inexplicable to a Northerner—or dismissed as weird and ill advised—are often composed of such sentiments as Eugene Gant had in *Look Homeward, Angel*: "His feeling for the South was not so much historic as it was of the core and desire of dark romanticism—that unlimited and inexplicable drunkenness, the magnetism of some men's blood that takes them into the heart of the heat, and beyond that, into the polar and emerald cold of the South as swiftly as it took the heart of that incomparable romanticist who wrote *The Rime of the Ancient Mariner*, beyond which there is nothing."

On this occasion the South had General Braxton Bragg, with boils on his butt and rage against mankind in his heart. He seems more like one of Lincoln's misplaced generals of the Army of the Potomac than a dashing hell-for-leather commander in gray. He was far from being daring like Lee and Jackson, and he had nothing of the foxy, careful nature of Retreating Joe Johnston. Despite it all, though, a bit of fantastic luck fell on the Confederates before the sun set this Sabbath—something almost unheard of in the military history of this war—and it didn't matter for a while who was in command. Lady Luck had come calling.

6

The Fatal Gap

William Starke Rosecrans had everything going for him—a military bearing, the affection of his men, a stout heart, and a facile mind. At the time of Chickamauga, he enjoyed being (and was forced to live up to being) one of the most esteemed commanding generals on either side. He could deal with the known and expected. Throw what you would at him, he could handle it—if he knew what it was. Call for a parade, call for an enfilade and a bold quick move, and Old Rosey was your man. However, it was the unexpected that would put him under the gun, the sudden bolt out of the blue that would test his mettle. It would do it in a flash.

We know Rosecrans from official reports, battle accounts, and reminiscences. We have pictures of a bearded fellow with a Roman nose and a sly half-grin. We can only speculate about his interior life. Why did he talk so much, keep himself in perpetual motion, and fight off sleep? To evade a hard look at reality? *Poor Garesche! He was right there beside me when his head was blown away!* Why was he so explosive one moment and a sea of calm the next? Was he teetering on the edge of a breakdown? We know his origins, and we know his fate. He failed. In the end, it may be asked if he wasn't simply unlucky, for unlucky he was in the end, even more unlucky in a way than snakebit Braxton Bragg. In one catastrophic moment Rosecrans surpassed in magnitude all the really sour misfortunes that befell Bragg. For one decision, and one decision only, Rosecrans fell from being one of the most admired Federal generals to being one who could be truly pitied.

George H. Thomas, like the consummate corps commander that he was, had kept badgering Rosecrans for reinforcements. He had kept a steady barrage of couriers flowing Rosecrans's way, all with one message: Where are my reinforcements? The feeling of urgency was catching, and Rosecrans soon got in a dither over the need to move more and more troops to the left, to help old reliable Thomas. Events were proving Thomas correct, of course, as they nearly always did. It seemed that all the Rebel action, all that was to be, would be directed toward the left and that the left must be held at all cost. Otherwise, the Federals were in danger of being sealed off, of having a door slammed on them—of being caught in an abattoir—if they didn't watch out. Rosecrans raised his eyes to heaven and proclaimed to one and all that Thomas would be sustained in his present position "if he has to be reinforced by the entire army." Old Rosey became transfixed with shoring up his left: Alexander McCook was to move two of Philip Sheridan's brigades, other brigades were to follow, and Rosey was aiming to put eight divisions on the left, leaving but two to guard the middle and the right.

And then the catastrophe was put in motion. Captain Sanford C. Kellogg, a good soldier from New York, a staff aide to General Thomas, was reining his horse over the Glenn-Kelly road, to impart to the commander of the Army of the Cumberland one more time the need for more men. "Compliments from General Thomas, sir. He requests more troops." As Kellogg kept his horse at a steady pace, he saw, in the broad daylight of morning, something he took to be unusual. He saw a gap in the Federal line. A *hole*! He passed on Thomas's troop request to Rosecrans and then he quite alarmingly noted the gap he had discovered. Rosecrans's nerves nearly gave way. What, oh what, was going on? A Federal line of defense with a gaping hole in its center? Perhaps he should go out and check it himself, to make sure Kellogg was seeing straight, but now two other couriers rode up with the same sighting and message: There were no troops between those of Brigadier Generals Thomas J. Wood and Joseph J. Reynolds. There was a gap in the center of the Federal line. They had seen it!

It was a mistake, though, something impossible to anticipate—the unexpected. John M. Brannan's Third Division was there all the time. Like a magician's sleight of hand, it was hidden in some woods down from the Glenn-Kelly Road. A whole division was down there engulfed in the forest, two steps into a jungle that hadn't been trampled by man in eons and now shrouded a whole division. Brannan's division lay deep in the woods. There was no gap.

And then a series of unlikely events occurred, one after another, in rapid order. Headquarters was in a state of high excitement, with shouts, commands, and the nearby exploding shells rattling the timber. It was not a sea of calm, and Rosecrans was not a calm deliberator in the calmest of times. Believing there was a gap, he fired off an order: General Wood was to take *his* division and close up on General Reynolds "as fast as possible, and support him." Rosecrans had the ill luck then to turn to Major Frank S. Bond, his aide-de-camp, to relay this order—not stolid, surefooted James A. Garfield. Garfield *knew* where Brannan was. He knew where nearly every man in blue stood; it was his job, a job of knowing who to count on, a feel for where the strength lay, an ability that would later bring him to the White House. Garfield studied and wrote out every order for Rosecrans that day, every single one save this fatal one. In the creaking, explosive headquarters, he was busy with something else and didn't overhear this order being given. Bond wrote out the simple message, and it was delivered immediately to General Wood. Of all men in the U.S. Army at the moment, it had to be Wood, straight-as-an-arrow, West Point Regular-Army Wood. It was all the apotheosis of bad luck. Scarcely two hours before, the nearly out-of-control Rosecrans had given Wood a nasty tongue-lashing, the heat of it lingering in the minds of those who heard it forever. Rosecrans had blamed Wood for James S. Negley's not hav-ing moved promptly to aid Thomas. At the time, in Rosecrans's feverish mind, it all made sense. Negley was dawdling, he was needed, and it was all Wood's fault. Thomas needed men, and Wood was holding up the works. Rosecrans had let loose, his invec-tive rising to a shout. His words were later put down on paper by an observer, but undoubtedly some of the choice adjectives and adverbs were cleaned up or stricken, as was customary in the nine-teenth century. "What is the meaning of this, sir?" Rosecrans had bellowed, according to the observer. "You have disobeyed my spe-cific orders. By your damnable negligence you are endangering the safety of the entire army, and, by God, I will not tolerate it. Move your division at once, as I have instructed, or the consequences will not be pleasant for yourself." Rosecrans could curse—all contempo-rary accounts affirm it. The actual words were probably more on the order of, "You goddamn son of a bitch, you've disobeyed me for the last goddamn time. Move your men over there on the double, or I'll bust your ass to private. Try me and see!" He had been in a purple-faced rage. He had surely said more than damn, and he had said it right in front of Wood's men. Wood was stricken to the core, but he was a good soldier and had sucked in his gut. Now here came a direct order from Rosecrans again. It came scarcely an hour after his dressing down from Rosecrans, at 10:55 A.M.: "The general commanding directs that you close up on Reynolds as fast as possible, and support him."

What was a man to do? Wood did not mull over the command, did not call aides for advice—he acted. There was that phrase, *as fast as possible*. He moved his troops straight back in order to skirt Brannan's rear, and then he moved crisply to connect with Reynolds. By the book. And he took no chances for any foul-ups along the way. He was out front himself, scouting the terrain, making sure there would be no hindrances. On the road he suddenly and surprisingly came across the redoubtable Thomas, who was also out front, batting down the hatches, personally making sure that everything in his domain was on the ready, all set for when the Rebels charged. Thomas was delighted, of course, to find more men in blue coming his way, but he was somewhat nonplussed that Wood was heading to support Reynolds. Reynolds? No, sir, Reynolds wouldn't be needing any support. Absolutely not. But he, Thomas, could certainly use some more flesh. Wood should keep right on going and give Absalom Baird some help there. Wood allowed his horse to paw the ground a moment and then said that if General Thomas would personally take full responsibility for this change in his orders, he would do so. By the book. Thomas was more than happy to take that responsibility, and so Wood moved his division far to the left. It couldn't have helped the Confederate cause more if Bragg had ordered it, and thus the Union defense line was set up for one of the greatest Federal debacles in the war. Hardly ten minutes after Wood moved out, all hell broke loose.

It now came time for General James "Old Pete" Longstreet, Robert E. Lee's warhorse and a man of all seasons and many sorrows, to enter the picture. He was a man cherished, with good reason, by his troops. He looked after them, and he was a good tactician who learned from past mistakes. He did not want to repeat the foolhardy charge of the third day at Gettysburg. On the other hand, Bragg—

his titular superior—never forgot anything, especially a slight. Bragg became exasperated with Bishop Leonidas Polk that morning and finally, with a sort of masochistic glee, sent out the order to forget everything; everybody should just go out and *attack*. All division commanders were simply to take matters in their own hands and fling themselves on the enemy. When Alexander P. Stewart went in and was immediately hurled back, with the rapidity of a returned tennis serve, Old Pete took to the front to calm down the other generals, in effect, to take charge of the battle. First, he saw to it that John Bell Hood was restrained. The Kentuckian was ready to go into the jaws of hell at the slightest goading. Longstreet understood that urge, but also understood that valor and impetuous bravery alone would not win this battle, but cunning and nerve might. He studied the terrain that morning, got a good look at his fresh troops, and decided that an armed glorified "column" should be able to break through the Federal breastwork, fling itself across the center, and then slaughter the foe. Long lines of Confederates, all spread out, charging in, one after another, had not worked, and would not work. Remember Gettysburg, remember poor George E. Pickett and his greased perfumed locks. No, Longstreet was going to line up his mighty left wing and go in narrowly like a battering ram. Just shove it right up 'em. And use every bit of cunning he had come by.

Longstreet had discovered the lively Brotherton household the night before, when he had been on the scent of any loyal Southerners in the area who could furnish intelligence. Use every advantage, leave no stone unturned! The Brotherton farm was on relatively flat land, with its 700 acres only partially darkened by woods. It turned out to be smack-dab in the middle of the adversaries. It was open to visitors. The night of the nineteenth, wily Old Pete introduced himself to Tom Brotherton, a son in the family—one a West Pointer, someone who had fought with Lee, feuded with Jackson, and experienced the war from the near beginning, the other a frontier farmer, someone who had seldom encountered anyone he didn't know and now had thousands of strangers to contend with. They were two Southerners, two Georgians, and they spoke the same language. They weren't fighting for states rights, plantation privilege, or the purity of Southern womanhood; they were fighting for their very lives. Brotherton showed Longstreet around and made him familiar with an overlooked path and road and where the bramble was too thick to penetrate. He gave him a perfect picture of the ground that was soon to become a battlefield. He turned out to be a valued scout, and Longstreet wouldn't let him out of his sight. "Hit's right over chere, gineral, that the road turns. You got to watch her." Brotherton stayed the night with the general and was with him through the fighting the next day. Years later, when a much more tired Longstreet returned to visit the battlefield, he asked immediately to see Tom. Tom unfortunately was dead, so the general never got to see again the man who had been so much a part of how the fight went in those obscure woods in northern Georgia.

On the morning of September 20, fed up with Bragg, Longstreet put all his ducks in a row—as if setting up a parade on the plains of West Point or going forth for a review at Richmond. He took care of details and became the quintessential version of what he had always been, a soldier. On a half mile front he set up a gigantic column that spread backward for miles and miles: eleven whole brigades. At the very front were the brigades of Bushrod Johnson, and behind and near them were those of E. McIvor Law and Joseph Brevard Kershaw; in support were the brigades of Thomas C. Hindman and William Preston. Here were 16,000 men set to attack, stretching back and back and back. The number was over five times the population of Chattanooga then. And because of the woods and foliage, the Yankees had no idea what was in store for them. The Yankee pickets had no idea that this gigantic column was poised to strike. At a little after eleven this Sabbath morning, just about church time, Longstreet gave the nod to start. Through the dense dark forest the Southerners began to scurry, arms flailing out front, crouched over, trotting where the brush wasn't too thick, coming on strong. On the right—boys from North Carolina, Arkansas, and South Carolina; on the left, all Tennesseans save for a Georgia artillery battalion, with a second line of Tennesseans, Texans, and a Missouri battery. This was not Gettysburg and Longstreet's charge of the third day. Here he had about half again more than he had then. And these weren't shot-up troops. These were fresh boys, primed to fight, and sure now of their leadership. Old Pete emanated full self-confidence; his very beard—full and luxurious—seemed to announce it; there was nothing scraggly and tentative about it. To Hood that morning he had said, without a bit of hesitation: "*Of course* [we will] whip and drive [the Yankees] from the field." Hood hadn't heard anyone else talk of victory that way since he had come to Georgia.

The Rebels didn't have far to go before they found a fight. Within ten minutes of Longstreet's nod for the action to commence, Bushrod Johnson's lead brigades had crossed dusty La Fayette Road, a Rebel yell in their throats, their muskets popping. The battering column—which might be considered the whole might of the South at this point—advanced toward the Brotherton farmhouse, a log cabin, and began receiving fire from behind the farm's split-rail fence and the Federal pickets who held ground slightly beyond it. They fired in each other's faces, the Federals and the Rebels, but there were far more Rebels now than Yanks—and they were coming forth with no one able to stop them. Many Southerners were charging on empty stomachs because supply wagons had been lost in the woods the night before and only skimpy rations had been handed out earlier that morning as they had listened to Polk's right wing shatter the Sunday air. They now charged hell-bent, casting the Federals aside; they swept them away like rows of wheat and plowed around both sides of the Brotherton cabin, trotting across the slight rise of cleared land beyond. A Federal battery from up front then opened up on them—*bam, bam, bam!* Puffs of smoke broke and washed over the field. The clatter of heavy fire shook the earth, and then the Southerners, slowly one after another, noticed something a little strange. The fire was coming at them from the *sides*, not head-on. It was as if they were charging through a chute—and, in effect, they were, for this battering column had picked the one hole, the one gap: the space that Wood had held just ten minutes before. Talk about luck! The column kept coming—trotting, cursing, screaming, shooting—passing over the cleared Brotherton land and plunging once again into some dark woods. They climbed and leaped over abandoned breastworks and overtook the last of Wood's men who were poking along for other parts, each man following the man in front, taking it easy. The blueclads thought they were marching to where the action was, when suddenly, out of nowhere, came these wild savages in butternut, scattering them left and right like tenpins, heralding a tornado that was set to roar through.

This rolling sea of Rebels hardly paused, flinging Federals aside, until all at once they left the second line of dark woods and emerged into a blue-sky clearing. Some miles away they could make out Missionary Ridge, although they didn't know it by name. This was uncharted territory, well before paved highways and green tinted folding maps. The first tourist had yet to descend. It looked like the Promised Land. The commander, Bushrod Johnson, later filed a report in these words: "The scene now presented was unspeakably grand. The resolute and impetuous charge, the rush of our heavy columns sweeping out from the shadow of the gloom of the forest into the open fields flooded with sunlight, the glitter of arms, the onward dash of artillery and mounted men, the retreat of the foe, the shout of hosts of our army, the dust, the smoke, the noise of fire-arms—of whistling balls and grape-shot and of bursting shell—made up a battle scene of unsurpassed grandeur."

He had won a spectacular view, but could hardly savor it. A

rider immediately trotted up, holding the reins of his horse with his one good hand, his other arm useless and in a sling. He wore the gold braid of a general: Hood, with his luxurious brown beard catching flecks of sunlight through the smoke and dust. "Go ahead," he advised Johnson, "and keep ahead of everything." It was one of his last commands that day. Only a few more minutes were left for his services.

Bushrod Johnson moved quickly to silence some Federal guns and to open up a battery against fleeing Federal troops. His men had exploded through and over one mile of ground, right through the enemy's center. The Rebels claimed nineteen pieces of Federal artillery and had sent a whole brigade of bluecoats flying. For those who lived to tell it, it might have seemed a lifetime, but in fact it took but forty-five minutes—from 11:15 A.M. until noon. When they called a halt, Johnson sent out skirmishers to feel where the enemy strength lay and what he might expect in the way of a Federal attempt at retribution. And he let Longstreet know that he could use some reinforcements in case the Federals decided to do their own surprise attacking, for a quarter of Johnson's troops had been put out of commission during the fight.

Thousands upon thousands of men, in both blue and gray, were now intent on killing each other or avoiding being killed, and they were right in the middle of nowhere, no one quite sure what was going on. The Brothertons, who had played host to the heaviest concentration of fire, might be sure where they were, but they weren't exactly sure what they should do. Something like this didn't happen every day on the farm. The Brothertons' four cows kept right on grazing while grape and canister whizzed past, and they were miraculously spared when the fighting moved farther north. In fact, daughter Adaline Brotherton returned while the battle flared elsewhere and milked the udder-heavy cows. The Brothertons' log cabin wasn't leveled either. Although all the Brothertons—the mother, father, and seven siblings—had fled down the road to relatives when it seemed prudent on the afternoon of the nineteenth, after Stewart had plunged his forces their way, they returned to their home as soon the fighting left their backyard. They found nine dead Federal soldiers in their front yard.

Farther up on the battlefield, Bushrod Johnson paused a moment for breath, as the Federals lay in disarray all around him. He had captured nineteen pieces of Federal artillery, there were no guns trained on him, and he could now kill the enemy almost at will—if he had the will to do so. He called a halt on Dry Valley Road. A dark good-looking man in his photographs, Johnson was distinguished by a full head of hair on the sides, an apparent comb-job over the pate, and a high forehead. He seemed to have a little twinkle in his eye, as if he might have had an easygoing nature and perhaps a sensual side. He was not a Southerner. Ohio born, he was teaching in Kentucky when the war broke out and decided not to complicate matters by going North but to stay put and join the Confederacy. He had graduated in the same class at West Point as William T. Sherman and Thomas. After the war, he went back to teaching, in Nashville, but the school ran out of funds, and then he moved to southern Illinois, where he failed as a farmer and businessman. Everyone for miles around took advantage of him—this nice, easygoing ex-Confederate. He lent books that he never got back, he overlooked loans of money that he gave, and he was always ready to pass on avuncular advice to a new generation who hadn't fought and knew nothing of combat. He made friends with former generals who had fought on the other side. Johnson was bookish and genial and, by all accounts, a marvelous teacher and extremely well liked. Like Grant and a few other successful generals, he might be inspired on the battlefield but got whipped to unconditional surrender by merciless nineteenth-century business practices.

On Johnson's left that Sunday, Major General Hindman was pushing the Federals back, too. He didn't get as far as Johnson, but he took on more blueclads. Johnson had sent a brigade fly-ing—Hindman fought two divisions. Hindman sent Federal Major General McCook's division into a wild, let's-get-the-hell-out-of-here retreat. McCook's men felt that panic which comes when the bottom falls out of one's perceived world, and nothing causes a soldier more panic than to witness a whole panoply of fellow soldiers breaking into a run for the rear. "You expect me to stand then? Me, *alone?*" It happened at Shiloh; it was now hap-pening at Chickamauga. Even the generals were fleeing—getting the hell out. Confederates were everywhere, breaking through, showering lead, whooping it up. Black curling smoke and a deaf-ening roar permeated their ranks. It was as if a primeval beast, the ultimate nightmare, had suddenly appeared out of the woods. And the Federals weren't set up for this kind of charge; their breastworks were no match. "McCook's corps was wiped off the field without any attempt at real resistance," a Federal colonel testified later. He reported seeing artillerymen leave their guns in fright, carrying along infantrymen in their dash for safety. Some of these infantrymen might have made a stand, but they got pushed into the sea of retreaters. No one was blowing the bugle for retreat; nothing was orderly—everyone got caught in the ter-ror of a mob. It was a rout.

Hindman, the attacker, was a fine figure of a man. He com-manded in a well-tailored uniform, and in civilian life outfitted himself in a certain rakish style. Among items he favored were pink gloves and a rattan cane. Nifty, somewhat arrogant, he was an aris-tocrat who was sure of his place. He had been born in Knoxville, Tennessee, but had been educated at the elite Lawrenceville Academy in New Jersey. He held a secure social position in the Razorback State of Arkansas when war broke out. He had long curling locks like Pickett—and, not unusual among fierce and determined men, was on the short side. He might never have had the vision to lead an army and think up grand strategies, but given good solid leadership—Longstreet in this case—he could be counted upon to deliver. He proceeded to knock the hell out of the enemy. At first.

Phil Sheridan, no fashion plate, but as much a bantam rooster as Hindman and as feisty as any man on either side, got caught in the backward Federal flow. Under orders from Rosecrans, he had been marching two of his brigades across the rear of Jefferson C. Davis's division, on his way to strengthening Thomas and the famous Union left wing—as everyone seemed to be doing—when holy hell broke loose. Caissons creaked and men backstepped and then ran—and he could do nothing. He could think of nothing. Uncharacteristically, Sheridan sank into a depression and came up with no military answer. His spirit merely said that he should flee to fight and love and eat another day—for all living things want to live. It was not a unique sensation. Davis, his fellow division general, had no time to think rationally either. If your breastworks fail, if your defensive line breaks, if your men are flying backward under a mighty wave of gray, you haven't got time to pull out a map, suck on a pipe, and try to figure out what Wellington or Napoleon might have done. Davis's backpedaling men swept over those of Sheridan, and all of them mingled together in a knot of humanity reeling backward. This day was done!

But no, not quite yet, for General William H. Lytle, commander of Sheridan's First Brigade, was still on the field. He had been the last in line to move to the left toward Thomas, the ever-moving procession to give aid to the left, when he saw the mass of Hindman's division chugging up the gentle slope that led to Widow Glenn's cabin, the once-flourishing and active Union headquarters. God almighty, here they came! It seemed like the whole population of Georgia was massed and rushing forth—intent on only one thing: to kill and dismember every blueclad in its way. This procession hardly paused, it didn't have to, before Davis's breastworks. It leaped over them, braying for blood, coming on—the whole Confederate Cause, it seemed, about to push its argument down the

Federals' throats. Lytle saw that his position was untenable: grayclad soldiers were overlapping both his sides, rushing forth like a stream of water around a boulder. It was unthinkable that Lytle would do anything but hightail it for the rear like everyone else. It was all hopeless, lost. It was then that Lytle borrowed a gesture that might have come straight from the other side, the Cavalier South. He pulled on his riding gloves, turned to one of his staff, and announced, "If I must die, I will die a gentleman." He ordered his brigade to stand—to die if necessary, "with their harness on."

Of course, Lytle was a poet—a recognized one at the time. Countless schoolboys, north and south, could recite his colorful "Antony and Cleopatra." He was of a mixed nature. His mother was a literary lady, a writer herself, and she cast a gentle, romantic glow over his persona. Lytle came from Cincinnati, a hub of commerce and a reservoir of military memories, and he was drawn by the desire to fight in the army and to argue before the bar. He became a lawyer. His father, who had been a general, was now a U.S. congressman, and Lytle had once yearned to go to West Point. When war broke out, he quickly volunteered and was readily given his wish to fight. He was wounded almost immediately—first in Virginia and then at Perryville. At Perryville, he was left on the field apparently dead and then was captured, nursed back to health, and later paroled to fight again. Now at Chickamauga, at noontime on this late September day, he wore a dark overcoat without an insignia but with a gold cord around the crown of his hat to show his rank. His fine horse, though, was decked out in finery as might bespeak a mount of a knight of the Round Table. It was caparisoned. It drew attention.

Lytle started his brigade on a counterattack against the horde and was quickly wounded—in the spine. He agonized in pain but stayed in the saddle. The Rebs might push them back, but he was going to be out in front of his men, leading them, as long as he could hold the reins. Then a fusillade hit him—three deadly shots simultaneously. He went down—smiling, it was later reported, to those of his staff who were gently easing him to the ground. They were trying to get him somewhere, anywhere, where the minié balls and shells weren't flying. Two hovering orderlies were shot dead trying to move him. The best the survivors could do was to lay Lytle beneath a large tree on a far knoll where his troops were making a final stand. They placed him down in the heart of the battle. Speechless, the life force ebbing away, he motioned weakly for his troops to leave the scene and save themselves. He moved his hand as long as he could, and then he died.

Then came the Southerners. Learning who Lytle was—a brigade general and a recognized poet—they stood guard over his body. A Major Douglas West secured Lytle's pistol, spurs, sword belt, scabbard, and memorandum book. He was a fan of "Antony and Cleopatra." Brigadier General Preston, who commanded the division on the Confederate left, passed by and saw the attention being paid a slain figure. "What have you there?" he asked.

"General Lytle of Cincinnati," the answer came.

"Ah," said Preston, "the son of my old friend Bob Lytle. I am sorry it is so."

Next a curious visitor came to pay homage. It was Confederate surgeon E. W. Thomasson, who had served with Lytle in the Mexican War, and he positively identified the body and had it taken to his private tent. There, in keeping with a nineteenth-century ritual, he snipped off a lock of Lytle's hair, which he sent to Lytle's sister. He also sent Lytle's wallet and a poem he had found in the general-poet's pocket. Thomasson dressed Lytle's wounded face with green leaves and placed a transparent silken net over it. Lytle lay in state. That night officers sat around campfires and recited favorite lines from "Antony and Cleopatra." Many an eye was misty. Not many throats stayed dry.

While the fighting went on, though, the Southerners showed no sentiment save to kill. They had swept romantic Lytle out of the

way and expected no one else to be so foolhardy. But someone else
was there, someone on a slight rise of ground, someone who was not
ready to run home either: General John T. Wilder and his mounted
brigade of men with Spencer rifles. These men let loose a fusillade
of rapid fire on the left flank of Hindman's division, and the Southern attack stalled for the moment in wonder. What the hell was
this? These blueclads weren't flinching; they were stepping forward,
their rapid-fire carbines popping, not intending that the Southerners would make them flee. Here the Southerners began to take their
own medicine and backpedal. They scurried back, hunched over,
zigzagging as best they could to dodge the hail of bullets until they
could get behind the safety of the La Fayette Road. It happened in
minutes. Holy God, what were those Yankees firing? You couldn't
raise your musket before they had got off three rounds. It wasn't
fair! And it came to more than one that if every Federal had held a
Spencer, the outcome might have been different. But Wilder's
brigade did hold the Spencers and knew how to use them, and they
saved a lot of the honor, if not the lives, of Union soldiers that
bloody day.

On the other hand, the South had Longstreet. Old Pete coolly
sat in the saddle, surveying the scene, expecting reversals every so
often—and knowing what to do about them. He hadn't been at
Fredericksburg and Gettysburg for nothing! Longstreet gave the
signal for Preston's reserve division to swing into action. More cautious than many Southern commanders—Hood for one—Longstreet
liked to keep some reserve forces hidden until he needed them. Preston
and those who had just been retreating overwhelmed the Lightning
Brigade, their Spencers and all. The sheer force of the Rebels' numbers drove Wilder's brigade back, and Wilder's men joined the other
Federals who had lost heart and were racing for the safe green
glades of McFarland's Gap. Dirt was flying everywhere, screams and
shells and chaos were all over. The Widow Glenn's cabin, where
Federal officers in shiny boots and gleaming brass had only hours

before been sending messages and receiving reports, took a direct hit. It burned to the ground in the noonday sun, like a hay-filled loft, and went right off the map. Bam!

Coming up now, through the center, were the Rebel brigades of Law and Kershaw. These brigades widened the gap in the Union line and, in doing so, found Brannan's forces, which had been swung like a gate, hinged on its left, to face them. It all happened in minutes—men rushing, commanders barking orders, the roar of the battle deafening. No one knew what he might expect at any given moment, so quickly was everything changing. Law's troops were now leaping over breastworks, screaming the Rebel Yell. They charged right into the confused blueclads of Brigadier General Horatio P. Van Cleve's division, men who were trying to march to Thomas's aid on the Union left, where Thomas didn't need help at the moment. Something startling, something abrupt, was occurring every second now. Colonel Charles G. Harker, commander of Wood's third brigade, was also marching toward Thomas and heard the furious battle erupt and ordered his men to about-face. He knew what fighting sounded like, and he was going where it was—and he was not the first one that day who acted instinctively. Harker, only five years out of West Point and a colonel at age twenty-five, had been tested at Shiloh. His men lunged into Law's highly surprised soldiers and sent them back. The Rebels had been *charging* just seconds before. Now they were rushing back.

They were Texans mostly, people with a certain shyness about retreat. They were far more comfortable blasting ahead on sheer nerve. These were Hood's men, Hood who was born in Kentucky but who qualified to the core as a Texan. Hood could be counted on to be in the thick of things, and he didn't disappoint this day. Massive in build and somewhat sleepy eyed, he had just finished his confab with Bushrod Johnson, finding Southerners on the move everywhere. Now he came across his beloved Texans fleeing in the face of Yankees, and the only ones in the throes of panic. What's happening here? Hold on, boys; turn around and *attack*! As his horse grappled with the bit between its teeth, jerking its head from side to side, Hood motioned his large head toward the front, toward the action. His right hand held the reins, his left arm—shattered at Gettysburg—hung useless at his side. The Texans couldn't help but pay attention. *Their beloved Hood!* Then a bullet that didn't respect name or rank or national origin found Hood. It hit his upper right thigh, shattering bone and flesh and causing the giant Hood to weave in the saddle. Texans came swiftly to his side, ignoring the whiz of lead by their heads, tenderly easing the general from his saddle to the ground. Hood was delirious by now and kept repeating, "Go ahead, and keep ahead of everything." It was what he had told Bushrod Johnson only minutes before. Hood was still fighting when he came under the battlefield surgeon's knife. His leg had to be amputated fairly close to the hip, and it was feared that even this remedy would not save him. Already his men were recounting his last words—*Go ahead, and keep ahead of everything*—as if they were the finishing touches to a great warrior's life. The Texans stood, their line ceased moving back—aided, in no small measure, by the timely arrival of two of Kershaw's brigades. Now the Texans were really fired up. "Look what they done to old Hood!" But it would take a lot to kill Hood. He recuperated from the loss of his right leg and went on to fight once again, having to be strapped in the saddle to do so. He cannot be pictured behind a desk, thinking up strategy. He liked to fight and be out front in the open. His side lost, but a fort is named after him in Texas. Although he lasted through the war, he ended up being crushed as a failed businessman in New Orleans. He died in bed in 1879, a victim of a yellow fever epidemic that also took his wife and a child.

It was now well past noon at Chickamauga, and Longstreet was taking reconnaissance of all that his mighty left wing had accomplished. Bushrod Johnson had blitzed up the center, Hindman had blasted the Yankees to kingdom come on Johnson's right, and Law and Kershaw had broadened the path to the right of Johnson. Longstreet had predicted that "we would of course whip and drive them from the field," and he was doing so. Now what? Bragg, still down at his headquarters near Reed's Bridge, away from the screaming Rebels and the scampering Federals, had drawn up the Confederate battle plan that was now working in reverse. Instead of Bishop Polk beating back the foe and wheeling *left*, Longstreet was swinging them *right*. Bragg had said for his forces to pivot on Preston; Longstreet changed the order of business to pivot on Stewart, in the opposite direction. A horde of blueclads were fleeing toward McFarland's Gap, and Little Joe Wheeler and his cavalry were called up from below Lee and Gordon's Mills to give them chase. The troopers were happy with the assignment, for they had been reduced to exchanging shots with Federal sentries and had crossed the Chickamauga at Glass's Mill. Everyone was now getting into the act.

However, because thousands of men were involved, sheer exhilaration was not enough to make them pivot and charge on a dime. Some units had to rest; others had to quick-march a few miles to reach a new position. Commanders had been lost, and new ones were yet to be chosen. Also, in the pell-mell rush of attack, regiments and brigades had intermingled. They needed to be sorted out, and ammunition boxes had to be refilled. There were about six hours of light left in the day, enough time to get things done. Important, too, was the fact that everyone was panting and hungry, especially hungry, and especially Longstreet, who wasn't exactly slim in the haunches. Longstreet ordered that lunch should be cooked and then left on a quick inspection of what he would face afterward. Hearing bullets whiz by his ears, he found that the Federals were reduced to setting up a defensive line that was well behind their previous one. It looked like a makeshift, last-gasp effort— along some slopes on a spur of Missionary Ridge. He saw some Yankees crowded together on one wooded slope in particular, and Bushrod Johnson told him its name: Snodgrass Hill. It didn't look like much. Hell, they'd been making the Yankees run over hill and dale. Longstreet chortled: "They have fought their last man, and *he* is running." Then he trotted his horse back to his headquarters at Dyer Yard, and dug into his hot lunch: Nassau bacon and Georgia sweet potatoes. The lunch was spread outdoors on a table, picnic style, and for a man who appreciated his stomach, it was fine fare. Nassau bacon might be considered ordinary by most troops (dubbed "nausea bacon" in some quarters), but those hot sweet potatoes, Georgia grown, umm, umm—moist and succulent and giving off a mouth-watering aroma as the crisp outside was split—could cause the eyes to go dim. Thirty years later Longstreet could still vividly recall the meal: "We were not accustomed to potatoes of any kind in Virginia, and thought we had a great luxury." Some later wondered why Longstreet took time to indulge so rapturously in a meal when the battle was but halfway fought. The answer may simply be that Long-street liked to eat about as much as he liked to fight.

Anyhow, an armistice hadn't been called. Minié balls still creased the air, and exploding shells shook the ground. One shell landed so close, in a nearby copse, that splintered wood ripped through a book one of Longstreet's men was reading and sent a staff colonel at the table reeling over backward to end up lying spread out on the ground, gasping and clutching his throat. All rushed to him, ready to staunch the flow of blood and ease the poor man's passage into the next world. Wise old Longstreet, never a man to make a quick judgment, looked closely. The man had only been grazed by a fragment of the shell and clutched his throat for another reason: He had wolfed down some of that delicious sweet potato too quickly, and a lump had got stuck in his throat. He was belted on the back until the lump broke free; then he sat back in his chair with dignity to polish off the rest of his meal.

Longstreet thankfully began to eat again himself, when there was another interruption. A courier rode up, dismounted, and swiftly presented a message from Bragg. Bragg wanted an immediate meeting. Were there to be new tactics? Was there new intelligence? Longstreet hadn't been in touch with Bragg since the night before. He took a mouthful of sweet potato, rose, and mounted his horse. When the commanding officer called, you went. And it was much better to bring good news than bad. They were whipping the Yankees, whipping them good. Longstreet rode through Federal wreckage to dismount and face Bragg once more. He found Bragg not much different from the night before, before today's battle had begun—a gaunt man who was hardly the picture of a cheerful, ebullient spirit. Longstreet rattled off what he had accomplished: The capture of forty big guns, thousands upon thousands of small arms, and bereft prisoners. He had wrested two whole square miles from the Yankees. He had whipped them, sir, *whipped* them.

Bragg's gray, skeptical eyes didn't seem to register the news. Something was eating him. He kept fidgeting and waiting his turn to speak. Longstreet's extraordinary speech was lost on him. When Longstreet cleared his throat and began sensibly to advise Bragg that Polk's right wing could perhaps best be utilized now if it joined Longstreet's victory parade on the left, Bragg let loose. "There is not a man in the right wing who has any fight in him!" He was lost in a thicket of hate, frustration, and petulance—all wrapped up in ill humor, terrible health, and near exhaustion. He couldn't get it out of his mind that Polk hadn't done as *he was told*. Bragg wanted *his plan* to work, his and his alone—where the old swinging gate on the right would send the Yankees scurrying into McLemore's Cove. Why, oh why, couldn't the goddamn bishop do something right? The matter at hand now was not a subordinate's victory, Longstreet's, but the sorry performance of Polk in sabotaging his, Bragg's, scheme. All right, if his plan wasn't going to work, he'd just retire and let nature take its course. He'd throw a masochistic cloak around himself and suffer alone. Poor Bragg. "If anything happens, communicate with me at Reed's Bridge," he said in parting, and rode toward the rear.

Longstreet, the old warhorse, was now in charge. He cantered his horse back to the new lines and prepared to mop up what little Federal resistance there might be. It was some day, this twentieth of September.

The commanding general of the Army of the Cumberland had already fled. Rosecrans had been unfortunately on the move—but fortunately away from his command center when the cabin was leveled—when Longstreet broke through the center earlier. With Garfield, Charles Dana (the assistant secretary of war), and a few of his staff in tow, he was inspecting near the heart of where the raging Rebels were headed. He sat on his horse, looking over the landscape, trying to determine by sight and sound what might happen next. Just before that horrendous clamor and the breaking forth of the Rebels, it had been quiet, a sort of Sunday quiet. It was, for a moment, so peaceful that Dana decided to dismount and catch a few winks in the grass. No sooner had he stretched out than the Rebels came—firing, hollering, shells blasting. "Never in any battle had I witnessed such a discharge of cannon and musketry," he later recalled. Bolting upright, he rushed to his horse, at the same time catching a glimpse of his commander. God help us, Rosecrans was crossing himself! Now they were in deep trouble. Dana also saw that the line of Federal troops was breaking in every direction. Even Sheridan—stout Little Phil—was lost in the panic. Sheridan might be a fierce warrior when he outnumbered the foe, as was the case later in the Shenandoah, but for now, he was simply one small fat person trying to save his hide. Davis—with an illustrious namesake on the other side, a man who had flattened a fellow general with a point-blank pistol shot—also wanted out. McCook, who was doomed to ill luck and wrong choices, hit the road. Lytle, the romantic, the one previously mentioned, was the only general in the immediate vicinity on the right to stand—and be shot dead for his bravery and insouciance. The unholy Rebels came charging, and absolutely nothing was stopping them. Suddenly, for the moment,

Rosecrans ceased being a commander and became a potential survivor. He turned to his staff, his eyes bright as if in a trance, his voice unnaturally calm, and said, "If you care to live any longer, gentlemen, get away from here."

In the moblike confusion on the Federal right, a young colonel on McCook's staff decided to take matters into his own hands. He rode through bramble and thicket and clusters of men and wagons, turning south after a while, and miraculously reached General Thomas on the left, who was going to stand, no matter what. Thomas didn't have time for any pleasantries or welcoming words. He told the young officer to make haste back where he had come and to bring up what he could from Davis and Sheridan's division to aid him in his stand. They were going to have to stem the Rebel thrust, or the whole army was going to perish. Think of it: The whole Army of the Cumberland. A Virginian with the accent of Robert E. Lee was speaking. The officer rode back along the heavily clogged Dry Valley Road, running across so many blueclads that they seemed one organism—shoulder to shoulder, dust rising to their chests. "Stop, stop," he said, "Thomas needs you over there. We must make a stand." Those who could, laughed. Hellfire, was he crazy? Those Southern devils were about to kill them all! Go back? Hell, no. "See Jeff, Colonel," one said, meaning Davis. "Take it up with Phil," said another, meaning Sheridan. "We'll talk to you, my son, when we get to the Ohio River," said a veteran, getting guffaws all around. At last the officer got to McFarland's Gap, where he found Davis and Sheridan. Davis gave a weak answer, that he might consider going back to make a stand. Sheridan, on the other hand, couldn't bring himself even to focus on a return to fighting right now. The whole battle had been thoroughly screwed up, and only a madman would reenter it. The colonel observed that Sheridan "had lost faith"; then he lost faith in those two generals and rode to find the column headed by Rosecrans.

Rosecrans and what was left of his staff had reached a crossroads. They had come, literally and figuratively, to a fork in the road:

> *Two roads diverged in a wood, and I—*
> *I took the one less traveled by,*
> *And that has made all the difference.*

One dirt road led northwest to Chattanooga and away from the battle; the other turned east toward Rossville Gap, then south to the spur of Missionary Ridge, where Thomas was holding out (they hoped). The battle-weary men all dismounted, and first one and then another placed his ear to the ground, like an Indian, to try to discern what was happening in the distance. They heard the reverberations of small-arms fire—which meant that Thomas was still engaging the enemy. But there were no heavy thuds, no hint of any big guns in operation. Thomas probably was having no better luck than the rest of them. How could he? The prevailing wisdom was that everyone—Thomas included—should withdraw and throw up a straggler line outside Chattanooga, the noble Tennessee River at their backs. Stand or perish there. But Rosecrans wasn't going. He was going to stay and find out what Thomas was doing. Rosecrans told Garfield to go on to Chattanooga and take charge. Prepare for the defense. He began, in his rapid-fire speech, his faculty for administration coming back, to explain to Garfield in detail all he should do in Chattanooga: select good defensive ground, assign the proper units in place, and set up supply routes and communication lines. On and on he went until Garfield's head swam. Garfield was helplessly confused. What unit where? What sort of ground for a defensive line? No, no, he would be completely lost going to Chattanooga. *General Rosecrans should go to Chattanooga. He, James A. Garfield, would go to Thomas.*

Rosecrans considered the proposal. Should he turn left for Chattanooga—and, let's face it, save his sweet life—or should he turn right to tie up with Thomas and more fighting on this hellish ground? This modern, genial commander, this military Prufrock, was caught in a dilemma, the correctness or incorrectness of his decision sealing forever his fate in military annals. And he could delay no longer. He could not light a cigar and ponder the question. He could not have an all-night staff meeting. But no matter how long he considered his choice, or how little, the mind has a way of making a decision without conscious thought; it hears what it wants to hear. *Poor Garesche!* Wasn't Thomas suffering, or about to suffer, the same fate as Davis and Sheridan? What made Thomas any different? Surely, the whole might of the Confederacy was about to fall on him. There was nothing to stand in the Rebels' way. What earthly good could Rosecrans do there? Garfield was a born messenger anyhow. Rosecrans would take care of business in Chattanooga and see about that new defensive line by the Tennessee. Of course. "Well," he said to Garfield, a future president of the United States, "go and tell General Thomas my precautions to hold the Dry Valley Road and secure our commissary stores and artillery. [Tell him] to report the situation to me and to use his discretion as to continuing the fight on the ground we occupy at the close of the afternoon or retiring to a position in the rear near Rossville."

Thick-chested Garfield, alive as any man to life's possibilities, struck to the right for Thomas's last stand before the terrible Confederates. His ride, as he slapped his foamy-mouthed horse on both flanks for speed, took him into the hearts of his countrymen, took him finally into the White House, where, of course, the ultimate hand of fickle fate pulled the trigger and halted his ride into history forever. In the opposite direction, Old Rosey, the army's favorite general, went off toward a Sunday evening in sleepy Chattanooga. The nearer he got, the greater the weight on his shoulders of what he had done—which was to have abandoned his army. Rosecrans's sin was that he was all too human, and war's requirement is that its generals be superhuman if they can't be lucky. At around 3:30 P.M.

he sadly drew up before Chattanooga's military headquarters, an imposing three-story building. No more the hustle and bustle of Widow Glenn's modest cabin. No more the shells whistling and the floor shaking. But Old Rosey could not dismount. He weaved in the saddle, by now, either unable to decide to swing down or physically unable to do so. He was psychically paralyzed. Fellow officers had to aid him. A nearby observer said, "The officers who helped him into the house did not soon forget the terrible look of a brave man, stunned by sudden calamity." He went on: "In later years I used occasionally to meet Rosecrans, and always felt that I could see the shadow of Chickamauga upon his noble face."

The indomitable Dana soon followed Rosecrans into headquarters. Whereas Rosecrans was now turning to the Almighty for instructions, Dana, the former newsman, was turning to the modern instrument of choice for disaster: the telegraph. The key was immediately clicking, the wire humming to Washington and fat-faced Edwin Stanton, secretary of war (and gloom): "My report today is of deplorable importance. Chickamauga is as fatal a name in our history as Bull Run." *Clickety click click.* "They came through with resistless impulse, composed of brigades formed in divisions. Before them our soldiers turned and fled. It was wholesale panic. Vain were all attempts to rally them." *Clickety click click.* "Our wounded are all left behind, some 6,000 in number. We have lost heavily in killed today. The total of our killed, wounded, and prisoners can hardly be less than 20,000, and may be much more . . . "

Surely, Chattanooga lay in danger of being swept away in the Rebel tidal wave. Who could doubt it? And straining the ear, one could hear in the far distance the report of gunfire. Some sort of fighting was still going on. Somewhere down there stood General Thomas of Virginia.

7

★

The Granddaddy of All Elephants

George H. Thomas, burly and tough and thoroughly good-natured, a Tidewater native who now was ironically placed in charge of what remained of the Union forces in this all-important godforsaken hinterland, had no doubts about what he should do. The Rebels were coming; he would hold them off. Like a competent surgeon, scalpel in hand, patient spread out before him, he could be counted upon for quick wits and an aggressive stance. Successful generals come in all sorts of packages, short and tall, crazy and sane, but one quality that all have in common is decisiveness—they brook no interference, and they know they're right. Hamlet could make a speech, but would have made a lousy general. A successful general may lose more men than his enemy and sometimes may technically "lose" the battle or engagement—as Stonewall Jackson did in his first one in the Shenandoah Valley Campaign at Kernstown, Virginia on

March 23, 1862—but he doesn't hem and haw and lose sleep over it. He acts. He recoups. He focuses. He keeps going. "This army doesn't retreat," Old Pap Thomas had said once before when the Rebels had come pounding at his gates.

Thomas threw together what he could from the half-organized, flying Federals. John M. Brannan, who had been connected with the action from near the beginning, had swung his weary troops up to a rise in the ground along the eastern spur of Missionary Ridge. Scattered brigades from the decimated commands of Thomas J. Wood, James S. Negley, and Horatio P. Van Cleve then took up arms with Brannan's men to try to form a new line. Thomas took a brigade each from Richard W. Johnson and John M. Palmer and detached them to aid Brannan. Here they were, this improvised collection, getting set to stem the might of the Rebels. Thomas did not like to see loss of life; he was not a butcher. Like Wellington (and later Erwin Rommel), he liked to chose his terrain and then counterpunch. If the others wanted blood, let them come. He wanted the best cover and the best rise of ground, and then he wanted to beat the hell out of anyone who came after him. He had no time for niceties now, no time for a wire to Washington or a chit-chat with his staff.

In what time he had left before James Longstreet threw his might at him, Thomas rode among his troops, offering words of encouragement. Actually, just the sight of him in the saddle was soothing and helped create a sense of security. Thomas was easy to spot—at six feet (not so usual in those days) and weighing over 200 pounds (not so unusual). He rode slowly, not from any slackness in purpose, but because his back was killing him. An old injury caused shooting darts of pain to course up his spin when he was on a horse. He sat squarely and rigidly in the saddle and was impossible to miss—and his nickname for this kind of pace was Old Slow Trot. He rode up to Charles G. Harker, who was as tough as old leather, and said, "This hill must be held and I trust you to do it." Harker didn't miss a beat: "We will hold it or die here." He came to Colonel Emerson Opdycke, a regimental commander. "This point must be held," Thomas said. Again on the beat: "We will hold this ground," Opdycke said, "or go to heaven from it." All around Thomas the men who would do the fighting, who stood behind these defiant words, nodded and spit in the dirt and gave Old Pap a cheer. The only sign of nervousness on Thomas's part was that he kept fidgeting with his brown, gray-streaked beard, absently drawing his fingers through it.

On the other side, the Southerners had reason to feel confident. Hadn't they been driving Yankees before them all day? This was the final push, a mopping-up operation, in which they would drive the final nail in the coffin.

Here now was the decisive moment in the war. Since the start, Lincoln had adhered more or less to the Anaconda Plan, which had been thought up by that shrewd old warrior, Winfield Scott, the ancient Virginian who was nonetheless a patriot for the Union. His beautifully conceived strategy (which was ridiculed by the press at first) was to strangle the rebellion as quickly and painlessly as possible: Cut off the South by a blockade from Chesapeake Bay to down around the shores of the Gulf, on the east, and down the length of the Mississippi from Cairo to New Orleans, on the west. Squeeze the South to death as if by a boa constrictor. By now, after more than a few setbacks, the pieces were falling into place. Vicksburg had fallen; New Orleans was in Federal hands. Lee was stalemated and checked in Virginia. Shortages were being felt in the South. Back in April there had been a near-calamitous bread riot in the Confederate capital of Richmond, where only the presence of a bareheaded Jefferson Davis, standing in the middle of the rioters, stating he was ready to shoot the troublemakers, had restored calm. Gettysburg had been a rude shock to the Southerners in July. Now the center, the *heart*, of the rebellion was at stake. As Lincoln wired a general, "The great object to be attained is to drive the enemy from Kentucky and East Tennessee. If we cannot do it now we need never to hope for it." Either do it now and hope for total victory or lose and expect a settled peace. It was that simple. The late afternoon of September 20, 1863, on Snodgrass Hill, was that important to both sides—whether they fully realized it or not.

Joseph B. Kershaw from South Carolina started his brigade, together with some doughty Mississippians, up the steep hill to engage the Federals—and to push them back, he believed. Not long before, in the heat of summer, these same men had taken the Wheat Field and the Peach Orchard at Gettysburg. They knew how to fight. They had seen "the elephant"—meaning, as the soldiers back then put it, that they had seen war at first hand; they had been to the circus and had seen the elephant. They were going to prevail. Up the slope they came, digging into the dirt and bramble, moving briskly and in close order as if trained for warfare in the previous century. All they had to do was gain the top, and victory was theirs. Shots rang out above—a deafening clatter. The Federals didn't move, but their rifles spoke—one after another the crackle of fire sounded. Harker, Palmer, William Babcock Hazen, and the men of Brannan's left brigade loaded and reloaded, and did it with the precision and the methodical mien of carpenters hard at work. They coolly fired and didn't even consider falling back. The gray troops slowed their ascent, comrades sinking around them. They stopped, they stood, they tried to inch up another bit of ground—and then they slowly began to descend. Kershaw wasn't in the mood to accept the result. He realigned them, put them closer together, and sent them up again. They got no farther. Back they came. Kershaw was hard to convince. He tried it a third time, and then he called it quits. Men were gasping for breath, clutching their throats, exhausted. One regimental colonel came across a beardless boy who was weeping and wailing. It was no time to be scared, he told the

boy, he must fight like a man. "That ain't hit, Colonel," the boy
said, still sobbing. "I'm so damned tired I can't keep up with my
company." Kershaw himself was pretty much exhausted at this
point. Whatever it was at the moment—concentrated troops above
or the steep slope they must climb through a rain of minié balls—it
was enough to make the Southerners slack off on their right. When
the time came for Bushrod Johnson and Thomas C. Hindman to
begin *their* further assault on the left, then they would try once
again. That assault should come pretty soon. The Yankees couldn't
defend both flanks at once. It stood to reason.

It did look grim for the Yankees.

Military life, even in war, is lived on the battlefield only in short
bursts of time. There are long, deadly stretches of boredom; rumors
of war; youthful exuberance pushed to the extreme; deep hungers
and thirsts; and feuds and personal conflicts (sometimes resulting in
maiming or death). Army life is an eccentric way of life. Union
Major General Gordon Granger, in charge of guarding Rossville
Gap as a possible escape valve for Federal troops into Chattanooga,
was military to the core and a type all too recognizable by those
who have known barracks life. His kind are called disciplinarians—
in Granger's case, strict disciplinarians. They enforce the rules; they
go by the book. This attitude does not endear them to ordinary soldiers, and their orders often go under the heading of "chickenshit"—unnecessary and disruptive. "That's a chickenshit thing to
do," or "He's nothing but chickenshit."

Granger was a West Pointer, class of 1845. He had fought in
Mexico and in the Indian Wars, and he was grizzled, tough, and
efficient as a Spencer repeater. Life in the army hadn't made him a
philosopher. He talked little, and his commands were curt and
brisk. Fellow officers didn't cotton to him any more than did the
enlisted men. He didn't join in whatever fun was at hand, had a
gruff answer for most things, and believed he could reach people

more easily through pain than through pleasure. Known for having a fondness for the whip, he came, paradoxically, from Joy, New York.

Granger's division commander, James Blair Steedman, was a man of a different stripe: sunny and robust and highly popular with his men. Nicknamed Old Steady, he used his bonhomie and good humor after the war to gain a seat in the Ohio Senate and to be elected chief of police of Toledo. He began as a poor orphan and ended a successful publisher of the *Northern Ohio Democrat* in Toledo. He had but one dread: the misspelling of his name. He left a clause in his will that newspapers should be watched in their obituaries of him, that his name should be spelled "Steedman," not "Steadman."

Of course, the midwesterners in the outfit favored Old Steady over Granger, who went without a nickname. For some reason, the 115th Illinois Volunteers was composed principally of Methodist ministers—hardly the sort to warm to Granger's brand of soldiering. They were, by and large, a sunny group, their hands primed to press the flesh or catch a passing chicken wing. Their civilian life had been conditioned by belting out hymns, passing the plate, and savoring dinners in someone else's home. Others in the outfit were down-home country boys from the southern part of Illinois, who were just as robust in their appetite for hearty lip-smacking food.

When Granger's men first reached Rossville, in their role as security guards, foragers spread out to liberate what victuals they could from the countryside. They hit a bonanza when they discovered well-stocked farms as yet untouched by the war. They roped in meat and fowl and bushels of vegetables—in vast quantities. The "cattle brigade," assigned to bring in livestock, soon began popping off so many rounds that one observer likened it to heavy skirmishing. They were firing more lead into farm animals than they were into Confederates. Granger, whose ear was ever alert to musketry, took note and found out that his men were having a fine time and helping themselves to many a free meal. Such freeloading was, of course, against regulations. The grub, however, was succulent, and something that was inordinately pleasing to his men and many of his officers. His orders were swift. Men who had brought these contrabands in should be arrested. Those who were still out in the countryside foraging should be stopped by a cavalry charge. A hundred soldiers were thus tied to fence posts in front of headquarters with their booty piled in front of them. No one doubted that the whip would soon come out and that lashes on bare backs would follow. All this was too much for these midwesterners who were in the process of saving the Union. They would not take it. A large number of Methodist ministers, along with farm boys and Irishmen, began congregating in front of Granger's command post. They were not there for a prayer meeting. Granger looked out the window and judged the crowd's size; he then decided that the whip could wait and that he would use his ill humor later against the enemy across the trees. He turned the matter of discipline over to Steedman. Old Steady let the men know that it would perhaps be better if they were more discreet in bringing home the contraband.

Thus Granger's corps stood at Rossville Gap with full confidence and many a full belly.

During the morning of September 20, Granger fretted over the sound of gunfire, but this time he knew it didn't come from foragers. This was the real McCoy. Leonidas L. Polk was in the midst of making his attack, and Longstreet was gearing up for his. A mighty grounds-well of rumbling battlefield sounds reached his perch at McAfee's Church, two miles east of Rossville, at this early stage of the day's savage fighting. Granger was not a man to sit on the sidelines. He climbed the nearest available haystack and looked through binoculars toward where the sounds of battle were coming from. Way down La Fayette Road he saw a billowing cloud of dust and unmistakable gunsmoke, with here and there telltale yellow flashes of battery fire. Something big and important and terrible was now in progress. Granger slid down the haystack. He wasn't about to hold binoculars while the fight was reaching such intensity. Back in the case went his field binoculars, the case snapped shut. To his chief of staff, he said: "I am going to Thomas, orders or no orders!" His aide said, "If you go it may bring disaster to the army and you to a court-martial."

Granger, in fact, went against his bias. He was Regular Army, the definition. Built in his sinews was the reflex to do what he had been commanded to do. If he was ordered to guard the outhouse, guard the outhouse he would. If he was told to run naked up Broadway, run naked up Broadway he would. Now he had been commanded to guard Rossville Gap, and he had determined to leave the post and head for the action. Perhaps it was liberating, this sudden rush to take matters into his own hands. He had faced the Rubicon and had made his choice. He would forgo the safety and safekeeping of Rossville Gap; he would march to where the battle raged. He had made countless decisions in his life, but hardly one of such far-ranging effect. So battles are sometimes decided. After all the war councils, the maneuvering, the training, the weather, the brilliances and ineptness, the hate and ill will and bravery—luck has its say. Granger's decision can be looked upon in two ways: It was fated, determined by Providence—or it was the roll of the dice, the draw of the card. His decision was an integral part of how the battle turned out that day, but he was not fool enough not to hedge his bet. He left behind a third of his troops to guard Rossville Gap and then set off to aid Thomas. He had four miles to go, but before one mile was passed, he found trouble—in the form of Nathan Bedford Forrest. That old devil Forrest had set up batteries along the La Fayette Road, and they opened up against Granger's marching column—the spit of cannon fire causing the Federals to stop, duck, and run for cover. Nor was the sudden gunfire the only trouble the Rebels suddenly brought. Captain Ambrose Bierce, an officer in an Ohio battery then and later a chronicler of the battle, wrote, "Then away to our left and rear some of Bragg's people set up 'the rebel yell.' It was taken up successively and passed around to our front, along our right and in behind us again, until it seemed almost to have got to the place where it started. It was the ugliest sound that any mortal ever heard—to a mortal exhausted and unnerved by two days of hard fighting, without sleep, without rest, without food and without hope. There was, however, a space somewhere at the back of us across which that horrible yell did not long prolong itself; and through that we finally retired in profound silence and dejection, unmolested."

Granger's troops were forced, for the moment, to turn from an orderly march into a defensive line of battle. Skirmishers pressed forward after a while and then chased the outnumbered Rebels away. They returned to the defensive line, but Forrest's men also returned to their guns, which they proceeded to fire with alacrity. Granger didn't mull over what he should do. He swore a substantial string of curses and then called for his reserve troops from Rossville Gap to come forward for support. They held off Forrest's pesky horsemen while Granger resumed the march. We're coming, Thomas!

A short distance from their goal, while gunfire began to swell, Granger faced another impediment: The remnants of Negley's division were marching—fleeing—the other way. Negley's troops were leaving the flaming cauldron, heading for the safety of Rossville Gap, which Granger, of course, had just left. There were catcalls and mutterings between the troops—but Granger cared only for moving his men forward. He rode ahead of his column and reached Thomas before the Virginian knew exactly who was calling. The tall, bulky Virginian had been looking over his shoulder, fretting over who these approaching troops might be, marching toward his rear. Dust clouds moved above them, and a faint ominous rumble of many troops issued forth. If they had been hostile, then Thomas would have been surrounded and inevitably annihilated. One can but imagine his relief to find that the outfit was commanded by the stiff-backed, die-hard Granger—usually not a gratifying sight, but today most welcome. A firm handshake, a greeting, and then down to business. They must contain the Confederates. Kershaw was then in full throttle, trying to smash Thomas on the left. Hindman and Johnson were coming out of the woods on the right. Patrick R. Cleburne had thrown his batteries forward—pushing, pulling, straining—then blowing Federal breastworks to pieces. Afterward his infantry had clambered over them. But the blueclads were holding as best they could. Musket barrels turned so hot that they burned flesh in the reloading process. Minié balls were fast running out, and the snap of bayonets locking into place sounded. Granger saved the day in that respect, too, because his men brought not only themselves, but cartridge boxes, ammunition. After pumping Thomas's hand, Granger pointed to a crowd of graybacks he saw congregating on Horseshoe Ridge. "Those men must be driven back," he said.

Thomas couldn't agree more. "Can you do it?" he asked.

"Yes," Granger said. "My men are fresh, and they are just the fellows for that work. They are raw troops, and they don't know any better than to charge up there."

A shell fragment tore through Granger's field hat, and he hardly noticed, didn't step back. He watched as General Steedman—"a great hearty man, broad-breasted [and] broad shouldered"—personally led his men forward. Steedman was exactly the sort of man you wanted now. He had only had one verbal command to make to his staff: "Spell my name right in the obituaries." Astride a fine horse, he signaled the charge to begin and trotted forth at the head only to find his troops wavering at the sight of Confederates who were not backing off but raising muskets. Steedman knew what to do. As the Federals moved through brush and waist-high weeds, as if wading through a pounding surf, their bodies exhausted, their minds gripped by terror, faltering, about to give up, Steedman tore the regimental colors from a pale Illinois bearer's hands and waved it high, still on his mount. Minié balls buzzed all around. "Go back, boys, go back," he thundered, "but the flag can't go with you!" That gesture was all that was needed. No one backstepped; all continued forward, Steedman in front. His horse was shot from under him, and his large bulk bounced on the ground. He got up, shook himself, and continued, still holding the colors aloft, into a rain of minié balls. "Follow me!" Here was a certified general trudging up an exploding hill, lugging the colors. On the other side, a wrenching mood passed through the Southerners: These Yankees were crazy, were madder than hornets—and coming to get them! The Southerners who had thought they had a lock on craziness, what with their wild yell, wild hair, and patched-up clothing and often no shoes, fell back, mulled it over, regrouped, and then staged a counterattack. But the Federals held the ridge. It had taken but twenty minutes of combat and the loss of one-fifth of Federal troops. It was only the beginning.

Longstreet did not like what he saw. He had good reason to expect that, by now, the Federals would have given up and turned tail. Just a slight nudge, and they should have been on the run. But here they were, fighting like alley cats. Longstreet was a soldier's soldier, though, and couldn't waste time thinking about what should be or what might have been better planned and executed. Deal with what you have. Kershaw had jumped the gun on the right, eager to get at the Yankees, but before Johnson and Hindman had been in position to strike on the left. By the time Johnson and Hindman had struck, Kershaw was already beaten back. There must be coordination. They must strike all at once, every man jack, in one solid blow. Kershaw was on one flank, and Johnson and Hindman were on the other. Now Longstreet brought in a fresh general to attack the middle, someone he had met for the first time that day: William Preston. Longstreet had scarcely laid eyes on this fine figure of a man before deeming him "the genial, gallant, lovable

William Preston." Preston had been a U.S. congressman and diplo-
mat and now he wore gray with gold braid—a brigadier general of
the Confederate army. He was a Kentucky aristocrat, a Harvard
graduate, and the brother-in-law of the late and exceptional General Albert Sidney Johnston, on whose staff he had once served.

The sun was starting to sink now, a little before four o'clock,
and Preston, tall in the saddle, sent two brigades in echelon out of
the dark woods and up the slope of Snodgrass Hill, holding one
brigade in reserve. He sent the brigades directly against the center
of Brannan's line, a valiant do-or-die charge reminiscent of Pickett's
Charge on the field at Gettysburg. The men marched straight
ahead, heads up, as if in review; goddamn everybody, here they
came, muskets in hand, up after the Yankees! On the hill the Federals were moving everything that wasn't nailed down—stones, brush,
logs, and dirt—to give themselves cover and impede the advance.
They fired well-aimed, direct fire down on the Southerners, knocking them off left and right, but not stopping them. About eighty
yards short of the top, where blazing yellow bursts came from the
Federal line, the Rebels stopped. They then raised their own muskets and returned the fire. In essence the two lines stood frozen, firing into each other's faces. The Federals had the best of it, for they
were partly hidden and were firing downhill. The Southerners had
to raise their muskets to fire uphill, and their aim was necessarily
not as good. But they did not flinch. They stood. And for nearly an
hour the two sides fired right into each other's ranks.

The two Confederate brigades had two somewhat unlikely commanders. Brigadier General Archibald Gracie, Jr., was New York
born, a Heidelberg University and West Point graduate, who had
been doing business in his family's mercantile firm in Mobile before
Alabama seceded. He joined the Southern cause while his father
and other members of his family remained loyal to the Union. (The
white wood-framed Gracie Mansion, which looks out majestically
over the East River in Manhattan, was his family home and is now

the dwelling place of New York City mayors.) Colonel John Herbert Kelly, the other brigade commander, was but twenty-three and had men serving under him who were twice his age. At the start of the war, he was a cadet at West Point, which he left to return to his native Alabama to join the cause. He had risen rapidly in rank, fighting at Shiloh, Perryville, and Murfreesboro—and now on September 20, 1863, his men stood poised to break the Federal center and send Thomas's blueclads into catastrophic ruin. But if the Federals held, they could well save the vital Army of the Cumberland. The rough-hewn cabin on the gently rising hill, the Snodgrass farmhouse, had that much importance today. Before the hour had passed Preston's two brigades—led by Gracie and Kelly—lost 1,054 out of 2,879 effectives, nearly half.

They did not reach the crest, but their furious, disciplined attack woke up their fellow Southerners. Polk, who had been fuming at Bragg or praying to the Lord (or waiting for supper), decided to join the battle, hurling his divisions against Thomas's north–south line. Now Thomas was completely pressured. He could not relax. He could not call for one unit to move to the aid of another. The Federals were being charged on all fronts—from the east end of Snodgrass Hill to the west face of Horseshoe Ridge. A breakthrough at any point spelled disaster. In the parlance of the ring, they were on the ropes, sagging, being pounded all over, hanging on by a thread. A crucial fact, though, was that they were firing *down*, not *up*, and they did have some, although not much, cover. Even so, Thomas's men were perilously near being out of ammunition. The battle caused an almost constant sheet of flame—as more than one observer noted. One Ohio regiment, composed of 535 men at the start, fired around 45,000 rounds of bullets. Thomas's ordnance train was gone—long gone—shelled and blown apart like a tree stump. Granger's fresh supply of 95,000 rounds soon left the rifles, as if in one grand fusillade. The Northerners picked over the cartridge pouches of the dead, and when they came up empty, cried to their commander for instructions. "Use your bayonets," Thomas said simply. He sat in his customary square stance on his horse, head held high, while bullets snipped off the leaves of trees above him. Longstreet later claimed that there had been twenty-five separate charges that afternoon to overpower Snodgrass Hill. Those involved may not have known when one charge ended and another began. It finally took on the appearance of one all-out desperate surge of the Southerners to break through—anywhere. As the Rebels dug their boots in near the summit, rifles and heavy guns fired directly into them. They staggered and fell back, time after time. Then they re-formed at the foot of the slope and moved right back up to take the same resounding blow in the face. The woods caught fire. The heavens seemed to have exploded. The North held.

And the common soldier, who was nobody's general or grand tactician, may have seen the elephant before, but nothing like this. This Battle of Chickamauga was the granddaddy of all elephants. Here again is Thomas Wolfe recalling an old Confederate's story of what it was like to have been there in person:

The fight began upon our right at ten o'clock. We couldn't find out what was happenin': the woods thar was so close and thick we never knowed fer two days what had happened, and we didn't know for certain then. We never knowed how many we was fightin' or how many we had lost. I've heard them say that even Old Rosey himself didn't know jest what had happened when he rode back into town next day, and din't know that Thomas was still standin' like a rock. And if Old Rosey didn't know no more than this about hit, what could a common soldier know? We fought back and forth across that cedar thicket fer two days, thar was times when you would be right up on top of them before you even knowed that they was thar. And that's the way the fightin' went—the bloodiest fightin' that was ever knowed, until that cedar thicket was soaked red with blood, and thar was hardly a place left in thar where a sparrer could have perched.

. . . Hit was like fightin' in a bloody dream—like doin' somethin' in a nightmare—only the nightmare was like death and hell. Longstreet threw us up that hill five times, I think, before darkness came. We'd charge up to the very muzzles of their guns, and they'd mow us down like grass, and we'd come stumblin' back—or what was left of us—and form again at the foot of the hill, and then come on again. We'd charge right up the Ridge and drive 'em through the gap and fight 'em with cold steel, and they come back again and we'd brain each other with the butt end of guns. Then they'd throw us back and we'd re-form and come on after 'em again.

Around four o'clock Brigadier General James A. Garfield at last showed up. He had taken a perilous ride since leaving General William Starke Rosecrans—through briar patches, over high rocky land, and across wet marshes. The future president had even galloped past a quarantined house where Confederates kept smallpox cases. Garfield had the presence of mind to toss money to the unfortunates as he whipped by, and he had to ask directions more than once. On reaching the field where bullets flew, he didn't slow or change course. His two orderlies were shot dead, and his horse received a bullet wound. He jumped his horse over a high fence, raced over a farm field, zigzagging to avoid sniper bullets, and came up to Thomas in a clump of trees not far from the Snodgrass house. His horse took its second bullet, just as he arrived, and fell dead beside Thomas's mount. Garfield rose and relayed Rosecrans's order for "retiring to a position in the rear."

Rosecrans had, of course, set the example and was now himself on the way to a strong drink in Chattanooga. Thomas, on Snodgrass Hill, wasn't considering a fallback in daylight. "It will ruin the army to withdraw it now," he said. "This position must be held until night." However, the sharp slope of the mountains caused deep shadows to fall over the area before the sun had actually set, and at around five o'clock in the faint mountain light, Thomas began to withdraw, first on the left, where Polk was making a racket, then on the right, where Kershaw, Hindman, and Johnson were more hotly pressing. Thomas drew his troops back in sequence: first Joseph J. Reynolds's; then Johnson's; and finally Absalom Baird's, which served as a rear guard. It was right out of the textbook. Afterward, the units on the right were to perform the same kind of sequence. Reynolds's men began the first movement at around 5:30 P.M., but no sooner had they reached the northern rim, ready to move through McFarland's Gap on the way to Chattanooga, than they ran across Confederates from St. John Richardson Liddell's brigades. As happened time after time at Chickamauga, commanders had to go it on their own, often against orders, and do what needed to be done. Reynolds didn't hesitate. He took on Liddell's troops and drove them from the field, thus allowing a safe zone for the other units to pass through. Rebel pressure from the divisions of John C. Breckinridge and Cleburne soon became so insistent and intense, though, that Reynolds had to pull back before he could care for his wounded, let alone bury his dead. He had to leave the field littered with those crying in pain and bloodied by the fight, trusting that the onrushing Rebels would care for them. He raced for the safety of Missionary Ridge, far outstripping the Rebels' pursuit of him. In war, the one who is running often has more to gain than do those who are after him. When Reynolds at last reached safety, the sun had set behind Missionary Ridge.

When it came time for Steedman to pull back from Horseshoe Ridge in the pale light, the Rebels were more than ready to continue dishing it out. The Yankees had been frustrating them all through the late afternoon there. Maddeningly, decisively. Cool-headed, aristocratic Preston threw his one reserve brigade into the gap that Steedman left and let his boys charge right over the crest of the hill they'd hungered for and into hot pursuit. Kill 'em! The inspired and fresh Confederates turned east and slammed right into three Yankee regiments, who fought as best they could and then waved the white flag. The battle then evolved into who wanted the most first: Did the Rebels want to annihilate the Yankees more than the Yankees wanted to make a beeline for the ultimate goal of Chattanooga? The Yankees wanted to survive more than the Rebels wanted to smash them. Thomas marched his men out—thanks, in large part, to the rearguard action of Reynolds's do-or-die troops. Two Indiana regiments among them came across a broken-down ammunition wagon that had been abandoned in an earlier route and helped themselves to the fare, loading up. Seemingly everywhere, knowing all, Thomas came upon these men who were grabbing up bullets as the parched grab for water. Thomas didn't waste time marveling at the sight. He told them to countermarch immediately against the Rebels and hold them off while the remainder of the great Army of the Cumberland made its retreat. These Hoosiers didn't tarry. They made the Union army's last stand. In the first moments of the deep night, firing volley after volley of red-glowing fire into the growing darkness and shadows of the advancing gray line, they never knew what they had hit, but the Rebels didn't reach them. Finally, they about-faced and marched away—the last blue troops to exit the Battle of Chickamauga.

Then came the trip back. They went through McFarland's Gap to Rossville, as near defeat as they would ever be save with death, shoulders slumped, spirits broken. They had been whipped, shorn of honor, chased from the field. Those were the sentiments of those who recalled the moment. "Weary, worn, tired and hungry," a Federal captain later remembered. "We sullenly dragged ourselves along, feeling a shame and disgrace that had never been experienced by the Old Sixth before." When someone sank to the side, he left the sad march and wasn't carried along. Survivors had a hard enough time making their own legs move, one numb leg after another. There could come nothing worse, they all thought, than this miserable retreat. They were wrong. Soon they heard the Rebels on the other side of a ridge—celebrating, goddamn them. Those Rebels were hooting and hollering in an unholy manner, the worst sound that could ever strike the human ear, worse, by far, than their inhuman Rebel Yell. Ambrose Bierce, who was in the retreat, called the sound "the ugliest any mortal ever heard."

The Rebels apparently were more interested in whooping it up and enjoying the possession of the bloody battlefield than in any further fighting with the Federals. The Southerners wanted to savor their victory as they would fine whiskey. They'd beat them! They'd turned them back! Come to our homeland and see what you get, you sons of bitches! Longstreet described the whooping as "a tremendous swell of heroic harmony that seemed almost to lift from the roots the great trees of the forest." Beyond the merriment, the Rebels picked among the loot, which, when officially counted, included 51 guns, 23,281 small arms, 2,381 rounds of artillery shells, and 135,000 rifle cartridges. All armies prize exactness, and the Confederate report included other items: 35 pounds of picket rope, 365 shoulder straps, and 3 damaged copper bugles. In the dark they could not fully comprehend a litter of another kind: bodies broken and mangled and many dead. Even though the Confederates built fires near the wounded of both sides, to warm and cheer them, they had little sense of the complete tableau until day broke. There had been no rain for a month preceding the battle, and fires had erupted throughout the carnage. Where fires hadn't come from shelling, the Federals had started them when abandoning their breastworks. Those who went on burial details reported that the clothing of the dead had burned off many bodies. A Southerner reported that the night after the battle, "The dead and wounded lay in heaps, literally piled upon each other, and in many instances the fire had burned them to a cinder, and many of the wounded had their clothes burned off, and their bodies were a perfect blister." The wounded often took sticks and frantically raked back leaves and brush by them, hoping to escape the flames. The next day many were found scorched to death, still holding the sticks.

Sam Watkins, of the First Tennessee, wrote in his account of women who combed the battlefield with lanterns. These were the kinfolk and wives of soldiers who had not returned or been accounted for. He witnessed one woman scream, "O, there he is! Poor fellow! Dead, dead, dead." The woman put the soldier's head in her lap and began to kiss it. "O, O, they have killed my darling, my darling, my darling."

War does not end because of pity, though. War ends because one side quits. The Yankees had not surrendered, and even though the bodies were piled high in awesome rows—General Daniel Harvey Hill claimed he had "never seen the Federal dead lie so thickly on the ground, save in front of the sunken wall at Fredericksburg"— the thinking among the Confederate generals was that the victory should be followed by quick pursuit, that the fruits of victory shouldn't be allowed to slip away. Longstreet began assembling ammunition and putting things in order for a quick march at first light. Polk, who might have been suffering from a bad conscience because of his slackness in battle that day, didn't wait. The Episcopal bishop sent out scouts to see what shape the retreating Federals were in, preparatory to slaughtering them. The scouts reported back that the Federals were in full headlong flight, which caused Polk to ride headlong to Bragg's headquarters tent in the rear.

Bragg had been roused from slumber the night before by burly straight-talking Longstreet. Now the apparition of Polk hovered over his cot. Polk was hardly a welcome sight to Bragg at any time because he brought memories of missed assignments and cunning defiance. One can only imagine the lack of enthusiasm with which Bragg rose in his long johns, unwound his scrawny limbs, and left the warmth of his covers. What is it now? An aide who stood next to Polk that night reported one version of what took place. Polk said that "the enemy was routed and flying precipitately from the field, and that then was the opportunity to finish the work by the capture or destruction of [Rosecrans's] army, by prompt pursuit, before he had time to reorganize or throw up defenses at Chattanooga." In his accustomed role as the recipient of bad news, Bragg had trouble drinking in this news. He was not comfortable with winning. He did not believe Polk. On the other hand, Polk had never had an enjoyable interview with Bragg, and tonight was no exception. He left feeling terrible, as usual.

The next day a Confederate private was brought to Bragg's tent. This soldier had been captured by the Yankees and later escaped in the hubbub of the Federals' flight. He had something interesting to report. The Yankees not only were retreating, but were so whipped and demoralized that they were leaving their wounded behind. Bragg was a hard man to convince about anything. If he had witnessed the Yankees' flight in person, he well could have disagreed with his eyes. He glared balefully at the private and said, "Do you know what a retreat looks like?" The private said—or was supposed to have said—words that endeared him to Southern soldiers near and far, repeated and embellished and refined over campfires for some time to come: "I ought to, General; I've been with you during your whole campaign."

Still Bragg would not move. He had, in one sense, sound reasons not to: His army was exhausted, and there were few horses to haul his artillery. But wars are won by people who go against reason—what reasonable man would go to war in the first place?—and no one wins who doesn't sometimes go against the odds when ultimate victory is worth the attempt. If—if—Bragg had boldly pursued Thomas, the ultimate fate of the Confederacy might have been different. The Confederacy could conceivably have lasted, and a settled peace might have resulted. Forrest had no doubts about what to do. The morning after the battle, he took off with 400 troopers to see what havoc he could wreak on the retreating Federals. He found the Federals soon enough, when he stumbled over an outpost that fired one volley at him and then fled. The bluecoats fled so rapidly that they left lookouts stranded in an observation platform atop a tree on the crest of Missionary Ridge. The Yankees' aim was fairly accurate, though. One bullet hit an artery in the neck of Forrest's steed, and the blood spurted up. Then followed the chain of events that has helped create the Forrest legend. The intrepid Tennessean simply put his finger in the hole, stopping the flow, and rode on. When he came to the foot of the observation post, he removed his finger and the horse collapsed. He called for the lookouts to get the hell down in a hurry, and then he questioned them sharply, after which he climbed the tree to have a look himself. He saw the blue-clads in haste to reach safety, and he saw the grayclads dillydallying to his rear, as if on a holiday. On the ground he immediately dictated a dispatch to Polk:

> We are in a mile of Rossville. Have been on the point of Missionary Ridge. Can see Chattanooga and everything around. The enemy's trains are leaving, going around the point of Lookout Mountain.
>
> The prisoners captured report two pontoons thrown across [the Tennessee River] for the purpose of retreating.
>
> I think they are evacuating as hard as they can go.
>
> They are cutting timber down to obstruct our passage.
>
> I think we ought to press forward as rapid as possible.

Forrest didn't stop with that dispatch. He moved to within three miles of Chattanooga, carrying his guns to throw shells down on any defense of the town below. He was almost beside himself that reinforcement hadn't shown up yet. The delay was costing them men. Then came word that no infantry was on its way—none, zero. Bragg was holding his forces back. Far from giving up, knowing the importance of quick movement now, Forrest rode back to confront Bragg in person. He didn't do things halfway. Bragg always had an answer, though. He informed Forrest that the army could not move far from the railroad line because of a critical lack of supplies. "General Bragg, we can get all the supplies our army needs in Chattanooga." Few could change Bragg's mind short of pulling a gun on him. Forrest returned to his men, beginning to experience the slow burn that would, in a few days, explode in spectacular fury. "What does he fight battles for?" was all he could say.

By late the next day it became too late for an attack. Rosecrans had awakened and was back in the saddle, completing a defense of Chattanooga. Bragg wouldn't listen to anyone. He would have it his way. He ordered the occupation of Missionary Ridge and Lookout Mountain on the outskirts of Chattanooga. He was going to try something new on the Yankees, something diabolical. It would have to go some distance, though, for the battle that had just been completed near the Chickamauga River had been the bloodiest of the war so far.

The whole war had, indeed, changed. What had begun in a bloodless way at Fort Sumter had now become an abattoir. At First Manassas (or Bull Run) there had been, at least at the beginning, on the Federal side, a celebratory mood. Congressmen and wives and various notables congregated on hillsides, picnics spread out before them, to observe the contest—as if it were no more than a pageant or a game. Now the beast had popped out. Now the canker that held every lust, hate, and demoniac urge seemingly in the human soul had been lanced. The setting was perfect: primordial woods, the outback of burgeoning American civilization. Whatever was darkest in the American psyche came out: hate, vengeance, and self-preservation at all costs. A U.S. surgeon who went across the battlefield to care for the wounded reported that "on part of the field there was a head of a soldier on every stump." W. W. Lyle, who had served in an Ohio outfit, gave a graphic picture of the battlefield in a book called *Lights and Shadows of Army Life*: ". . . many of our wounded were buried alive, horrible as it may seem, for bodies were found partly consumed, where the contraction of the muscles, and the clenched fingers, seemed to indicate an attempt to grasp something, while the general appearance gave evidence of a violent struggle of some kind. In one place, the body of a Union soldier was found, with both ears cut off, and in another, several bodies from which the heads had been removed. These had been set up on stakes and rails of the fences, or fastened on limbs of trees . . . The details are sickening."

All who've studied the battle agree that the Confederates lost more. In his 1961 book, *Chickamauga: Bloody Battle of the West,* historian Glenn Tucker listed the losses of the Army of Tennessee as 2,673 killed, 16,274 wounded, and 2,003 missing, a total of 20,950 casualties. (Longstreet's losses alone that Sunday afternoon, principally in the hell-and-brimstone attack on Snodgrass Hill, were 1,856 killed, 6,506 wounded, and 270 missing, or 8,632 of the 22,885 grayclads in the battle.) Tucker figured that the Federals lost in total 1,656 killed, 9,749 wounded, and 4,774 missing—in sum, 16,179 casualties.

But figures themselves are bloodless. It takes an individual example or two from the battlefield itself to bring the savagery home. In his book *With Sabre and Scalpel,* John A. Wyeth, an Alabama private on the Confederate side who would later become a physician and the first president of the American Medical Association, described the scene at one field hospital where the wounded lay stretched out on blankets: "One fellow was walking up and down holding the freshly amputated stump of his forearm with the remaining hand. His jaws were firmly set, and his face wore the hard fixed expression of pain, yet he made no complaint. In fact, I do not think I heard a groan or cry in all that experience. . . . Fragments of arms and legs completed the gruesome picture."

The wounded had to travel many miles to field hospitals, over rutted roads in swaying wagons and then often on creeping railroad cars. At their final destination, they had to wait interminable hours for treatment. This was a part of war that knew no glory, no chivalry. Medical treatment then may seem medieval by today's standards. The bullet that pierced and shattered flesh and bone traveled at a slow speed and did not create sufficient air friction to be self-purifying. It also came contaminated with germs from the hands of the man who fired it and took with it into the wound any bits of filthy clothing it passed through. If the bullet or clothing didn't do it, then the surgeon's grimy hands and instruments were almost sure to bring calamity. The body not only had to withstand the assault of a lead bullet, it also, in treatment, had to contend with toxemia, septicemia, pyemia, tetanus, and gangrene. Recovery from the wound was possible, but fighting infection required a Herculean effort.

Surprisingly, the "backward" South, with far less medical sup-plies than the North, proved better able to fight infections. The Southern surgeons didn't know why their methods worked, but they did—boiled rags instead of contaminated sponges, sterile cotton baked in ovens, and boiled horsehair instead of silk in ligatures and sutures. They had come by the basic principles of asepsis and didn't know it.

But General Thomas knew that an ungodly number of souls had left this earth at the battle. He did not favor burying any Federals at Chickamauga, since the Southerners had technically carried the day there and it had seen enough deaths anyhow. By the time the carnage in the area ended, he set up, under General Order 296, a National Cemetery near Orchard Knob, Tennessee. Bodies that had been hastily buried elsewhere were dug up and laid to rest there. Veterans of American wars continue to be buried there, and the cemetery holds around 12,000 today. Only one soldier who fought at Chickamauga remains on the battle site—Private John Ingra-ham, Company K, First Confederate Regiment, a Georgia volun-teer. He had been engaged to a daughter of the Reed family, of Reed's Bridge fame, and the Reeds came across his body by chance while walking over the field after the smoke cleared. They buried him on the spot, and there he remains.

* * *

Among those who fought at Chickamauga was John Lincoln Clem. Johnny Clem fought in Company C, Twenty-second Michigan. He was twelve years old, and weighed sixty pounds. At age ten, he ran away from home in Ohio to tag along with the Twenty-second back in Michigan and was not officially on the rolls at the time of the battle—so company officers were in the habit of chipping in to give him a private's pay of $13 each month. He began the war as a drummer boy. At Chickamauga, when the battle began to cross all civilized boundaries, when every shot counted, Clem picked up a musket and went charging. He shot one Confederate officer off his horse as the officer raised his saber and shouted for the beardless boy to surrender. Clem kept charging and took a shell fragment in the hip. Some Rebels quickly captured him—but not for long. A very small target, he rolled out of view when no one was looking and into some tall grass. He rested while the action traveled elsewhere and then crawled to safety behind Union lines. He recovered and lived to fight again under Thomas and in the Atlanta campaign. Although wounded a second time, he kept going back for more. After the war, he tried to get into West Point, but failed the written examination. When Ulysses S. Grant became president, he made Clem a second lieutenant in 1871. Clem retired in 1916 as a short major general, the last man on active duty who had served at Chickamauga.

Some who fought at Chickamauga curiously came under the spell of the place and returned to live there. Union Second Lieutenant Charles Edwin Stivers was one. He was a pivotal player in saving Snodgrass Hill on the Confederates' last charge. Just as they were gaining a foothold near the top, Stivers had charge of bringing in the Eighteenth Ohio, which was being held in reserve for such a moment, and threw the exhausted Rebels back and saved the day. Stivers had come up through the ranks. He had proved his ingenuity and his steady nerves on earlier occasions. At Murfreesboro he got caught alone between two long lines of Confederate cavalry. He didn't panic, but kept his head up defiantly and his horse moving smartly. The Rebels took him for one of their own, since he acted as if he belonged and his overcoat was similar to theirs. He escaped. When Thomas pulled back from Snodgrass Hill on September 20, Stivers was one of the last to leave. He continued to serve in the Union army until September 16, 1864. After the war he and other former soldiers from Ohio returned to live in Tennessee. (The distinguished Montagu family in Chattanooga is descended from Ohio soldiers who fought for the North there.) Stivers became a successful banker in Chattanooga and fathered four daughters. The descendants of this Ohio soldier speak with Tennessee accents.

On September 24, 1863, few had a sense of how the battle was going to turn out. Bullets, shells, lucky charges, and do-or-die charges hadn't persuaded the Northerners to return home. Wild yells hadn't turned them back. Now Bragg was going to try one of the oldest games in warfare. He was going to try to starve them out.

8

Another Kind of War

Some things never change. The attitude of the Army of Tennessee, officers and men alike, toward its commander, Lieutenant General Braxton Bragg, remained the same. The men hated Bragg—with a hatred that was in the form not of irritation, but of deep, abiding contempt. You almost have to feel sorry for him; he couldn't seem to do anything right. Now his lieutenants fumed over his failure to charge after the depressed and humiliated Federals. At Shiloh it had been different. At Shiloh (Pittsburg Landing) Bragg had ordered charge after senseless charge against the Yankees' strong fortifications in the Hornet's Nest—against all reason, charge, charge, charge—and *now*, when the Yankees were apparently whipped and bolting, he wouldn't move a finger against them. How could you win a war this way? There were, of course, sound reasons for Bragg not moving on the Yankees after the victory: He had suffered terrible casualties, he did not want to move too precipitously away from the rail line and supplies, he was uncertain about the Yankees' intentions, and so forth. But one thing is certain after all the explanations, after all the latter-day memoirs and second-guessing: Separated by a simple ridge on the night of September 20, the Southerners were whooping it up, nearly insane with delight, while the Yankees could barely crawl away. Why not go after them?

In one respect, Bragg showed a lifetime consistency: Again, according to him, it was the other fellow's fault. Two days after the battle, Bragg sent a curt note to Leonidas Polk, his old nemesis, demanding to know why Polk's attack on the morning of September 20 had been delayed. Polk mulled the matter over for a week and then offered a lengthy explanation, placing the blame on Daniel Harvey Hill. Bragg replied that this explanation was not good enough by far and suspended Polk (and Charles C. Hindman for good measure, although Hindman had done nothing wrong), sending them to Atlanta to await further orders. Polk departed, but the fireworks did not end. Polk, who had a certain flair as a letter writer, got off a blistering message to President Jefferson Davis, charging Bragg with gross incompetence: "The troops at the close of the fight were in the very highest spirits, ready for any service. . . . General Bragg did not know what had happened. He let us down as usual, and allowed the fruits of the great but sanguinary victory to pass from him by the most criminal negligence, or rather incapacity . . ." Polk suggested that Robert E. Lee should take over, but getting Lee to leave Virginia, his home country, for frontier Tennessee was a large order. You might as well suggest sending Lee to the Crimea. Polk mentioned Pierre G. T. Beauregard, the hero of Fort Sumter, as another possibility, but Beauregard was, and always would be, in disfavor with Davis. Davis and Beauregard had a personality conflict, perhaps because Davis was Puritanically inclined while the Creole Beauregard had a sensual and rococo nature. Who, then, could take over for Bragg if Bragg was a disaster? James Longstreet might be reticent, but he wasn't shy. He became ipso facto the one in charge of doing something about their commander—preferably getting him sent elsewhere. Longstreet called a secret meeting on October 4 with the ever-increasing list of dissidents to see what could be done. The upshot was a message fired off to the president calling Bragg unfit to command. It softened the call somewhat by blaming Bragg's health and not his heart and brains.

Davis was not the sort of man to move against old friends. Bragg had come to his aid in Mexico and had shown a world of bravery then. And, anyhow, hadn't they been through this once before? It was getting tiresome. Davis pondered away in Richmond. Meanwhile, Bragg indeed showed his bravery (or his innocence) by taking on someone only the fearless dared attack: Nathan Bedford Forrest. Bragg might lash out with impunity at Polk and be abrupt and rude with Hill and Longstreet, but care was needed in handling Forrest. But in a fit of ill humor, in a meeting with General St. John Richardson Liddell, Bragg made these remarks that Liddell had the presence of mind to record quickly in his journal: "I have not a single general of cavalry fit for command—look at Forrest . . . The man is ignorant, and does not know anything of cooperation. He is nothing more than a good raider." You could say that, sure. Go right ahead. In fact, more than one critic made similar disparaging remarks about Forrest (and some critics continue to do so today). It was better to wait until the man was certifiably dead, though.

A short time after his broadside to Liddell, Bragg made his move: He ordered Forrest to turn over all of his corps to Little Joe Wheeler and left Forrest with only one regiment and one artillery battery. Why? No one could be sure. It didn't make any tactical or strategic sense. It would have only one surefire result: It would cause an explosion. Forrest did not cotton to Wheeler. To Forrest, the Alabaman cavalryman was little more than a strutting bantam rooster. He had almost come to blows with Wheeler once after Fort Donelson, and he was in no mood to bow to Wheeler now. Forrest's fuse was ignited and began its slow burn. He protested the order with a blistering letter of his own, the likes of which Bragg had never received before, and followed it up with a brief confrontation with Bragg in which the commander of the Army of Tennessee assured Forrest that his troops would be returned to him just as soon as they completed a maneuver to cut off the Federals' line of supply above Chattanooga. Don't worry, General, these troops will come back to you. Cooled down somewhat, Forrest requested leave and went to La Grange, Georgia, to visit his wife. While there, he received word that he was being put under the command of little Joe Wheeler.

There are several conflicting accounts of Forrest's subsequent encounter with Bragg, and once again some of the language of what transpired has obviously been cleaned up. The most accurate account would probably have to come from Dr. J. B. Cowan, Forrest's chief surgeon and kinsman, who was present at the event. Cowan passed on the details to Dr. John A. Wyeth and Captain Harvey Mathes, who later wrote biographies of Forrest. Forrest marched into Bragg's headquarters, brushing aside a sentry and having no time for salutes or pleasantries. He strode right into the face of Bragg who, in his abiding innocence, had risen and was courteously extending his hand. Forrest jabbed his index finger toward Bragg's scraggly bearded face and kept doing so while he said:

You commenced your cowardly and contemptible persecution of me soon after the battle of Shiloh, and you have kept it up ever since. . . . I have stood your meanness as long as I intend to. You have played the part of a damned scoundrel, and are a coward, and if you were any part of a man I would slap your jaws and force you to resent it. You may as well not issue any orders to me, for I will not obey them, and I will hold you personally responsible for any further indignities you endeavor to inflict upon me. You have threatened to arrest me for not obeying your orders promptly. I dare you to do it, and I say to you that if you ever again try to interfere with me or cross my path it will be at the peril of your life.

One can imagine the shock to Bragg's nervous system—he may have paled or turned beet red, sat immediately down or didn't know what to do with his hands. He watched Forrest and Cowan depart, and he had nothing to say. As Forrest and Cowan rode off smartly, the doctor said, "Now you are in for it."

"No," Forrest replied, accurately predicting what would follow, "he'll never say a word about it; he'll be the last man to mention it; and mark my word, he'll take no action in the matter. I will ask to be relieved and transferred to a different field, and he will not oppose it."

Forrest had abided by a cardinal rule of the frontier: never let an insult pass. When Bragg didn't stand up and fight back, Forrest dismissed him. In Forrest's eyes, Bragg was no longer a man worthy of any consideration.

And then President Davis made the long trip from Richmond to try to settle the mishmash of quarrels that hovered around Bragg's command. Perhaps he thought he could calm the ill will that had spread far and wide from it. On October 6 he left in his presidential train and wound his way through the Carolinas to Columbia and then over toward Atlanta. He passed through sleepy southern villages, still untouched by the cannonade of war but nonetheless threadbare because of it. It was a slow, bumpy, and curving ride, through crisp fall weather. Davis got to see more of the southern landscape this trip than he had the last time he had come to soothe ruffled feathers that lay in the wake of a Bragg operation, for in the short time that had elapsed since his last visit, the Federals—Ambrose E. Burnside in command—had secured Knoxville and Davis had to take a more roundabout route. In Atlanta Davis conferred with Polk, who stated emphatically that he would never, under any circumstances, again serve under Bragg. Shoot him, cashier him—the bishop would never again do service with that bearded and dour general from North Carolina.

Davis then wound his way to the top of Missionary Ridge, where Bragg had pitched his headquarters. The old comrades, who had memories in common of Old Mexico, pumped hands and slid into business. They knew each other well. Bragg immediately turned to his sorrows: All his supporting generals either had betrayed him or were incompetent. All, *tout le monde*, were against him. Davis had a suggestion. What about having the stalwart John Clifford Pemberton, who had stood at Vicksburg and was now more or less unemployed, come aboard as a replacement for Polk. Bring the veteran in and add some stability. No, not Pemberton. Bragg wouldn't hear of it. Then why not let bygones be bygones and take Polk back—think about winning the war. No suggestion ever elicited less enthusiasm from Bragg. Keep Polk away from him. Then Bragg magnanimously offered his resignation. No, no, Davis would not hear of it. He called a council of war that evening for all Bragg's lieutenants, with Bragg sitting in. He would present the commander now with masochist heaven. Ringed around Bragg at this council loomed all the dissidents, with Bragg in the center and Davis directing the choir. Was Davis a bit of a sadist, or was he simply insensitive? In attendance stood Longstreet, Hill, Simon Bolivar Buckner, and Benjamin F. Cheatham (who had taken over from Polk). After some preliminaries, which was the same as flicking the whip about in tantalizing fashion, Davis struck home rather bluntly. What did the generals think of their commander, Braxton Bragg, who was cornered right here with them now? General Longstreet, give us your opinion, if you would be so kind. Longstreet at first tried to sidestep the issue, but Davis kept pressing while Bragg sat squirming. All right; Longstreet said that Bragg "could be of greater service elsewhere than at the head of the Army of Tennessee." The whip landed. *Crack*! Then Davis went around the circle, exquisitely letting each one savor the administration of the lash. All delivered a whack, Hill apparently relishing the moment most when his turn came. Bragg should leave; he was a disaster.

Davis buttonholed Longstreet the next day and sounded him out about taking Bragg's place. Oh, no, Old Pete would have none of it. Secretly he believed the whole shebang was shot to hell, and he wanted no part of the colossal disaster he saw coming. He suggested that the eminent Joseph Eggleston Johnston come down from his perch in Virginia and take over. At the sound of the name, Davis saw red. Johnston had been offered the job once before and had refused it. He had even refused it after he had been *ordered* to take it. Davis exploded, and Longstreet submitted *his* resignation, which was not accepted. Then Davis sought out others, right down the line. If Bragg was more of an asset to the Yankees than to the cause, who was going to take his place? Not me, William J. Hardee told him. And Hill, Buckner, and Cheatham didn't race forward to take over either. All said Bragg should leave, but no one wanted his job. They knew a calamity when they saw one. Something had to be done, though, and Davis cleverly acceded to Bragg's wish that Hill be blamed for any delays that caused the mistakes at Chickamauga and gave Bragg the green light to remove Hill. Bragg did so with hand-rubbing satisfaction on October 15, ordering Hill to report to Richmond. Hill angrily demanded to know why, but Bragg continued his punishment by giving him no reason. And now Bragg would do what he had wanted to do from the beginning: He would keep the Federals penned up in the small town of Chattanooga, cut them off, and slowly and pitilessly starve them to death. His official report stated that "we held [the enemy] at our mercy, and his destruction was only a question of time." It was time for revenge.

After Bragg missed his golden opportunity to attack the Federals and allowed them to stagger back to Chattanooga, he started a siege of the town in almost a pique. Let's see how they like that! The only trouble with the plan was that it soon became difficult to determine who was the besieged and who was the besieger. Bragg's Southerners were slowly but surely starving to death along with the besieged Yankees. One after another Southern soldier wrote home his complaints. From a Florida infantryman: "Some of the boys that were lucky enough to steal some ears of corn from the horses last night are busy grating it and making mush out of it for we are almost starved to death."

In the Confederate ranks, on the outskirts of Chattanooga, sights of misery lay all around. The wounded and maimed of the recent battle were still being reckoned with and cared for as best the medical teams could, and the able foraged around for firewood, firearms, and blankets that had once covered those who were no longer alive or around. Some played cards with greasy torn decks. Others turned to religion. One badly wounded Confederate, who was passed over for treatment and any hope, kept crying, "Are you Christian? Do you love Jesus?" And exhorted all who passed to convert to the teachings of Christ and make way for the Hereafter. Those whose minds were more on the moment joined the line that wove into the house of ill repute at the base of Missionary Ridge. It rained, it was cold, it was a desperate and wretched time. Yet in the stillness of night a sparkling view spread out before them that few ever forgot, even years later. Brigadier General Arthur Middleton Manigault, of South Carolina, recalled in his memoir after the war, "At night just after dark, when all the campfires were lighted, the effect was very grand and imposing, and such a one as had seldom, I take it, been witnessed." Even Bragg took time out from his endless wranglings and testiness to be moved by the scene. He wrote his wife: "Just underneath my headquarters [on Missionary Ridge] are the lines of the two armies, and beyond with their outposts and signal stations are Lookout, Raccoon, and Walden Mountains. At night all are brilliantly lit up in the most gorgeous manner by the myriads of camp fires. No scene in the most splendid theater ever approached it."

And no soldier in his ranks ever suspected (or would have cared probably) that Bragg had a poetic side. Bragg had let them all down, men and officers alike, in a most grievous way. It was a burr under every saddle. He had not pursued the whipped Yankees when he had the chance to ruin the whole Federal army. As a letter from a Confederate named John W. Harris expressed it: "Everyone here curses Bragg, and if he is removed it will put our troops in much better spirits."

William Starke Rosecrans was beloved by his troops, even after the recent debacle in the woods of northeast Georgia. He was a man who was partly defined by the rosary in his pocket and the salty language in his mouth and would surely have been one of the North's outstanding generals save for the gap in the line at Chickamauga and his precipitous flight to Chattanooga. After all, he had never suffered a defeat in the war before then. He had wrestled Bragg out of Tullahoma and had feinted him from Chattanooga. He had not lost a man in taking Chattanooga, and the North had responded by making Old Rosey a hero for a day. Before Chickamauga Rosecrans could do no wrong. On the evening of September 20, the picture changed dramatically, for then he wired Washington: "We have met with a serious disaster; extent not yet ascertained. The enemy overwhelmed us, drove our right, pierced our center, and scattered the troops there." Lincoln, who was certainly as accustomed to bad news as to good, said, "Well, Rosecrans has been whipped." Lincoln, as he did time after time, pulled himself up and shot back a late-night telegram of cheer: "We have unabated confidence in you and in your soldiers and officers . . . We shall do our utmost to assist you." Old Rosey was sinking into depression, though, and general words of cheer could not ward off the black dog. In the morning

Lincoln received a more frightening message from him: ". . . after two days of the severest fighting I ever witnessed, our left and center were beaten. The left held its position until sunset. Our loss is heavy and our troops worn down. . . ." Then came an alarming coda, one that brought the president to attention: "We have no certainty of holding our position here."

East Tennessee was a bugbear to Lincoln, who was fixated on it. Was it because his forebears had traveled over it to get to Kentucky and Illinois when it was frontier country and he held it dear? If he could hold East Tennessee, he thought, the rebellion could be crushed. But if he lost East Tennessee, everything might be lost. The usually sunny Rosecrans could not have wired more disturbing news. "If we can hold Chattanooga and East Tennessee," Lincoln wrote to Rosecrans, "I think the rebellion must dwindle and die." Then Lincoln telegraphed him: "Please relieve my anxiety as to the position and condition of your army up to the latest moment." He got back this reply: "We are about 30,000 brave and determined men; but our fate is in the hands of God, in whom I hope."

Bringing in the Almighty at such a moment was a bad sign. It was all right to praise the Lord and thank His bountifulness after a victory, as Stonewall Jackson invariably did, but turning to God instead of the sword in time of peril spelled trouble. Also there were those disquieting reports from Secretary of War Edwin M. Stanton's undercover man in Rosecrans's camp—Assistant Secretary of War Charles A. Dana, who couldn't say enough bad things about Rosecrans. "I consider this army to be very unsafe in his hands," Dana wrote. "It often seems difficult to believe him of sound mind." But the president didn't need Dana's bad-mouthing. Rosecrans was doing the job himself. When Lincoln telegraphed him with some insights on strategy, Rosecrans shot back, "We must put our trust in God, who never fails those who truly trust." Rosecrans was sinking fast and was almost around the bend. Lincoln put it more kindly:

Rosecrans had been acting "confused and stunned, like a duck hit on the head."

The Federal army in Chattanooga was near disaster, but Rosecrans kept shaking himself awake, kept trying to feed his men and reach out for supplies. The Federals did control the railroad coming down north through Nashville, but its last stop was now Bridgeport, Alabama, a heartbreaking twenty-five miles downstream from Chattanooga. Supply wagons that ventured out were cut down by Rebel sharpshooters on the south bank of the river, and crude and makeshift roads over the tops of mountains were used to try to circumvent the Rebel musket fire. If you weren't cut down by minié balls, you had a good chance of falling off the side of a mountain. Soon the treacherous path to Bridgeport was littered with dead animals and broken wagons. Mules, the workhorses of the army, suffered greatly. They survived on the bark of trees only to plunge 200 to 300 feet off a precipice. And the supplies that did reach the town were woefully inadequate.

The name "Chattanooga" is of Indian origin. It comes from the Cherokee *Chatta* (crow) and *nooga* (nest). Those who wish to give it a loftier ring call it "eagles' nest" or "hawks' nest." The aboriginal name was originally given to Lookout Mountain, which overlooks the town, before the town took it for its own. In pre-Revolutionary days Catholic priests from St. Augustine came to the region to spread the gospel and began a school for Indians of the ridge to the east of Lookout. This ridge became known as Mission Ridge, later changed to Missionary Ridge. Some say that the Indians sniffed some trouble brewing in this advance of civilization and goodness and designated the ridge as a point beyond which the do-gooders could not cross. In any case, Chattanooga, at the time Rosecrans and his army took up emergency quarters, was a small town of 5,000 that still had strong frontier roots. It was located in a beautiful natural setting, and it boasted some fine residences before they were overrun by the Confederate and Union forces. But Chattanooga hadn't been settled long, having chased the Indians out only a few decades before. It had the proud Crutchfield House, a hotel of three stories, but it did not proclaim any English origins in a clarion call as did Richmond, Savannah, and Charleston. The frontier was bred into the bones of Tennesseans, whose main concern was to last through the winter and whose first instinct was to shoot an intruder first and ask questions later. Deep down the Tennesseans never ceased worrying about getting scalped. Many of the quick witted left town when the Yankees first appeared in early September, women and children taking refuge in caves. Into the town of Chattanooga then came 45,000 soldiers in blue.

Soon every living thing was approaching starvation. Full rations for the soldiers dwindled immediately to half, then to quarter, and finally to whatever could be found to appease the stomach. Hollow-cheeked men followed straggling commissary wagons, fighting over any scraps that fell. The lucky ate hardtack and parched corn. Horses were grudgingly fed three ears of corn a day, but starving men robbed the troughs until guards were posted to head them off. Before long, no animals were found strong enough to pull artillery and guns, and supply wagons stood unused. Farm cattle went down to skin and bone, but were still slaughtered for their flesh. Starving men roamed the abattoirs picking over the garbage, looking for hoofs, tails, heads, and entrails—anything of animal origin that could be cooked. A stray dog that wandered into one regiment's camp was cooked in short order. One ingenious soldier found a discarded tin can that had once contained grease and a rag as a makeshift candle; he mixed some flies in with the grease and wolfed the concoction down. "I ate them all and relished them very much at the time."

Although Rosecrans's troops were starving, their morale strangely remained relatively high. They continued to joke and sing and became tough as nuts left to dry in the sun. Time, however, was running out, even for those who could rustle up an entrail and a laugh. It was soon apparent that, even if they were willing, the men were becoming too weak to make a breakout. They depended for what little they had on the roundabout supply line, and cunning Bragg took the opportunity to send Wheeler's cavalry out to demolish even that. They almost did, too.

Wheeler's raid through the Sequatchie Valley and Walden's Ridge has been passed down as lore through generations of Tennesseans and is still held in awe for its violence. The five-foot-five Wheeler was twenty-seven and a major general. He had recently inherited three scarecrow brigades from Forrest, and many were poorly armed, ill nourished, and with mean dispositions. Forrest had protested their going on the raid, saying they were in no condition, but Wheeler took them anyhow. He didn't care that they held him in contempt, as Forrest did, and he didn't care if they could barely ride; he had his orders, and he had his sights set on Yankee scalps. On October 3, he led one column down the Sequatchie Valley and quickly overtook thirty-two supply wagons. An hour later he caught the mother lode at the foot of Anderson's Gap—an enormous train of Federal wagons estimated at 800 to 1,500. (Rosecrans later claimed there were 500.) The front of the train was near the crest of Walden's Ridge, and the rear five miles were down the road. As Wheeler's men descended on the wagon train in a whoop, total confusion broke out on both sides. The Confederates dived into the booty—the cases of liquor and the pyramids of cigars—and threw away their slouch hats for expensive felt ones. They forgot about destroying or capturing anything and began to indulge in whatever met their eye. Wheeler personally had to pull some of them off the wagons by their heels.

When the men were finally brought back to some degree of comportment, the mules in the wagon train took the opportunity to go berserk. After untangling them and calming them down, the men selected what wagons and mules they wanted and then put the torch to the other wagons and shot or sabered the remaining mules. It took eight hours. One in the party later wrote, "The destruction of the ordnance trains presented a fearful spectacle. The noise of bursting shells and boxes of ammunition so resembled the sound of battle as to astonish and alarm the enemy in Chattanooga, who were in doubt as to the cause until the ascending clouds of smoke told them the food and ammunition upon which almost the vitality of their army depended were actually destroyed."

While Wheeler was causing mischief and mayhem at Anderson's Gap, his other column, composed mainly of Forrest's troops, overpowered the Federal garrison at McMinnville. They may have caused even greater havoc than what was done to the wagon train. The Union commander said that after his surrender, "there occurred the most brutal outrages on the part of Rebels ever known to any civilized war in America or elsewhere." When Wheeler appeared on the scene, the commander appealed to him to stop the pillaging. Wheeler begged off. He might be able to surprise and whip Yankees, but he could not control Forrest's men. He told the commander that they went about doing as they pleased.

Wheeler pressed on to Murfreesboro, destroying a stockade and burning a bridge over Stone's River. By then the Federal cavalry had been alerted and was coming to the rescue. The cavalry broke upon Wheeler suddenly and recaptured 800 mules. In trying to get away, Wheeler's men threw away whatever slowed them down— knapsacks, bundles, guns. At Farmington, it was nearly a rout because Confederate officers were unable to set up an orderly retreat. Discipline broke down (if it had ever been in place), and the Yankees took full advantage, sabering fleeing Confederate riders in the saddle and throwing up roadblocks before them. The raid was the most famous one Wheeler ever carried out, and though he inflicted a great deal of damage on the Yankees, he suffered greatly in casualties in the process. When he was finally able to get back across the river just below Chattanooga, he displayed as many aspects of defeat as he did of victory. It was almost like Chicka-mauga. He had caused serious damage, but he had almost destroyed himself doing it. He had earned a great victory, but had almost crip-pled his outfit. It would be a while before he was able to fight again.

Meanwhile the conditions in Chattanooga were becoming truly alarming, and Dana telegraphed Secretary of War Stanton, who happened to be staying at the Galt House in Louisville, Kentucky, that Rosecrans was on the verge of pulling up stakes and retreating. Rosecrans may have been calling on the Lord still, but not to help him retreat. As well as he could function now, he was trying to hold on and devise ways of besting the Southerners. But Dana was deter-mined to do him in, and nothing could save him now. Stanton immediately called for a certain general who happened to be in Louisville, too, with his wife, visiting her relatives. Stanton greeted the general in his voluminous dressing gown and waved Dana's tele-gram excitedly in his face. What were they to do? The general was a man of few and precise words, and he knew what to do—for he was the man who was going to win this war.

He seemed an unlikely candidate. He was a professional soldier who did not much like soldiering and detested Napoleon and his kind of flamboyant generalship. He was a West Pointer who claimed that "a military life had no charms for me" and that one of the happiest days of his life had been when he left West Point. He was a most decided failure in the garrison life of the pre-Civil War regular army. He began to shine only in the Mexican War, as a junior officer, showing bravery and inventiveness in tactics—but he disapproved of the war, much as a Vietnam vet might disapprove of the Southeast Asian adventure. He read volume after volume of romantic fiction while at West Point, but for the rest of his life would not discuss the matter or reveal the names of the books. He wrote beautifully himself, in a lucid, straight manner—with a style and insight that the finest writers of the nineteenth century might well envy. He was made of heroic material, at least as seen by a new kind of American who was beginning to emerge around this time. Americans could love such a man and make him a hero because, essentially, he was so much like them. Lee was always somewhat removed from the ordinary fray of Americans—too aristocratic, too much a holy Virginian, someone who could always be sure of receiving a free meal and a sinecure because of his blameless reputation—but not this man. After being let go by the army for drinking, he was reduced to clerking in his father's leather goods store (and hating it). He married the woman of his dreams, who was cross-eyed; in financial trouble just before the war, he sold firewood and Christmas trees on the streets of St. Louis. For those who were going to make the new America great, he could well serve as the guide (and not too well at times, it should be noted). He was short and slight, someone who never stood out in a crowd. He could take a punch. He could be knocked down and cast aside, but he would come back. Americans like those who can come back from failure. They like those who persevere and stick to their guns. They like them, that is, when they are ultimate winners, like Ulysses S. Grant. His cronies called him Sam.

Grant was never an immediate success, even at the start of the war in which he would later become the master. No one seemed to want him at first. At one point he thought he might have a chance of getting on the staff of the great George B. McClellan, with whom he had served in Mexico and studied at West Point. Grant went to visit McClellan in Cincinnati, where McClellan had his headquarters; he came with hat in hand, a supplicant, the scent of failure about him, an aura of the unclean. Grant hoped, as someone who might have had his dreams enlarged by the bottle, that once McClellan saw him and recognized him, the good old days of comraderie would return and McClellan would immediately take him under his wing and into his inner circle. Grant showed up at McClellan's office for two successive days, but the busy man would not see him. He went home, and there, at last, the hand of fate fell

kindly on him. He was commissioned a colonel of Illinois volunteers because of his West Point bona fides. He was given command
of a regiment, one that was in about the sorriest state in the military, one that was hobbled by an almost complete lack of discipline—one, it would seem, that Grant might feel comfortable in.
The colonel before him had the habit of getting lonely at night and
barging into town for a few snorts, often dragging some soldier off
guard duty for company. Grant did not buddy-buddy with anyone,
and whipped the outfit into shape in whirlwind fashion. He had
seen his chance, and he had jumped at it. His first foray into enemy
territory was most revealing and goes a long way to show why
Americans took so readily to Grant. He and his men were moving
against a Confederate force under a colonel named Harris. Here is
what happened, in Grant's own pithy way of putting it:

As we approached the brow of the hill from which it was expected we
could see Harris' camp, and possibly find his men ready formed to meet us,
my heart kept getting higher and higher until it felt to me as though it was
in my throat. I would have given anything then to have been back in Illinois, but I had not the moral courage to halt and consider what to do; I
kept right on. We reached a point from which the valley below was in full
view. I halted. The place where Harris had been encamped a few days
before was still there and the marks of a recent encampment were plainly
visible, but the troops were gone. My heart resumed its place. It occurred
to me at once that Harris had been as much afraid of me as I had been of
him. This was a view of the question I had never taken before; but it was
one I never forgot afterwards. From that event to the close of the war, I
never experienced trepidation upon confronting an enemy, though I
always felt more or less anxiety. I never forgot that he had as much reason
to fear my forces as I had his. The lesson was valuable.

Grant went on to prevail at Fort Donelson and at Shiloh.
When he kept hammering away and finally prevailed at Vicksburg,

he became America's favorite general, the toast of the North. He was promoted to a Regular Army major general—the only one of such elevated rank on active duty save Henry "Old Brains" Halleck in Washington. He looked after his own, too, another trait that endeared him to the populace (before "cronyism" took it to extremes and became a bad word). He saw to it that his sidekick William Tecumseh Sherman was made a regular brigadier, and he looked after his fellow townsman and chief of staff, John A. Rawlins, promoting him from lieutenant colonel to a brigadier when he had power to do so. Grant, the peacetime failure, was feted when he became a military hero. In Memphis he was the guest of honor at a huge banquet, where he was compared to Hernando de Soto and Robert Fulton, two legendary figures in Mississippi River history. After wild cheers, Grant stood, said thanks in two brief sentences, and sat down. They loved him for that. He sailed down the Mississippi, being celebrated along the way, and ended up in New Orleans, the guest of general Nathaniel Banks, the self-made orphan boy from Massachusetts whom Stonewall Jackson had whipped and humiliated in the Shenandoah Valley of Virginia. Now ensconced as the Federal commander in the Crescent City, he wanted to put on the dog for the new American hero Grant. Banks relished pomp and parade—the in-betweens of actual fighting—and the festivities that awaited Grant were grand. There were elements of the fun-loving Creole society at work here, too—people who knew how to whoop it up and never found the moment, night or day, when it was out of order to take a little toddy.

Banks staged a review worthy of the war's finale at Carrollton, a suburb of New Orleans, in honor of his esteemed guest. All who knew anything about Grant knew his love for horses, and this day Grant's hosts selected for him a frisky, high-stepping charger—the best horseflesh around. Grant appreciated the gesture, for his feel for horses dated back to his childhood. He could practically talk to them like Dr. Doolittle. As a toddler, it has been said, hardly old enough to walk, Grant had moved among the legs of corralled horses—unharmed, instinctively sure of their movements and designs. He sat well on a mount and enjoyed few things more. This day he watched veterans march by him with banners flying, proclaiming all of his (and their) recent victories upriver. It was a prelude to the end of the war itself—stirring, emotional, and liberating. If ever there was a time for a drink, it was now—and let us not forget we are in New Orleans. Grant's wife was not there; neither was the usually omnipotent Rawlins. Either could stay with a glance Grant's hand from reaching for the bottle. Grant knew better than to drink around either of them. Now he was free. And on the ride back to New Orleans, an uncharacteristic event took place. Grant lost control of the horse, which shied at a hissing locomotive and bolted, smacking into a carriage coming the other way. The horse and rider tumbled over, but the horse was able to rise and trot off. Grant lay as if shot; he didn't come to until an hour or so later, when he looked up from his hotel bed to see several faces hovering worriedly over him. He described the result of the day later: "My leg was swollen from the knee to the thigh, and the swelling, almost to the point of bursting, extended along the body up to the armpit. The pain was almost beyond endurance. I lay at the hotel something over a week without being able to turn myself in bed."

At last he was able to travel, but painfully, to Louisville, where he had his meeting with rotund Stanton. The secretary of war made it official: Grant was to be in charge of all the Western armies. Let us not fool around now. Grant had proved himself a dogged fighter and a winner over adversity. Let him win the war. Besides his Army of Tennessee, he was now to command Rosecrans's Army of the Cumberland and Ambrose E. Burnside's Army of the Ohio. It was left up to Grant whether Rosecrans or George M. Thomas was to be in command of the Army of the Cumberland. Grant didn't cotton to either. He was a man who either liked you and was loyal or didn't like you and found ways to diminish or leave you. After Grant read

Dana's dispatch, he handed it back to Stanton. Rosecrans must go. It was Grant's decision. He sent a wire to Chattanooga replacing Rosecrans with Thomas and instructing the Rock of Chickamauga to hold the town at all costs. Thomas sent back his reply, which became part of Civil War lore: "We will hold the town until we starve." Which might not be that far off, the way things were going. The hero of Vicksburg was hefted aboard a train bound for Tennessee. He passed south into Alabama and then had a meeting with the former commander of the Army of the Cumberland. Military man that he still was, Rosecrans concisely outlined the situation in Chattanooga and suggested some ways to alleviate the problems and win the battle. Later Grant acknowledged that Rosecrans's suggestions were excellent, but wondered that "he had not carried them out."

A Union soldier caught sight of Grant on a train platform the day he met Rosecrans and described him so: "He wore an army slouch hat with bronze cord around it, quite a long military coat, unbuttoned, no sword or belt, and there was nothing to indicate his rank. . . . When the boys called for a speech he bowed and said nothing."

Grant moved on crutches, a lame little man. But there continued to be some gritty and ineffable quality about him that set him apart from other men while he still seemed part and parcel of the common throng. He continued his travel by rail to Bridgeport, the last stop before Chattanooga territory. Then he began a sixty-mile trip on horseback over frontier country with his crutches strapped to the saddle like rifles. Ten miles outside Chattanooga he stopped with his party for a visit with Major General Oliver Otis Howard, a veteran of Chancellorsville and Gettysburg, who had been sent west because of the emergency. Howard had never met Grant before. Here is his description: "Rather thin in flesh and very pale in complexion, and noticeably self-contained and retiring." Howard was not a drinker; in fact, he was something of an old fogey, noted for his fervent stand for temperance. It happened that Grant's eye went to a bottle that stood solitary and upright on a nearby table. It was as if Grant had become transfixed. Howard said quickly, to save his reputation, "I never drink." Grant at last turned and said with a poker face, "Neither do I." He swung out of the tent on his crutches and then had himself lifted back on his horse as if he were a child.

As Grant wearily and painfully trudged by horse up the Sequatchie Valley and over Walden's Ridge, he got a firsthand taste of what the Union forces were facing in trying to run their meager supply route from Bridgeport. He had to take a rough and circuitous path to avoid being seen by the Rebels who were up on Raccoon Mountain with their guns pointed his way. For the last stretch of his journey, rain turned parts of the road into knee-deep quagmires of mud or landslides of rock and dirt. At times, when the going was terribly rough, Grant had to be taken from his horse and carried. His horse slipped in the mud, and Grant fell once more, now doubly bruised and battered from a fall. He kept going. He passed the carcasses of animals that littered the route—for, by the time Grant was there, ten thousand mules and horses had died, either by Rebel fire or starvation. Grant rode on, or was carried, and although he might harbor pity or the tugging thoughts of surrender, his will never flagged. His will didn't lessen when he descended on Chattanooga itself on October 23 and saw the horror there. It was like a death camp, soldiers emaciated and somewhat crazed and more dead animals and signs of defeat everywhere. And at dusk, as his horse clomped over the lone fragile pontoon bridge into the town, Grant looked up at the dark, looming mountains around him. He used his field glasses to get a better view and took in the array of guns on the slopes, peaks, and ridges, aimed down on the town. He could actually see the Rebel cannoneers lounging about, confident and perky and all too ready to unload volleys. Their campfires became pinpoints of light on three sides as Grant, in company with his small entourage, rode as if into an amphitheater of doom. He didn't slow.

Grant had arrived, and he was there to take on the wily, dyspeptic Bragg, who, against all odds and reason, somehow managed to stay alive and in command. The two men were about as different as two men could be in military prowess, but startlingly similar in other traits. Both had deep and mysterious conflicts with their mothers. In all his correspondence, Bragg never once mentioned his mother; Grant kept his at arm's length, never inviting her to the White House when he had attained the highest office in the land.

There was always something guarded about Grant, some restraint that was possibly of a Puritan nature—not an uncommon trait in an American, then and now. Bragg, of course, kept to stern moral strictures, so stern that he was practically incapacitated. Neither man was given to cursing or the telling of bawdy yarns, qualities that set them apart from the majority in the old army. Both verged at times on being somewhat prissy. Grant could not abide hunting or the mistreatment of animals—the very idea turned his stomach. The consummate irony was that he was the fieriest practitioner of killing men in the Civil War. He may have later regretted the bloodbath of Cold Harbor in 1864, but he directed the battle and, some say, well earned the title the Butcher. Is there any wonder why he drank? He was raised a Methodist. He had a touching modesty about his person. When it came bath time in the field, Grant always took his in the privacy of his tent, all flaps closed tightly, while others of his staff ran around naked as jaybirds happily throwing buckets of water on each other.

It would be hard to imagine any other general arriving as Grant did at headquarters in Chattanooga that cold rainy night in November. Longstreet and Burnside being carried? Their circumferences would have ruled it out unless a team were brought in. Lee? Hardly; a lot more braid and deference would have been on display. Grant was lifted off his horse by two aides and limped into Thomas's billet—cold, wet, hungry, and covered in mud.

Thomas and Grant did not like each other. Thomas was from the patrician South, a Virginian to the core except in one deciding aspect—he wanted to save the Union. Grant was the new man in America—out for the main chance, not concerned with appearances, sensitive to change and opportunity, and as stubborn as any man in the Union. Thomas greeted Grant, and then the two men sat at either side of a glowing log fire. It took some newly arrived aides of Grant to notice that something was wrong. Grant, the commander of all forces, was sitting there silently while a puddle of water spread beneath him. A Colonel Wilson, of Grant's staff, entered and was shocked. He cleared his throat and spoke: "General Grant is wet and in pain . . . ," causing Thomas to stir into action, to call for a meal and dry clothing to be given to Grant. This account is at variance with what we know of Thomas, who was, in nearly all reports, courteous and thoughtful of others in private. Another version of the event has Grant *refusing* any food or fresh clothing upon entering and wanting to get right down to business, simply taking a seat before the fire, shaking whatever hand was proffered and not rising. In all versions, Grant soon cut through protocol and got down to the matter at hand, as was his nature. He was not a man, like Rosecrans, for bonhomie and flights of fancy. Lighting a cigar, one of his few visible pleasures, he requested that each of Thomas's officers assess the military pickle they were in and offer what suggestions they might have as to how to get out of it. Thomas himself had thoroughly and efficiently reorganized the army that he had inherited from Rosecrans. That was all to the good. Grant was also informed that there was just one day's supply of ammunition. Not only might they starve to death, but they now had little means to fight their way out of encirclement.

Around the room, the fire crackling, the gray cigar smoke curling, the officers spoke of materiel and tactics. Grant made few, if any, comments and was seemingly inattentive, just biding his time for the voices to end. Horace Porter found him "immovable as a rock and as silent as a sphinx." Actually, Grant was adept at hiding his emotions. He was alert, though—looking for any word or gesture that betrayed someone's desire to retreat or surrender, or perhaps he might find someone who had an idea about how to get out of this mess. He perked up when a bald man, deferring to no one, began to talk forcefully in engineering terms about a solution. This was an old West Point classmate, Brigadier General William F. Smith, and Grant hadn't run across him since those days on the Hudson. Old Baldy, as he was nicknamed, had always been contentious, a little out of step, sure of himself, different from the crowd. In other words, he was a lot like Sherman and, in fact, like Grant. Grant liked him. Smith clarified the topographical lay of the land and how the two armies faced each other. In clear, precise language, he explained how a new supply line could be made. It would mean crossing the Tennessee at three places: first, across a pontoon bridge to the north; second, at Brown's Ferry opposite Moccasin Point; and third, at Kelly's Ferry, which would lead along the banks of the river to the oasis at Bridgeport. The route would be much more simple and direct than the old one. It was guaranteed to relieve the siege. One problem remained: The Rebels held Raccoon Mountain with pickets stretching to Brown's Ferry. They would have to be eliminated.

The next day Grant and Smith and an entourage went out on an inspection tour. Grant was known for his power of concentration—focus in on something, let others jabber, let nothing distract you. Grant dismounted near Brown's Ferry (or was lifted off) and hobbled along the bank of the Tennessee, looking over the terrain. Perhaps he had a cigar clamped between his teeth; he certainly was in clear sight of the Rebel pickets on the other side, who strangely saluted, rather than fired. It was that kind of war. The outcome of the war might have been different if they had fired. Someone commented on Grant's appearance at this time: "He wore his uniform more like a civilian than a graduate of West Point. His military coat was never buttoned up to his neck. . . . He walked with his head down and without the slightest suggestion of a military step. Neither his face nor his figure was imposing." Others have suggested that his peculiar high-stepping gait was possibly the result of something called a jake leg, the reward for having drunk too much bad whiskey. When he rode, his dark trousers came up to reveal wrinkled white socks that did not reach his calves.

Smith's plan for taking Brown's Ferry involved daring and surprise—a blitzkrieg. The honorable Joseph Hooker of Massachusetts would play a large part in it. Fighting Joe and his 20,000 Federal troops had recently arrived from the battlefields of Virginia and were now cooling their heels in Bridgeport, unable to make their way to Chattanooga. Let them help dislodge the Rebels who barred their way, opening up the supply route at the same time. Hooker, a well-barbered and handsome man, with apple cheeks and a salty, confident air, had impressed Lincoln as a general who thought more about winning than of losing and making up excuses. True, Hooker had been routed at Chancellorsville that past summer, but the victor there had been Stonewall Jackson—and who could prevail against him? It had taken accidental fire from his own men to bring Jackson down. Hooker, who was a hard-drinking soldier's soldier, wouldn't mind vindication as a general who could deliver the goods. He liked to brag and affect a menacing stance. He could use a victory. The plan called for Hooker, following railroad tracks and under the cover of night, to close upon Brown's Ferry from the rear. Meanwhile Thomas would arrive—also at night—noiselessly by boat down the Tennessee. At Brown's Ferry the two forces would combine, opening Cummings Gap west to Kelly's Ferry. In the process they would take out those fear-producing guns up on Raccoon Mountain. It would keep the passage below safe. There would be a new highway, a new secure route to Bridgeport—where bacon and bread and all the sweet goods for the inner man waited. There, too, were cartridge boxes and limber chests, the better to fight the

Rebels who would be reduced to holding Lookout Mountain and Missionary Ridge. The Federals would have opened the Cracker Line, so named because it would permit the abiding staple for appeasing hunger to pass through—the all-purpose cracker. Grant's single-mindedness and the Cracker Line would save Chattanooga.

9

★

The Beginning of the End

General William F. Smith found a most appreciative audience of one in Ulysses S. Grant. He led a delighted Grant to a sawmill, where workers were busily putting together pontoons and the flooring for the bridges that would be used for the assault. Everyone was in action, the saws humming. A steamboat, to be used for transporting supplies, was even being nailed together, the engine liberated from a nearby cotton gin. No one in command was carping and standing around now that Grant was here.

Grant, in fact, put Smith in charge of the amphibious attack that would come from Chattanooga. Here was not a swashbuckler with saber raised, set to race forward on a white charger. Here was a soldier bent over a drafting board, figuring weights and space and drawing upon his knowledge of Newton's laws of physics—given his job by a slight bearded man who couldn't hold a clerk's job under his younger brothers in the family store in Ohio and who now couldn't keep his socks up.

On the night of October 26, Smith crossed Moccasin Point with two brigades of infantry and a battalion of engineers, around 3,500 effectives; at 3:00 A.M., 1,500 skilled and daring men—who would be called commandos today—cast off from Chattanooga's wharves on sixty pontoon-transports, two dozen men and one officer in each boat. There was no turning back. If the Rebels caught them before they established a beachhead downriver, it could well turn into a massacre. They traveled a circuitous stretch of the Tennessee, a six-mile run, hugging the right bank to avoid detection. The current was swift, so swift that no oars were needed. A light bracing mist fell. They drifted on, boat after boat, noiselessly. They had been told that any man who fell overboard would not be picked up. They couldn't afford to take the time, couldn't risk being caught by the Rebels. One soldier lost his balance because of the rapidly changing current and fell overboard. He cried and whimpered for aid—to stop the boat, to lift him back aboard. His boat continued on. He sank in the dark Tennessee.

Smith's men came ashore at Brown's Ferry at five o'clock, one hour before sunup. They rushed ashore, surprising the Rebel pickets and quickly setting up a defensive perimeter. They did their work well, for a Confederate brigade that charged into the works in the gray dawn was thrown back in short order. "So soon as the skirmishers were thrown out from each command," Smith reported, "the axes were set at work felling an abatis, and in two hours the command was sufficiently protected to withstand any attack which was likely to be made." The Confederates could always be expected to charge bravely, but now it was coming to be expected that they would just as quickly be thrown back.

As the day heated up, the pontoon bridge across the river was beginning to take shape, a causeway for the large number of George H. Thomas's troops to pass over. As planned, Joseph Hooker and his men strode up from the South, ready to take on all comers. As Hooker traveled, he could see the vastness of Lookout Mountain looming dead ahead; about a mile and a half from the northern tip of Lookout, he left John W. Geary's division of 1,500 men to protect his rear. He left them at Wauhatchie, in the gloom of towering Lookout Mountain. Then he marched with Oliver Otis Howard's 5,000 soldiers, consisting of two divisions under Adolph von Stein-wehr and Carl Schurz, into Brown's Ferry on October 28. Smith's plan, it seemed, was beginning to work out in textbook fashion.

Hooker had no instinct for doing things on the sly; he was not the man to maneuver stealthily into a daring position and then strike with blinding speed. He was more at home astride a big glistening horse, uniform spotless, back straight, being the very model of the modern major general. He was tall and vigorous and sat well for portraits. He was well aware that those threadbare, glum Rebels up on Lookout Mountain were gazing down on him as he led his fine collection of men through the valley. Here's what real soldiers look like, boys! He might have been surprised, though, to learn that two sets of those eyes above—possibly bloodshot and bleary— belonged to the Rebel commanders themselves, Braxton Bragg and James Longstreet. An excited messenger had interrupted a meeting between Bragg and Longstreet at headquarters, informing them that Hooker's troops had been spotted moving through the valley. It couldn't be, Bragg said; it wasn't possible. The messenger invited him and Longstreet to come see—which Bragg reluctantly agreed to do. At the sight of Hooker's array of men, Bragg fell into his usual snit, which caused Longstreet to become more sullen and removed. All along Bragg had been pressing for Longstreet to take his entire corps and attack Brown's Ferry. Now here came Hooker up the valley, ready to reinforce that very place. The more Bragg fumed, though, the more Longstreet resisted. Bragg went back to headquarters and continued with his customary ill humor. General St. John Richardson Liddell was there and later recorded that Bragg "complained of Longstreet's inactivity and lack of ability; asserting him to be greatly overrated, etc."

After watching Hooker's parade through the valley, Longstreet did stir himself to fight that night—but not against pivotal Brown's Ferry, where Hooker ended up. He threw John Bell Hood's old division, now under Brigadier General Micah Jenkins, against Wauhatchie, which Geary guarded down below.

At midnight, Hooker and crew heard the loud booming of cannon at Wauhatchie. Yellow, lightninglike flashes broke through the dark night, and a hell of a fight seemed to be under way. Hooker could well imagine himself routed once again, as at Chancellorsville. Alarmed, he sent Schurz's division flying in relief. If the Confederates broke through Geary's defense, then Brown's Ferry might be next, and everyone would have to retreat to Chattanooga either to starve or to surrender. However, Hooker could have saved himself some worry. Stonewall Jackson was dead; no real surprises lay ahead. The Confederates' bad luck remained steady and on course, always under the shadow of the ill-fated Bragg. The attacking Rebels got lost in the dark and weren't sure who they were attacking. Complicating matters, some 200 mules on the Federal side broke free under the disquieting barrage and leaped and scrambled toward the Confederate lines in a crazed melee. The grayclads thought it was a cavalry charge and began to retreat. By the time Schurz arrived, the Confederate offensive was grinding to a halt. Two hours before dawn, the Confederates had drawn back across Lookout Creek, leaving the field to the Federals.

General Geary could not wholly appreciate the victory, for he was worried about his young son, an artillery officer in Battery E of Pennsylvania, the pride of the outfit. The battery was in the thick of the fight, taking casualties right and left. In the darkness, rammers and swabbers groped to find the muzzles in which to sink their staffs. Southern sharpshooters somehow sighted in on horses and men, leaving but thirteen of the forty-eight horses in the battery standing at the end. Men fell in comparable numbers, thrown down among the bleeding horses or by their guns. Battery E kept firing yellow-streaked bursts that pierced the blackness and briefly lit up the carnage. A Pennsylvania infantry colonel came running up to a promontory where young Geary manned a gun. He screamed, "You're shooting short! Your shells are bursting in my line!"

Lieutenant Geary called to his ammunition handlers: "Cut the fuses longer!" After the next round, he yelled, "How's that?"

"Right!" called the colonel, who then sprinted back to his men.

Soon young Geary took the place of a wounded gunner, aiming the piece as best he could in the mayhem and bad light, hoping to hit the charging, wild-firing Rebels. He leaned over, squinting down the barrel, and took a bullet through the brain. After the guns had stilled and the Federals had stood, his father learned of his death. He mourned but had to keep leading his men.

On Missionary Ridge the Confederate high command conducted business in its usual climate of hate, envy, and malice. So much ill will was directed toward Bragg that even when he gave an appropriate and well-advised order, it was undone somehow by the mean-spirited atmosphere he had helped to create in the first place. Longstreet had not attacked the Yankee bridgehead at Brown's Ferry as directed. As Bragg put it: ". . . your whole corps was placed at your disposal for the movement indicated against the enemy. It is still at your disposal. . . . The movement should be prompt and decisive." Somehow, some way Longstreet—out of contempt for Bragg, contrariness, who knows?—subverted that order. When Longstreet did at last attack at Wauhat-chie (and not at Brown's Ferry), he moved late at night and without his full force. All men deserve sympathy at times. Here is where Bragg, whom all men loved to hate, comes in for some compassion. If Longstreet had thrown all he had against Brown's Ferry when Bragg had wanted him to attack, when the pontoon bridge was going up and a beachhead was being planted, then the Cracker Line might have remained a figment of Smith's vivid imagination. Now the Federals had a supply route. It reached from Brown's Ferry across Raccoon Mountain to Bridgeport. Grant wired General Henry W. Halleck in Washington: "The question of supplies may now be regarded as settled. If the rebels give us one week more time, I think all danger of losing territory now held by us will have passed away, and preparations may commence for offensive operations."

Now that the Federals had a new supply line, and had, in fact, won a great victory, the Southern commander Bragg threw himself into a scheme that would seriously, irrevocably weaken his already short-handed army. He figuratively shot himself in the foot. He enthusiastically concurred with Jefferson Davis that Longstreet might be better utilized if he was ordered north to Knoxville, in the foothills of the Smokies, to pressure Major General Ambrose E. Burnside, who wasn't giving anyone any trouble. Davis's reason for the transfer was that Grant might be forced to send some men away from Chattanooga when he learned that Longstreet was at Knoxville. It might be a faulty reason, but it did have some basis. Also, Davis would be getting Longstreet back closer to Virginia from whence he came. But Bragg? What had he to gain by dispatching his most competent tactician and fighter elsewhere? Why would he agree to reduce his fighting force one-third by sending Longstreet away—by dispatching the general who had broken through the Federal line at Chickamauga and given the South its final great moment? Why? Because he personally detested Longstreet, and the feeling was mutual. Longstreet was shipped off, along with Joe Wheeler's Cavalry (later to be recalled), 20,000 veteran fighters. Gone. These men from the great Army of Virginia would indeed try to storm the upper East Tennessee town of Knoxville with their customary confidence and fierceness, the same qualities they had shown at Chickamauga—but they were summarily repulsed this time. Never again would this mighty collection of warriors, those who had chased General

William Starke Rosecrans into oblivion and General Philip H. Sheridan from the field, serve under Bragg.

When Washington learned that archenemy Longstreet had departed to fight Burnside, a strong request went out to Grant to lay into Bragg. It was easier said than done, though. The Cracker Line rejuvenated the men soon enough, but getting replacements for the starved and slaughtered horses was another matter. Grant told Thomas to do it somehow—get the artillery for attack moving with mules or officer mounts, if nothing else. Grant could come up with ideas. But Thomas was once again levelheaded, cautious. He convinced Grant that mules might run amok in battle, bolt at the first report of fire, and officer mounts were too sleek in the flank to haul caissons.

The war then took this moment for a holiday. No one had the wherewithal really to lay into each other—so why not take a break? After all, they were all cut from the same cloth. These farm boys from both sides crossed the river to pay friendly and curious visits to each other, warning one another when officers came near. All too soon they would be dismembering each other—but during a lull, why not share a neighborly moment or two? One of the Rebels in a blue uniform (not unusual in the Confederate army) chanced miraculously to come across Grant himself. They had a pleasant little chat and parted with offhand salutes. Unassuming Grant rode his horse by picket lines and could easily see the Confederate outposts on the opposite bank of the river—and be seen himself, right out in the open, by the Confederates. The Rebels saluted him just as politely as if he were one of their own generals—perhaps, truth to tell, a little more politely than if he had been Bragg. Up on the heights Bragg's men polished their cannons, whiled away their time bitching about the army and daydreaming about home, and believed that no one would ever be fool enough to attack their seemingly impregnable position.

Although Grant might appear ordinary, someone to josh with

and possibly dismiss, he was not to be denied. He meant to win. He had come to Chattanooga to prevail, and few in either army possessed his cunning and will. The day after he arrived, he called for the services of his closest lieutenant. Sherman and his 20,000 troops had been reassigned from West Tennessee to Chattanooga and were on their way. The two armies would not be mingling in quite the same way once Sherman got there.

General Sherman was red haired; fidgety as a colt; brilliant; mercurial, but steady as a surgeon when he set out to do something; and single-minded. Cump Sherman perfectly complimented his slight and unassuming commander: His uniform showed soup stains like Grant's, and he hadn't exactly shone at West Point. Sherman also came from another distinct group of generals with unusual backgrounds that served on both sides. Like Stonewall Jackson and Nathaniel P. Banks, he had been raised an orphan (he later married the daughter of the Ohio foster family with whom he had grown up). Sherman's excitable nature grew out of bounds early in the war, causing what may have been a mini nervous breakdown, and he had to retire from the command structure for a short time. He proved his steadiness at Shiloh and bonded forever with his sometime fellow outcast, Grant, at that memorable battle. The two men became like blood brothers afterward. (When Grant became president, some wanted Sherman to attack his Reconstruction ideas. "No," Sherman said, "Grant stood by me when I was crazy, and I stood by him when he was drunk, and now we stand by each other.") Now Sherman was coming to Chattanooga to join Grant, to begin one of the great adventures in American history that would end for Sherman when he reached the sea. He came as a grief-stricken father, for he had just learned that his favorite son had died. He had a difficult and unsatisfying marriage. He was coming to Chattanooga to fight.

Sherman reached Bridgeport on the night of November 13—well ahead of his troops. A message from Grant was put into his hands before he had time to remove his boots. "Hurry!" it said. Sherman rode into Chattanooga the next day and was greeted in person by his superior. Grant had been on crutches when he left Sherman in Vicksburg in September, and now he was more mobile, more engaged. He had a battle to fight. Soon Grant took Sherman out on a tour of inspection of the coming battlefield. It was a unique American panorama, like the Grand Canyon. The Tennessee River snaked beautifully through the valley; dark, seemingly impregnable promontories loomed above. Sherman, the fidgety redhead, gazed up at Lookout Mountain and then to the east where Missionary Ridge spread out in a long gloomy shadow. Chattanooga lay at their feet. It was a vista that could well please the eye of a Hudson River School painter, a Frederick E. Church or Thomas Cole. But Sherman did not have the eye of a naturalist. He looked up to where, right out in the open, hardly a thousand feet away, a continuous chain of Rebel sentinels walked their posts with no fear of disruption. They marched as if they owned the landscape. Sherman took one look at them, stood in his stirrups, swept his eyes around, and said, "Why, General Grant, you are besieged!" Grant replied, "It's too true."

But Grant was one man in the nation who could get these troops out of this mess. He could focus on it and bring problems down to their essentials. And he would rely most on those few whom he thoroughly trusted. Once you were down and out, especially in the new success-oriented America, you stuck with those you knew would come through for you. Sure, Thomas was a proved, capable commander—Grant would be the first to acknowledge his worth. Didn't he name Thomas to replace Rosecrans as head of the Army of the Cumberland? But Grant needed the assurance that one of his intimates would play the most crucial role in any battle plan. He had a great need for intimates. (His young son Jesse kept him company in his tent at the battle of Vicksburg.) He rationalized Thomas's less active role in the battle plans at Chattanooga by declaring that Thomas's troops "had been so demoralized by the Battle of Chickamauga that he feared they could not be got out of their trenches to assume the offensive." He said this at a briefing that Sherman attended, about the men who had recently saved the Union against a stronger Rebel force. In his simple logical plans, Grant determined that Sherman would carry the main thrust of the offensive, attacking the front of Bragg's right, which began at the front (northern end) of the all-important Missionary Ridge. All other movements—by Thomas, by Hooker—would be to support Sherman's attack. Sherman would ascend the ridge like a mighty fury and then muscle down its spine, knocking off Rebels left and right. Of course, Grant would use Thomas and his men; there was no question about that. They would attack Missionary Ridge's center from the west, fixing the Rebels in place, and serving more as a diversion than a threat. They would eventually, in Grant's scheme, combine with Sherman's warriors to sweep the Southerners completely from the ridge and valley and into Valhalla. Fighting Joe Hooker would be held in reserve on the Union's far right, prepared to strike wherever needed. Hooker wore his well-tailored blue uniform smartly, his apple cheeks aglow (from spirits or the bracing fall weather or both) and he was ready, as usual, to fight and shine. Sherman was always ready.

Sherman, Grant, and Baldy Smith stole as close as possible to where the plan called for Sherman to strike. Sherman liked what he saw. He saw where, with the element of surprise, he could ascend the unfortified ridge and undoubtedly beat back the Southerners. He could hardly wait. He hurriedly got on the road to Bridgeport, forgoing any more time in Chattanooga, so he could gather his troops for the assault. He hoped to get them in position by November 20—in five days—for a dawn attack, but, as often happens in war and life, circumstances didn't cooperate. The Cracker Line road was far too primitive for a quick march, and the bridge at Brown's Ferry was too frail to withstand much weight all at once. It was not until November 23 that Sherman got three of his four divisions in place and concealed in some woods behind some hills, ready to cross the Tennessee above Chattanooga, ready to take Missionary Ridge. Impatient, jittery, itching for action, Sherman cursed every drop of errant rain that fell, every moment of delay.

On the evening of November 23, while his tired troops ate a hot supper, Sherman, who couldn't sit still, was inspecting the 116 pontoon boats that would carry his troops across the Tennessee into Confederate territory. The boats had been constructed under the eye of Sherman's onetime law partner, Dan McCook, and at midnight Sherman sent his first boat with thirty aboard into the swift current, off into the unknown. The men had a simple mission: Clear the landing area on the other side of enemy pickets. They landed stealthily and silently worked their way behind the Rebel pickets. Knowing the groggy state of late-night pickets and how they yearned to return to their bedrolls, these Federal "commandos" called out, "Relief!" catching the Rebels by surprise and capturing all but one. A beachhead was secured. At 2:00 A.M. Sherman's troops began fording the river en masse. In the dark moonless night, an impatient man scurried from boat to boat at the dock, offering encouragement and goodwill. "Be prompt as you can, boys; there's room for thirty in a boat," Sherman said.

It took less than half an hour to send a thousand men across—an efficient irresistible machine. The blueclads scrambled up the bank on the Confederate side, wading their way through thickets, with a spade in one hand, a rifle in the other. It was difficult to see a hand in front of one, and no one knew the whereabouts of the main Rebel force. Were they being sucked into a trap? The word spread that one of the enemy pickets had escaped and then their imagination, which always works wonders in the dark, threw up many terrifying pictures. At any moment, many felt, they were going to be engulfed and swallowed alive. Strangely, nothing happened. Another Rebel trick?

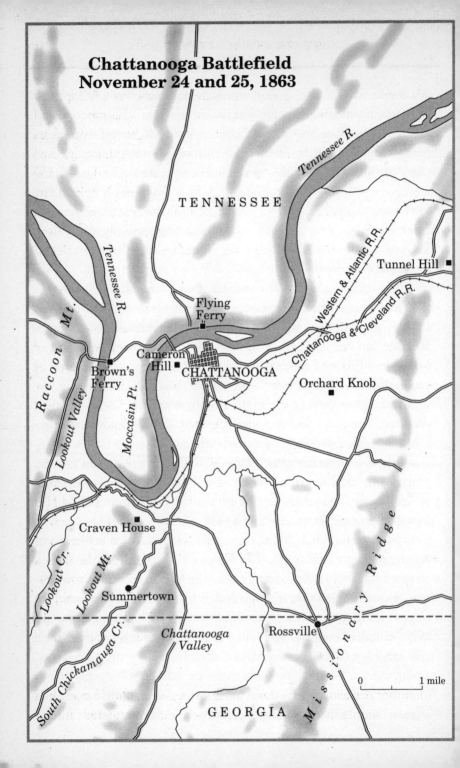

Chattanooga Battlefield
November 24 and 25, 1863

TENNESSEE

Tennessee R.

Tennessee R.

Western & Atlantic R.R.

Tunnel Hill

Chattanooga & Cleveland R.R.

Flying Ferry

Raccoon Mt.

Brown's Ferry

Cameron Hill

CHATTANOOGA

Orchard Knob

Lookout Valley

Moccasin Pt.

Craven House

Lookout Cr.

Lookout Mt.

Summertown

Mission a r y R i d g e

Chattanooga Valley

Rossville

South Chickamauga Cr.

GEORGIA

0   1 mile

Thousands more landed and entrenched themselves. A captured Confederate steamer, the *Dunbar,* sailed up from Chattanooga and carried more blueclads across the river. By daylight the worst fears had not been realized. In fact, no Confederate counterattack had come at all. By noon Baldy Smith had put a pontoon bridge—1,350 feet long—across the river. Sherman said, "I have never beheld any work done so quietly, so well, and I doubt if the history of war can show a bridge of that extent . . . laid down so noiselessly and well in so short a time. I attribute it to the genius and intelligence of General William F. Smith."

It was a foul day—misty and drizzling—a portent of winter in the mountains. Darkness fell soon. It was the kind of day where you long to cozy up by a fire. At one o'clock Sherman moved out to attack whatever might face him and to gain the northern end of Missionary Ridge, a spot called Tunnel Hill. He easily captured or brushed aside 200 to 300 Confederates who got in his way. At 3:30 P.M., as the first shadows of night began to fall, Sherman called a halt. In his After Action Report, he stated, "We gained, with no loss, the desired point."

Actually, he hadn't. He had gained two high points, but not the crucial Tunnel Hill that was the true northern prominence on Missionary Ridge. When he realized he was separated from Tunnel Hill by a deep ravine, one and a quarter miles from it, he told his men to fortify themselves and bed down. Little did he know that there was but a mere part of a brigade on Tunnel Hill—hardly more than a glorified band of pickets, hardly a force to repel Sherman's juggernaut. By calling it a day, Sherman allowed Patrick Cleburne and his troops at Chickamauga Station to scurry back and put up an inspired line of defense at Tunnel Hill. Thus, the stage was set for a real battle.

Grant, that cleanly precise and most focused of administrators, had a most simple plan. His troops, which now numbered around

75,000, would be used against Bragg's 43,000 this way: Thomas would be in the feint toward the center of Missionary Ridge, and Hooker would deliver a blow at Lookout Mountain on Bragg's left, and after clearing the Rebels (he hoped), would continue into the valley and swing up Missionary Ridge from the South. The main thrust, as Grant and Sherman saw it, was for Sherman to assault Tunnel Hill. It made sense. Bragg would be put in a vise, and the lifeblood would be squeezed from him. Bragg would seem to deserve a modicum of sympathy even from his severest critic. No one liked him—his own men and officers, the other side, and even fate. Now, facing this Federal onslaught, he took the time to offend deeply the slow-to-anger Thomas. Of all people to rub the wrong way, he picked the most unlikely one around. Thomas, the Rock of Chicka- mauga, was a quiet, steady man. He indulged in a few drinks, was held with great affection by his troops, and kept to his quiet code of honor. Bragg, only Bragg, had the wherewithal to change his demeanor and evoke a whiplash of anger from him. A letter had arrived in Thomas's camp for referral to a Confederate officer. On the ridge above him stood Bragg's headquarters. Bragg had been his battery commander in the old army and a supposed friend. As a courtesy, Thomas sent the letter along—a token gesture, of little import, a good deed on Thomas's part. It came back like a shot, a note attached: "Respectfully returned to General Thomas. General Bragg declines to have any intercourse with a man who has betrayed his state." *His state!* Bragg had hit on the one tender spot in Thomas's makeup, the one area of vulnerability that he kept guarded because to open it up might drive him crazy. He was from Virginia, but he was a loyal Union man. "Damn him," Thomas reportedly said. "I'll be even with him yet." Thomas was thought to be imperturbable. He wasn't exactly, and Bragg proved it.

And now that hunger ceased to override other passions, the Federals in Chattanooga found other ways to occupy themselves. Those from the west—more rough hewn—began to sense that the

easterners among them considered themselves superior. The easterners wanted to soldier in style; they liked their boots shined, their
campaign caps snapped smartly down, and a knapsack positioned
just so on their backs. They had been drilled well, their officers set
good examples of sartorial splendor, and they took for granted that
the upper east of the United States was the cradle of civilization—
the rest, frontier. Contrast Hooker—barbered and resplendent in
blue—with Sherman, wild and grizzled and not paying much attention to the outer man—one from the east, the other from the west.
Westerners sometimes referred to their fellow soldiers of elevated
stances as "Virginians," more because of their rarefied states of mind
than because of their place of origin. *Virginian* was almost a fighting
word. It was used in a pejorative sense. "Hey, Virginian, you sure
smell sweet. Won't you make a beautiful looking corpse," a farmer-
soldier from Illinois might call to one of Hooker's men, who was
taking a dignified, by-the-rule break along the road. To the well-
bred easterner, someone who knew the geography of Boston Common and where to find theaters and books in New York, the true
westerner wasn't all that different from a Rebel. Aside from the fact
that the westerners wore blue, there sometimes didn't seem to be
any difference between them and the Southerners. The westerners
liked to carry Confederate-type blanket rolls, rather than the neater
knapsacks. They strode about like ridge runners, hawking up
phlegm and tobacco juice to the four winds, paying minimum
respect to officers, and often displaying as much racial bigotry as did
Rebels from south of Tupelo. The easterners might well wonder
what beliefs brought these westerners into the fray. But fight, and
fight ferociously, the westerners did for the Union, and they had little reverence for how seriously and high-mindedly others might
take themselves. They liked to slip up on an easterner and verbally
goose him. "All quiet on the Potomac," one would call, the ultimate insult, a reminder of eastern pusillanimity, alarums, and excursions. Or they called "Bull Run!" a reminder of the granddaddy of

all eastern debacles. The easterners took the catcalling and derision as best they could, having little in their arsenal for reply. It would be vulgar to engage in name-calling. The best revenge would be to prove themselves in battle here in this wilderness, and they soon got their chance.

Hooker faced more of a mountain than an army. Lookout Mountain rises steep and rocky, seeming to be an obstacle more for a mountain climber than for a dog soldier who would have to fight at the same time. Hooker also faced the weather on November 24, a misty, bone-chilly morning. Finally, he faced his demons. As Hooker prepared to engage the Rebels on Lookout Mountain, to the west of Chattanooga, he faced the specter of Sherman and his seemingly chosen role in the whole campaign. Oh, how these generals, north and south, guarded their reputations and fought to maintain or enhance them! No Hollywood luminary ever fought harder for renown or felt so slighted over the smallest insult. A month after the battle Hooker wrote a "confidential" letter to Secretary of the Treasury Salmon P. Chase, saying, "You will perceive that the strategy and tactics of the campaign were to throw it into the hands of Sherman, to my exclusion. . . . Please remember what I tell you. It was natural for Grant to feel partial to his old companions, and do all in his power to enhance their renown. . . ."

At first Hooker had been instructed merely to feint at Lookout Mountain, so the Rebels wouldn't send men over to Missionary Ridge, where the real fighting would take place, where Sherman would give them a real head thumping. However, high water on the Tennessee River had broken the pontoon bridge at Brown's Ferry, and one of Sherman's divisions under Brigadier General Peter J. Osterhaus couldn't get across; it was stranded on the west bank. Grant didn't waste time. He pressed on with lightninglike decisions. He ordered this division to aid Hooker, which then raised Hooker's troop strength to around 12,000. High up, the few Rebel brigades that faced Hooker on Lookout Mountain began setting up impediments as best they could through the fog and the absence of clear directives. Hooker, ever aware of image, with additional troops under his command, requested that his demeaning feint be converted into a *coup de maître*. Permission granted. Hooker then forged ahead on that fall morning at around eight o'clock, first crossing a swollen Lookout Creek. In the lead surged Geary's division, followed by that of Charles Cruft—all easterners. They moved like men who knew precisely what they were doing and who were not going to be denied by man or steep, heavily timbered land. They quickly roped in over forty Rebel pickets who stood in their way and then plunged into the mist. No one could see them. Up on Lookout Mountain, the meager Rebel force heard some racket and began loping down to man rifle pits. Geary's lead column soon reached a bare vertical cliff, about halfway up, which presented the obstacles of a Matterhorn, and immediately began fanning out to seek a more convenient way up. They moved in the direction of the Craven farmhouse, later to become a landmark in the battle.

Down below, the Federals had captured one lightly guarded bridge and were busily constructing another. Blueclads from the divisions of Osterhaus and Cruft were pouring over rattling, creaking boards, on the way to tie up with Geary. A long line of Federals was now in the process of scaling Lookout Mountain. Brigadier General Walter C. Whitaker, who led the Second Brigade in Cruft's division, reported an advance "over steep, rocky, ravine-seamed, torrent-torn sides of the mountain," which became "laborious and extremely toilsome."

The field artillery rolled out heavy Parrott guns from Moccasin Point and tried to blast the Rebels out of the way. The caissons jumped and swayed and slowed as the incline up grand Lookout Mountain grew suddenly very steep. At first they couldn't slack off because they might slide backward with a horrible snowball effect. They had to keep pushing, and "Keep 'em rolling!" sounded through the trees. Artillery drivers bent low over pommels, whips singing, while their horses scrambled up by inches, bellies practically touching the ground. Later the "Field Artillery Song" would vividly recall such moments—"Over hill, over dale, as we hit those dusty trails, as those caissons keep rolling along!"—and all the while the westerners in other divisions watched such dogged military efforts with a touch of superiority. Easterners were on those caissons; they were part of the Army of the Cumberland. They were, of course, fools. "Look at 'em! They'll never get them blame guns back. Them Potomac boys have no sense and should have stayed at home!"

The batteries halted a short distance up Lookout Mountain, rocks placed under wheels to keep them from rolling back, the barrels of their guns pointing sharply up. There was consolation in the fact that if the Rebels pushed their infantry back, they could cover a retreat. Infantrymen surged around them, climbing up. The Rebels still held the advantage, though, for in war, those who hold the high ground—as Lee did at Fredericksburg—hold a mighty ace in the hole. On plateaus up Lookout Mountain, Southern batteries began taking aim, as best they could, on this array of blue coming for them. Welcome, Yanks! Their first volleys landed with precision into the Union ranks, but only slowed, didn't stop, the ascent. And the closer the blue army came, ironically, the harder it was to fire a gun into them because as the range decreased, the back ends of the guns had to be raised and raised to avoid overshooting. Finally, the desperate Southerners could not raise the back ends any higher and had to get their own artillery rolling to avoid capture. The Southern gunners on top of the mountain resorted to lighting the fuses on their shells and rolling them down the mountain. They did so more in anger and frustration than with any hope that it would impede the Federal advance. In any case, the Yankees hopped out of the way, and the sizzling shells caused little damage and no confusion. Hooker's men were coming closer and closer.

The Craven farmhouse, perched halfway up the sheer north face of Lookout Mountain, afforded the Rebels as good a view as any through the mist of the advancing Federals. The antebellum Cravens were a family with an advanced sense of the aesthetic. Their tastefully and, for the times, expensively furnished white frame home looked out over a wide majestic vista. It was secluded, situated miles and centuries from civilization's discontents. War now struck it—just like that—just as it had the Widow Henry's home at Manassas and the Brotherton farm on the La Fayette Road at Chickamauga. Their number came up.

Edward C. Walthall and his Mississippi brigade were taking the brunt of the Yankee attack, trying to block the narrow passage around the northern face of the mountain. Walthall tried everything he could with whatever he had at hand, but the Yankees kept coming. He threw four companies of sharpshooters to his rear and up the slope of the mountain, hoping they could make a dent in the Yankee advance. It didn't work. The sharpshooters cracked away, but proved to be only an annoyance, not a threat. Around noon Walthall's brigade was forced to draw back some 400 yards from the Craven farmhouse, hunkering down in some trenched breastworks. Wispy fog waved over the lines of men on both sides, clearing for moments to reveal raised muskets and bucking guns. It was nearly impossible to make out any object over 100 yards away, but anyone caught within that space was soon shot at. John C. Moore's Alabama brigade came to lend a hand, and not long afterward Edmund W. Pettus's brigade of fellow Alabamans followed suit. These three brigades fought hard to hold their position, but their ammunition was running low. They suffered, too, from not having on hand a general to give them overall directions. This day the division commander was as hard to pin down as the fog.

Brigadier General John K. Jackson, who was headquartered on top of Lookout Mountain, presented all the elements of an eccentric without any compensating charm (or victories). For example, he was dubbed "Mudwall" to show what some thought of him in comparison to his more famed namesake, "Stonewall." Mudwall Jackson was truculent, easily upset, and held to one telling distinctive imponderable: Out of all the Confederate generals at Chickamauga, he believed Braxton Bragg to be a great leader. Jackson did not get along too well with those under him, something he had in common with Bragg. He also had a way of making decisions while being removed from where the action was taking place. Throughout the hot fight around the Craven farmhouse, Jackson was a missing physical element. When Moore desperately needed ammunition and advice, he sent an aide flying aloft to find Jackson—*What should we do?* The aide returned; he couldn't locate Jackson. Then Pettus sent one of his staff officers to the summit who did manage to find Jackson. Jackson sent back word for the brigade to hold its position for "as long as possible." At that moment he was drawing up plans to withdraw everyone from Lookout Mountain. The three brigades, though, somehow held on that foggy day, no thanks to Jackson. The Mississippian Walthall was still furious with Jackson for weeks afterward. In his After Action Report, Walthall let loose: "At no time during this prolonged struggle . . . did I have the benefit of my division commander's [Jackson's] personal presence. After I was relieved, and while awaiting orders to move, I saw him for the first time on his way, as he told me, to see the general-in-chief [Bragg]."

Pettus and Moore chimed in with their own low estimate of Jackson. The division commander, smarting still over being dubbed Mudwall, exchanged blistering letters with his subordinates. Now he was the angry one. He was mad enough to fight, and consecutive duels with all three brigade commanders became a possibility. "Call them out, sir! Call them!" an at first sympathetic General William Henry Talbot Walker advised him. As Walker learned more details of the brouhaha, his ardor cooled. He finally advised that the matter should be dropped, which Jackson finally determined to be the more prudent policy.

On the foggy afternoon of November 24, the Federals finally drove the Southerners from the entrenchments back of the Craven farmhouse. By then, everyone was too exhausted to fight anymore. At two in the afternoon, Hooker sent out word to hold the ground they stood on and not to try to advance farther. Everyone lay back.

The oddity of this battle was that it was being watched, as a glorified form of outdoor theater, by Federal troops down in the valley, particularly by Grant and Thomas at Orchard Knob. These observers heard the roar of the battle rolling down through the valley, thunderous and crackling. Those closer saw red, white, and blue banners inching up the mountain to plunge suddenly into the mist. Then a gust of wind would lift the haze, and they would see the banners again. Some flags fell, only to be picked up quickly and thrust forward again. A color-bearer was a marked man, a shoot-me target, but no fighting soldier could bear to see a banner grounded. There was a practical reason for the flags to be out front, too, because men advanced toward one—rushing over breastworks or whatever stood in the way. Seeing one's banner on the ground could take the will out of a man. Carry one aloft, and you remained undefeated.

It was called the Battle Above the Clouds, a name that has survived in defining it. A correspondent who covered the event said that "there were no clouds to fight above, only heavy mist." No matter what the men fought through—fog, clouds, gunpowder, or all three—it was an unusual sight. No one hears the horrors of war translated into stirring, mythical moments without a certain uneasiness. Certainly, the aerial bombing of Abyssinia at night might have made Count Ciano think of the beauty of an unfolding rose, and Lee's quote about the seductiveness of war while his superiorly positioned guns prevailed at Fredericksburg is understandable, but one can be made a little uneasy by such feelings. One hears of the exploding radiance of muzzle fire of an armada of American tanks in Vietnam at night during the Tet offensive and feels a shameful recognition of war's power. Grant, that master of words, wrote afterward: "The Battle of Lookout Mountain is one of the romances of the war. There was no such battle and no action even worthy to be called a battle on Lookout Mountain. It is all poetry."

All poetry—how seductive the phrase. Yet thousands were engaged in combat, and many soldiers left this earth there. Hooker suffered a total of 629 casualties, including 81 dead and 8 missing. A burning building, a spectacular train wreck, and a bridge collapse wouldn't have caused so many. It was war. And Hooker's men bedded down that damp night, halfway up the mountain, fully expecting the Rebels to pounce upon them in the dawn. Their campfires blazed, and their fellow soldiers down in the valley and farther east could tell exactly how far they had gotten by these pinpoints of lights. Confederates looking down on the fires compared them to so many lightning bugs. The moon was in a total eclipse, and it was dark indeed.

Bragg now wanted all the Confederate troops to remove themselves from Lookout Mountain and rush to Missionary Ridge for its defense. Around two in the morning, these troops began a successful withdrawal, burning the single bridge over Chattanooga Creek in the process. The dark night aided them, and Hooker went to bed convinced he had a fight on his hands the next day.

At first light on November 25, Hooker was astride his big white horse, awaiting the conquest, he hoped, of the rest of Lookout Mountain. Through the damp cold night, his men had tried to rest for battle. Bone-weary drivers had coaxed heavily laden pack mules over craggy rocks and fallen timber to bring in food and ammunition. When the sun peeked up, they were ready. Six volunteers from the Eighth Kentucky scaled a cliff to see what Confederates might be on hand. They found an abandoned campsite, In one of the most dramatic moments in American military history, they raised the Stars and Stripes, its red, white, and blue colors fiery in the increasing sunlight, and waved it back and forth. Far into the valley below soldiers waved their caps in the air, yelled, and waved back. Lookout Mountain was now back in the Union.

10

★

"I Shall Take Those Guns for That!"

The battle of Lookout Mountain won, Joseph Hooker continued on. He moved to strike at small Rossville at the southern foot of Missionary Ridge. Then he planned to scale the heights, driving north along the crest until he majestically tied up with William Tecumseh Sherman, who would be coming down from Tunnel Hill from the opposite direction. For good measure, Hooker might also be able to seal off any Confederate retreat through Chickamauga Station. It was a big order. Ulysses S. Grant's idea was to squeeze Braxton Bragg—Sherman pressing one way, Hooker another, until the life was squeezed right out of him. One thing about fighting under Grant: You didn't rest on your laurels. Everything moved at a rapid pace. But a happy path to Missionary Ridge was not automatically assured.

After leaving a small occupying force atop the mountain,

Hooker's men wound their way down to the foot, traveling over a curving narrow road. They moved out at 10:00 A.M. on November 25, which was turning out to be a sun-kissed day unlike the depressingly wet and dreary day before. They were going fine, banners whipping, horses trotting, when they called an abrupt halt at the narrow Chattanooga River at one-thirty. They had come three-fourths of the way, and they could go no farther; the infuriating Rebels had blown the lone bridge up. No material was at hand to build another bridge, so scouting parties fanned out to bring in what was required. It caused a four-hour delay in their advance to Rossville, the starting-off point for their assault. Hard luck and a damned nuisance.

The men of the Cumberland—George H. Thomas's troops— poised to tear into the middle of Missionary Ridge, took the news of the delay badly. They had little patience for the theatrical Fighting Joe Hooker and his troopers anyhow. Sure, Hooker's men had unfurled a flag at sunrise on the summit of Lookout Mountain—but how could they march out without a few engineers and enough material for a makeshift bridge? How long had these paper-collar nitwits been in the war? Did they think they could walk on water? It goes to show you. Hooker was a blowhard.

Grant had sent word to Sherman to attack early. At seven that morning Sherman sent out skirmishers, who readily found some Rebel pickets who fired back. Soon Sherman was lobbing artillery shells onto Missionary Ridge, but the Rebels on Tunnel Hill were ready, Patrick Cleburne at the helm. Since he had returned to Missionary Ridge, called back at the last minute, Cleburne had been feverishly seeing to fortifications, positioning his men, and lining up his artillery. The eclipse of the moon conveniently covered his movements, but in the near-total darkness he had to do many things by feel, literally feeling with his hands where a gun should be placed and a rifle pit should be dug, like a blind man.

By mid-morning Sherman had his fill of skirmishing and

shelling. It was time to get down to business. Bugles sounded; drums rolled; and Sherman's men, victors of the bluffs at Vicksburg, sallied forth. Already, in pianissimo, lofty Lookout Mountain had fallen. Now, in fortissimo, these veterans of the Army of Tennessee raised their muskets and charged, cheering as they went. They reached the first line of Rebel entrenchments and were immediately thrown back. Cleburne had devilishly constructed a defensive front that was narrow, with no way to outflank it. The Federals had to charge straight into a space of narrow width that, unfortunately for Sherman's men, was manned by some of the most stubborn soldiers on earth—Cleburne's men. Thus, no matter how many divisions Sherman held, he could throw only three or four brigades at Tunnel Hill at a time.

As the blue line surged, the Warren Light Artillery of Mississippi let off some rapid volleys from the top of the hill. The Federal right flank slowed, stopped, and fell over, the living tumbling among the dead and wounded, all mixed together, a wave of humanity falling down the slope. The left kept charging, reached some small protective woods, and kept going up. The Mississippi battery got caught in a cross fire for a moment, but held. All its officers and sergeants took bullets and fell. A corporal took command and had gun muzzles swinging to where they could do the most damage. The guns clattered and jumped, and wide swathes of the blue left line disappeared. The Federals got to within fifty paces of the top, when a gray line loomed suddenly and countercharged. The Federal left fell and tumbled back down. Sherman had his orders from Grant—"Attack!"—so he sent another wave forward, and those men inched their way up, toes digging in, only to be flung back unceremoniously. Charge after charge after charge went up and came back down. The Confederates and Cleburne weren't going to give up Tunnel Hill even if the assailant was the celebrated and redoubtable Sherman, acting under the command of the man who had made *unconditional surrender* part of the lexicon. The

Southerners threw everything they had down on them, even boulders when nothing else was at hand. Cleburne held.

"You may go up the hill if you like," Sherman said in an offhand way to his brother-in-law, Hugh B. Ewing, who commanded a lead division. "And don't call for help unless you need it." Ewing took off and almost immediately called for help. Sherman gave it—first one division, then another. Before midday, two divisions of Oliver Otis Howard had joined him in the desperate fight, but nothing worked. Sherman tried to maneuver this way and that, feint here, attack there—but he couldn't prevail, couldn't plant his colors atop Tunnel Hill.

The crack Sixth Wisconsin flung itself up the slope and put its proud honor on the line. It went its own way and usually got its way. In its earliest moments in the war, it had discarded sabers as being too showy and too heavy. But it made sure it had a band, and to every battle it brought a fiddle, banjo, tambourine, and clarinet. Inspired by the likes of "Listen to the Mockingbird," its men started up. Squads of axemen cleared a new approach through some woods, and an extra pair of horses was added to each team that pulled a piece of artillery. The horses finally could not do it; the slope was too rough and too steep, and there was too much fire to take on the move. The Sixth wasn't easily discouraged. Limbers were unhitched, and the men themselves began to pull the heavy guns up by rope. Then, as if in a cruel practical joke, the unhitched horses—now not forced to climb up—began to slip and slide back down, knocking over an advancing blue line. Everything, everyone Sherman threw forward came back down. Tunnel Hill was proving to be impregnable.

Cleburne's men later remembered the fusillades from below as "one continuous sheet of hissing, flying lead." The Federals kept coming, even if they knew in their hearts that it was futile and that they would be thrown back. Every once in a while, a Yankee came close to breaking through the defenses, but would be sent backward, like a Sisyphus in blue. Before it ended, the inspired grayclads pried up any remaining boulders they could find and rolled them down on the horses, carts, and men. Still Sherman kept it up. Around three in the afternoon, after almost a full day's work and not an inch gained, Sherman had just about enough. Even Sherman had his limits. He'd suffered 1,500 casualties, including 261 of his men who had been captured in Confederate countercharges. He wasn't winning here—he was losing—and it was a novel experience for him. Well, he had caused the Rebels to reassign a lot of men his way—at least he had that for consolation. "Go signal Grant," he ordered a staff officer. "The orders were that I should get as many as possible in front of me, and God knows there are enough. They've been reinforcing all day."

In point of fact, he had been directed to take Tunnel Hill and drive down Missionary Ridge to tie up with Hooker, who was to come up from the lower end. Grant, at his station down on Orchard Knob, facing the center, signaled back to his old friend: "Attack, again!" So Sherman did. Grant thought if he put more bodies into the fight, the tide might turn. Wasn't this a battle like any other? Didn't numbers count? Grant kept believing that by throwing more and more men at the enemy, the enemy would have to give up. This thought process reached its apogee in the later horrendous fighting at Cold Harbor.

Grant dispatched Absalom Baird's division from Thomas's army to help, but the gesture proved superfluous. Since Cleburne's front was so narrow, only so many could assault it at one time.Thus, Sherman didn't need more men; he needed Cleburne to drop dead. While Baird was trooping toward Tunnel Hill, Grant called him back. Then Sherman began to think that there might be a communication problem, that he might be receiving the wrong answer from Grant. He asked that a signal be sent to supreme headquarters, asking if he had heard right: Was he still to attack while being thrown back like a shot? On the hill behind him, a signalman smartly snapped his flags around, so they could be seen by Grant's headquarters down on Orchard Knob. Was it true, should the attack continue? Signal flags snapped around on Orchard Knob in answer: "Keep attacking."

But Grant had begun to fret. He chewed on an unlit cigar and then took it from his mouth and examined it. A message had at last come from Fighting Joe. Hooker had reached Rossville, where he had the good fortune to capture some needed supplies, and he was now sending Charles Cruft's division north over the top of Missionary Ridge, with John W. Geary on the left and Peter J. Osterhaus on the right. Well and good—but late, too late. He would never have time to tie up with Sherman. The great plan of using pincers on Bragg was fast unraveling. And now, binoculars to his eyes, a cigar clamped between his teeth, Grant saw what he took to be Confederate reinforcements going to aid Cleburne. Bragg's headquarters stood out in the clear clean light, right up on top of Missionary Ridge, smack in the middle. The mountain rose 500 feet and was a mile and a half away. It was close enough for Grant, aided by binoculars, almost to see the flies worrying the tails of the horses. Grant saw aides scurrying away and horses galloping to and fro. He could well have spied Bragg himself, fretting and stomping around. A lot was happening up there, and Grant couldn't afford for anything terribly bad to happen to his old saddle pal Sherman. Sherman must be saved.

Grant turned to General Thomas and said, almost plaintively, "Don't you think it's about time to advance against the rifle pits?" A theoretical question was not what the Virginian wanted to talk over at this moment. He kept staring through his own binoculars at the enemy above. If Grant wanted action, he had to order it. Grant was in command. At around three-thirty that afternoon of November 25—late in the day for that time of year—Grant did just that, in a somewhat reluctant fashion. He was going to send an awful lot of brave men against a triple line of entrenchments, in the face of many guns looking down from the crest of Missionary Ridge. But he ordered it.

The charge that followed has gone down in military lore as one of the most magnificent ever. It has been mythologized, rhapsodized, told, and retold. According to Edwin W. Payne, of the Thirty-fourth Illinois, it was "a scene never to be forgotten—a panorama to stir the blood into wild tumult." Others in the line of assault called it "one of the grandest spectacles ever seen" and an experience "never to be encountered twice in a lifetime." One simply declared, "Our advance to the base of the ridge was the grandest sight I ever saw." For those who were there, those in the thick of it, it was St. Crispin's Day. They were bonded forever.

Four divisions in blue lined up: Baird's on the far left, followed by Thomas J. Wood's, Philip H. Sheridan's, and Richard W. Johnson's. Here were 25,000 men bunched together, ready to plunge across what was mostly a wooded, hilly plain and take out a row of Confederate rifle pits at the base of Missionary Ridge. Because starting points varied and the rifle pits were in an uneven alignment, the distance to be traveled differed from regiment to regiment. For some it was a long mile, while for others, it was a shorter distance— but all who made it that far had to manage the last 500 to 700 yards over open level ground, where the fire could be expected to be intense. The charge was a mammoth solid mass of blueclad figures, over two miles in width—more men than in Pickett's ill-starred charge at Gettysburg, a cautionary event that gave all men pause who had to transverse an open field, shoulder to shoulder, against an entrenched and murderous foe.

The troops cheered when word came that they were to attack. Orderlies, clerks, and cooks rushed to find rifles and to fall in line. It is hard to know the mishmash of resentments and anger that lurked beneath the surface in many men's hearts. Perhaps these men of the Army of the Cumberland weren't fully aware of all the emotions that now came into play when they were at last given the nod to go against the Southerners. They were mad and stirred up— against the Rebels and their lawlessness, against being run off the field at Chickamauga; they were smarting under the prevailing notion that Sherman's troops were somehow more battle hardened and wise, and they were irritated by the pomp and superciliousness of Hooker's easterners. They hadn't been used for over a day and a half, and now they had their chance. *Look out!*

The signal for the troops to advance came from the report of six guns fired in rapid succession. Ten minutes after Grant told Thomas to move out, the first gun went off. The signal was given by Gordon Granger, one of the heroes at Chickamauga, who stood on a high parapet at Orchard Knob. High-strung, jumpy, and thoroughly wedded to a strict military protocol, Granger brought his skinny arm down: "Number One, *fire!*" and the troops rustled but did not step forward; then came, "Number Two, *fire!* Number Three, *fire!* Number Four, *fire!* Number Five, *fire!*" The lead elements started to move. "Number Six, *fire!*" Granger yelled, and they were all off.

At first the Confederates were stunned. They were either seeing a splendid military parade and exercise—or they were seeing the world's largest army coming right at them. "Forward, guide center, march!" the regimental commanders called out. At first it was like a parade, with a glistening array of fixed bayonets catching the late-afternoon light. Then they hit gullies, jumped over felled trees, and wove around rocks and stumps—coming forward, yelling from front to back in one resounding cheer. The gray pickets up front ran like hell to take cover in the earthworks, screaming out in alarm. Confederate artillerymen on the crest of Missionary Ridge gaped and then came alive. They flung shells into cannons and started the fuses sizzling. Bragg had 110 guns on high, and before many minutes passed at least 50 of them were trained down and blasting away at the two-and-a-half-mile line of bluecoats coming forward. A tremendous, ear-shattering roar erupted as the shells landed. One soldier described it as "a crash like a thousand thunderclaps." Another said that "the whole ridge to our front had broken out like another Aetna."

In the clear sunlight, shells could be discerned leaving the muzzles of Confederate guns in a halo of crimson and puffs of white. Most of these missiles screamed over the heads of the Federals, while some landed in their midst, sending up showers of dirt and an occasional body. The random shell fell, did not explode, and caused terror. Horses reared and couldn't be controlled. A few of the Federals bolted; it was too terrifying, too much—what had happened to the parade? But the mass of blue did not take to its heels. The soldiers scurried about, continuing on in a zigzagging run, as if the shells were no more than an inconvenient thundershower. They went through woods and then hit the open field just in front of the rifle pits. They didn't pause. They charged, bayonets raised, yelling, "Chickamauga! Chickamauga!" Most didn't stop to load and fire, but pressed forward for hand-to-hand combat. They were mad—madder than even they knew.

Federal artillerymen on Orchard Knob and surrounding territory came alive and were soon in competition with the Confederates as to who could cause the most damage and effect the most terror. The cannoneers blasted away, emitting deafening concussions and spreading dirty white smoke. Pulses raced and adrenaline flowed as the blasts echoed as far away as Lookout Mountain. A lot was at stake. Reason was disappearing; savagery was taking its place in those who could swallow their fears. Granger couldn't restrain himself, couldn't stay in the role of an observer. The agile Granger vaulted from his safe haven on the parapet and ran to the fieldpiece of an Illinois battery under a Captain Lyman Bridge. Out of the way, General Granger taking charge! Granger sighted the cannon and sent a round lofting toward the summit of Missionary Ridge, where it sent a caisson into a thousand pieces. Another skillfully aimed shell landed smack-dab in, of all places, the very headquarters of Bragg. Gone, blasted away to rubble. (Bragg was elsewhere—fortunately or unfortunately for the Confederacy.) A third shell hit a gray mass of men, breaking it apart, as one observer put it, "as if it had been a wasp's nest."

Granger might have continued sharpshooting if Grant hadn't taken notice and come running. Pay attention to your troop movements, Grant advised; you're commanding a corps, not a cannon. Granger reluctantly went back to his post, and the North lost an excellent marksman. Shells from both sides were creating much terror and noise, but aside from those scattered hits—such as the bull's-eye on star-crossed Bragg's hut—the shells missed their marks and did not cause extensive damage. A duel did develop between a Confederate battery on the ridge and a Federal one on Orchard Knob. While shells whizzed over their heads, neither Grant nor Thomas ducked or seemingly took much notice. The rounds came near them, but did not connect. Up on the ridge some men of the Forty-fifth Tennessee had been mesmerized by the pageantry of the Federal charge, gaping in wonder, not moving for cover, when a shell landed among them, decapitating a soldier named Will Clark and ripping off the shoulder of his brother, Newt. That was the result of one of the shells that landed accurately that day.

The taking of the rifle pits at the base of Missionary Ridge was, of course, the purpose of all this shelling and the reason the mass of blueclads were charging forward. The Confederates in the rifle pits were well positioned, dug in, and witnessed ready targets coming forward, soldiers almost begging to be shot—but they sensed something more in this awesome advance: a possible diabolical thirst for vengeance by the Yankees. Normal soldiers didn't charge this way. When the first attackers came within pistol range—not discouraged by cannon fire or by round after round of musket fire—the front line of Southerners began to have second thoughts about sticking around. First one, then another, leaped out of a rifle pit and tried to save his skin. Before long it was a rout. A few tried to claw their way up the slope to safety, while many raised their hands and leaped to the side of the entrenchments to try to avoid the shells that were raining down from their comrades above. The Federals herded them to the rear, taunting them along the way: "You have been trying to get there long enough, and now charge on Chattanooga!" Not all Confederates fled by a long shot; not all were captured or clawed their way to safety. Some stayed at their posts—because they couldn't hear any command to retreat, because they saw no purpose in exposing themselves to fire by leaving, and because they were Southerners and too proud and stubborn to give up. Soon, though, all order was lost, and the Federals had captured this first line of entrenchment.

The Federals milled around at first, panting from the charge, still mad and itching to fight but unsure about how to go about it. Then they were suddenly denied the luxury of thinking. The Rebels at the second line of defense up the slope began taking deadly aim, and cannoneers who had trouble lowering their howitzer muzzles simply lit fuses and rolled sputtering cannon balls down toward them like bowling balls. "Terrible was the effect of this fire on the dense lines of the enemy," Confederate Brigadier General Alexander W. Reynolds, who was at the crest, later recalled. At the time, he was busily depressing his guns and blasting away with canister. Everyone from above was getting his chance to shoot a Yankee, one way or another.

Up above stood the corps of John C. Breckinridge and William J. Hardee—Bragg in overall command, Bragg planted in the middle of the ridge looking down. When his headquarters had blown apart, Bragg—and Breckinridge, too—began to have second thoughts about the "impregnability" of the Confederate middle on Missionary Ridge. Bragg's worry all along had not been about his middle, but about his flanks: on his right to the north, where Sherman was pounding away, and on his left to the south, where Hooker was getting ready to start mischief. What a mess. The Confederate middle on Missionary Ridge was a poor relation, a neglected child. It seemed that Bragg spent so much time worrying about his flanks that he didn't have any time left to consider his middle. The defense there hadn't begun until November 23, and then only with a small crew who were short on entrenching tools. In fact, they really didn't get to work until the night of November 24–25, when it was too late. Mistakes abounded. Rebel infantry weren't placed where they could do the most good. Cannons were misguidedly placed on the very top of the crest, not slightly below it, at the "military" crest, where they could have done more good. Thus, Federal infantry had a stretch of safe ground where they could catch their breath before surging over the top. Through some sort of whimsy, Bragg had christened his Napoleons on the ridge with names of his generals, reversing the genders—"Lady Buckner," "Lady Breckinridge," "Lady Lyon," and "Lady Gracie." He might have spent his time more profitably in positioning them. There were also spots where Confederate strong points became vulnerable to enfilading fire, distracting the men there from dealing with the assault coming right at their faces. And nature conspired with the inept Confederates to make defense a problem. Missionary Ridge runs narrowly down the crest from north to south—ranging in width from 70 to 600 feet—so that the Confederates had little room to maneuver, to draw back and regroup. It was either stop the assault completely or abandon ship. As the ridge rises steeply from the west, it sinks immediately to the east. In addition, the narrow crest meanders with varying elevations and sudden deep ravines. Actually, it resembles a series of hills more than one continuous ridge. Because of the uneven rugged terrain when the assault did come, it became difficult for the Confederates to respond quickly to any particularly threatened point.

The Rebels had 10,500 soldiers on the crest who were ready to meet the charge, and they set up a defensive line of around five miles. They faced around 23,000 Federals—but they commanded the heights, a not insignificant factor. Accounts differ on how close together these defenders were. Some Rebel veterans of the fight reported that they were positioned far enough apart to be able to swing their rifles without hitting one another. They were not shoulder to shoulder; there were gaps in the line. A further foul-up in the defense was the unclearness about how the three lines of defense were to be used. Corps commander Breckinridge favored holding the first line at the rifle pits below at all hazards. But various generals under him—J. Patton Anderson and Zachariah C. Deas, in particular—wanted those in the rifle pits to beat a fast retreat to the second line farther up in the face of an assault. When the assault came, General William B. Bate began withdrawing his brigade immediately from the rifle pits, the better to defend the crest. Breckinridge saw them coming, countermanded the order, and sent them back to the rifle pits. There was much more of the usual confusion in the Rebel ranks. Robert Watson from Florida was in the rifle pits when the Yankees got to within thirty yards of him. Next, he beat a retreat to the second line of defense, which also became untenable, so he broke for the crest. "Then came the worst part of the fight," he recalled, "for the hill was dreadful steep and the enemy kept up a continual fire. . . . Many a poor fellow fell exhausted and was taken prisoner." Like his fellow soldiers of the South, he carried a rifled musket, a heavy knapsack, three days' rations in his haversack, and a canteen full of water. "I stopped several times and took a shot at the damned Yankees and at the same time it rested me." One Rebel said his company hadn't suffered in the rifle pits, but took many casualties falling back and scurrying up the steep hill. "It seemed that every Yankee within a mile was shooting at us." John Ware from Tennessee presented not an uncommon sight: He wore no shoes and had to hop about going up, scraping, cutting, and bruising his bare feet.

After taking the rifle pits, the Federals darted around while dirt from exploding shells flew, smoke spread, screams and the thunder of fire erupted, and horses jumped about. They weren't having an easy time, either. In this bedlam company officers, who were always called upon to be the bravest and most coolheaded in the front lines, began waving their sabers and commanding that dirt be shoveled up to offer some protection. The Federals had captured the rifle pits, but they were now having great trouble staying there. Had all this been a wily trick on the Southerners' part? Lure them in and then kill them all like rabbits. They sure weren't going to retreat. First one, then another, began going up the slope toward the enemy. It was mostly spontaneous. No arm dropped to start the troops forward, no command had been shouted, and no bugle blew. There went a squad suddenly, hunkering down low, digging in, climbing up—then another, followed by a platoon here and a company there. Those junior officers who had been calling for dirt now yelled for these men to stop, but they soon caught the fever and joined the rush, changing their yells to, "Follow me!" It was now an army of inspiration, not deliberation. It was as if they were boys again, caught in a dangerous mood of directionless adventure. First colonels and then brigadiers joined in, and finally whole regiments were sweeping up. Color guards weren't aligned, the drums weren't rolling, but a freedom from restraint had caught hold. Colonels dug their boots in the dirt, trying to get to the front of their men.

Down below at Orchard Knob, Grant showed emotion—not elation, but profound anxiety. His cigar went in and out of his mouth, and he clamped down upon it strongly. He foresaw the makings of a gigantic disaster. Sherman, on his left, had been trying all day to go up Missionary Ridge, but had been foiled and humiliated. On his right Hooker was behind schedule and just getting started. *Now* the Confederates could well send the Army of the Cumberland reeling back in the middle. The blue army was without defenses, was trying to scale a wall in the face of overwhelming firepower. *Grant could see it!* He could see these men going up a fortified mountain—right out in plain view. If they came tumbling back, then his own headquarters, the might of the North, would be lost.

"Thomas, who ordered those men up the ridge?" he spat out.

Always the gentleman, always quietly spoken, Thomas said, "I don't know. I did not."

Grant wasn't satisfied. Granger, who was standing nearby, was a convenient target. Grant had reprimanded him only moments before for taking pleasure in firing his artillery and not spending enough time as a corps commander. Stiff-backed Granger was always a good one to hit in a time of tension. "Did you order them up, Granger?"

Granger might have wished he had. "No; they started up without orders," he said. "When those fellows get started, all hell can't stop them."

Grant began muttering, dissatisfied, on edge, his binoculars trained ahead. If those men got repulsed, somebody was going to pay, and somebody was going to pay dearly.

Several general officers were not as cautious as Grant. They had less to lose, of course, but they also sensed something infectious in the air, some mood that said the Confederates in their "impregnable" position could be beaten. General Phil Sheridan later said that Captain William Avery of Granger's staff caught up with him and indicated that if Sheridan thought the ridge itself could be taken, he should do so. Sheridan had his blood up and immediately gave the command for his division to storm the ridge. On his left, General William B. Hazen of Wood's division gave his men five minutes to catch their breath after taking the rifle pits, then, "receiving no orders, [he] gave the word forward, which was eagerly obeyed." Grant said the storming of Lookout Mountain was "all poetry." Here it was all improvisation.

Combat-wise veterans sensed that the safest thing to do was to charge uphill, not hunker down in the rifle pits, where they would turn into targets. No overall command was in effect anywhere; no tactical plan had been devised. Long after the battle, after Sheridan had become general in chief of the U.S. Army, he admitted that after giving his own improvised order to charge, he had ridden his horse through the rifle pits, forcing out skulkers and making whoever he found get out and charge. The men who charged up Missionary Ridge were not in gym attire either. Each carried a nine-pound rifle and around eighty rounds of ammunition, plus—because this was November in the mountains—a heavy winter overcoat.

The Federals kept pressing ahead on the ridge as if in a foot race, or, it should be said, a climbing race. A staff colonel later remembered that "at times their movements were in shape like a flight of migratory birds, sometimes in line, sometimes in mass, mostly in V-shaped groups, with the points toward the enemy. At these points regimental flags were flying, sometimes drooping as the bearers were shot, but never reaching the ground, for other brave hands were there to seize them." The colors must be held! Seven of the color-bearers who scaled Missionary Ridge to plant their flags won the Congressional Medal of Honor. When they captured an enemy flag, it became a rallying point. First Lieutenant Simeon T. Josselyn of the Thirteenth Illinois shot a Confederate color-bearer and wrestled the Stars and Bars out of his hands, causing nearby Confederates to flee or raise their hands. Ahead of all the color-bearers clomped a young adjutant of the Twenty-fourth Wisconsin, later to become known as "the boy colonel of the West." He waved his regimental colors back and forth as bullets whizzed around him, his face blackened like a minstrel singer's from the battle smoke, his uniform wet with mud and blood. "On, Wisconsin!" he cried. He made it to the top and was among the first, if not the first, to sink the staff of his flag in the ground. Miraculously, he was not killed; if he had been, we would not have had General Douglas MacArthur of twentieth-century fame. The color-bearer was his father—Arthur MacArthur. MacArthur père became a general who commanded troops in the Philippines. His son won his share of fame in the two world wars of this century.

At the base of the ridge, pudgy Phil Sheridan stood watching his men on the right trying to outstrip Wood's troops to the left. It was almost an athletic contest—with bullets. A staff captain, who knew what he was doing, held out a silver flask for Sheridan. Sheridan had romantic instincts—at least in this instance—and he lifted the flask in a salute to a group of Confederate officers he saw peering down on him from Bragg's headquarters at the top. "Here's to you," he called. He may not have known what he was doing, for a pair of gunners in a nearby Rebel battery swung their pieces and unloaded a near-direct hit on him. The round kicked up a shower of dirt, and Little Phil busily brushed himself off. He was lucky to be alive. "Ah, that is ungenerous," he yelled up. "I shall take those guns for that!" First he took a healthy swig from the flask, and then he started for the top on foot. In the advance over the plain of battle, his horse had been shot out from under him.

The second line of the Confederate defense fell, and those at the crest looked down with increasing horror on the onrushing mass in blue. Hindsight may say that the Confederate defenders should have been closer together, but then nature might have been more generous in making the ridge more even and easier to do so. Hindsight may also say that the rifle pits at the bottom should have been abandoned much sooner and that the second line should have been shored up immediately. But hindsight is hindsight. The Southerners kept fighting—they would, in one guise or another, for some time afterward—but their spirit was slowly breaking on the crest of Missionary Ridge. When their ammunition failed, they rolled rocks. When there were no more rocks and many more blueclads were coming up, they began to break for the other side of the ridge. For their lives. Confederate officers rode among them, cursing, screaming, begging them to return to their posts. The Yankees are exhausted—beat them back! Even poor Bragg was imploring them to stand. He wasn't threatening them now, he wasn't actually angry;

he was pathetically begging them. "Here is your commander!" he called. The Southerners were running. "Here's your mule!" they yelled back. Bragg didn't mean much to them anymore.

Wood's division is generally given credit for having been the first over the top, although the evidence is not clear. Lieutenant Colonel Bassett Langdon, commanding a regiment in the division, gave the order to fix bayonets just before the summit and then was shot in the face. He slumped over, but still had enough wits about him to give another officer some advice on how to proceed; he rose and yelled, "Charge!" Then he collapsed again, but lived to tell the story.

As the full force of blueclads swept over the crest, they witnessed an unbelievable sight, one that seemed dreamlike and improbable. The tableau said much about where the war had taken them. It was a portent, too, of a lot to follow. Rebels were tumbling over each other in wild confusion, beating their way down the slope on the opposite side. They were heaving to the side all that slowed or impeded them—knapsacks, muskets, and blankets. Batteries galloped down narrow, winding roads at breakneck speeds, not worrying about crashing, but concerned about Yankees. Horses fell, guns were abandoned, and those who couldn't flee moaned, sank, and were captured.

The Federals captured 3,000 prisoners, 7,000 small arms, and 37 cannon. Phil Sheridan, who had huffed and puffed his way up, now ran to one of the guns that had fired upon him not many minutes before. In a bravado move, he climbed aboard it as if it were a steed and waved his hat around like a cowboy, yelping all the while. It was a vindication for Chickamauga, and all were conscious of it, especially Sheridan. Colonel Charles G. Harker, who commanded a brigade under Sheridan, tried to follow in his chief's footsteps and leapt on another cannon. His ensuing scream was not from the heart but from the seat of his pants: The hot metal from the recently exploding gun almost took his hide away. Harker was a casualty for two weeks afterward, not able even to look at a saddle. Sheridan had not even winced while aboard his cannon. His butt was either thicker or he could withstand pain better. Granger came riding up soon, one of the first to arrive from the command post at Orchard Knob. He had his charger prance around, while he waved and whooped, showing some unexpected wit in his enthusiasm and good humor. "I'm going to have you all court-martialed!" he shouted, chortling. "You were ordered to take the works at the foot of the hill and you've taken those on top! You have disobeyed orders, all of you, and you know that you ought to be court-martialed!"

Bragg got away by the skin of his teeth, his only piece of good luck that day, and Breckinridge also escaped. They had extracted a price from the Federals, too. The fire that had rained down on the Federals had caused a woeful number of casualties, which was not entirely forgotten in the victory celebration. Wood suffered 1,035 casualties; Baird and Johnson, a combined 789, in their support roles; and Sheridan lost the most, 1,346, a little more than 20 percent of the 6,500 infantrymen he had sent out. As in all battles, some companies lost no men, whereas others lost nearly all. Those who had cover going up lost few, whereas those who braved the firepower of the dead center lost a startling number. One Indiana regiment lost 202 out of 337 it started with, almost 60 percent of the men in the 45 minutes it took to gain the crest. The Federals did it, too, without cavalry, which was beyond the Tennessee River because of the lack of feed.

The Federals who were now on top of Missionary Ridge were exhausted, depleted, and in no mood to strike out after the shell-shocked Rebels. None was in the mood save one. Little Phil still hadn't forgotten Chickamauga (and his own flight there) or how the guns had poured a round at him after his good-humored toast here, and now he wanted to put the spurs to them. Asking no one's permission, he led his division down the eastern face of the ridge, hammering away against the Rebel rear guard in the twilight. He captured nine pieces of Confederate artillery and a host of enemy stragglers, but before long, the Confederates threw up some delaying lines and drove him back. Night fell, and Sheridan had to content himself with the distinction of being the last to kick the Southerners on their way.

Over on Tunnel Hill Cleburne had continued to hold Sherman in place, like a wrestler who has pinned his foe to the mat, and these other Confederates were able to vacate Missionary Ridge in a less humiliating way. Alexander P. Stewart was holding Hooker in place down at the other end, too, so that when darkness started at 4:50 P.M., a large number of remaining Confederates relaxed into a more or less orderly retreat. An hour later, when the sun had fully set, Hardee rallied all the fugitive troops he could find and led them across Chickamauga Creek into eastern Georgia. Through a full moon that shone that night, the Rebels wound their way south, the outline of Missionary Ridge growing dimmer in their vision; Cleburne's division fittingly was the last to retreat. In the morning they were near Ringgold and still traveling, leaving charred supply dumps and broken wagons by the wayside. As soldiers of the Confederacy, they wouldn't see Chattanooga again.

11

Fare Thee Well, Cause

The battle for the small gateway town and railroad hub had cost both sides dearly. In the three days of fighting, November 23–25, Braxton Bragg had lost less than half of what Ulysses S. Grant, the innovator, had in casualties—361 Confederates to 753 Federals killed and 2,160 Confederates versus 4,722 Federals wounded. But another figure was perhaps more telling in who was emphatically winning the war. Bragg lost 4,146 men who were missing or captured, whereas Grant lost but 349. The total lost, then, was 6,667 for the Confederates and 5,824 for the Federals. Bragg had lost 15 percent of his army. He lost forty-one guns, a third of his arsenal. He lost Chattanooga, the culmination of all engagements since First Manassas, which proclaimed, finally, that the South was finished. Oh, sure, the war would go on for a while. There would be attacks and counterattacks and moments of dim hope, but here, at

Chattanooga, the South had finally and irrevocably lost all rational hope for a settled peace, one in which the South would have some bargaining power. The antebellum South of plantation and cavalier was finished. The North had the generals, it had the will to dictate the terms, and now it had the land.

If . . . if . . . et cetera, the South had done this, Bragg had done that, and so on and so forth, it might have been different. But the end of the script was as inevitable as the opening page at Fort Sumter. And perhaps, after all, the South had come up with the perfect candidate to command this pivotal engagement: Someone you could blame. Fate chose the perfect scapegoat—someone who, like the South itself, blamed everyone else. Bragg was intelligent (all attest to it), he could be charming, and he had seen his share of battles and come through with his skin and wits. But, like the South itself, he did not have the will or wherewithal to win. He was star-crossed and doomed. Yet what shape would the South have been in after the war if it had produced a Grant, someone competent and single-minded? It did produce Robert E. Lee, who nearly killed everyone with Pickett's Charge. A few more Lees and Stonewall Jacksons, and the South might have ended up a nation of widows and orphans. Remember that, at Chattanooga, many fewer of Bragg's troops than of Grant's were killed. Bragg was sometimes too incompetent to get men killed.

And until the end, he blamed others for his failures. How unlike the patrician Lee, who was willing to take the blame for everything. Bragg's final After Action Report, written on November 30, 1863, blamed the inherent nature of his soldiers for their defeat in the battle of Missionary Ridge. Bragg wrote in a fine style to reach a woeful conclusion: "No satisfactory excuse can possibly be given for the shameful conduct of our troops on the left in allowing their line to be penetrated. The position was one which ought to have been held by a line of skirmishers against any assaulting column, and wherever resistance was made the enemy fled in disorder after suffering heavy loss. Those who reached the ridge did so in a condition of exhaustion from the great physical exertion in climbing which rendered them powerless, and the slightest effort would have destroyed them. . . ."

Bragg was relieved of his command in Georgia a few days later and left for Richmond to renew himself under the comforting glow of Jefferson Davis and to serve as Davis's chief of staff. The president soon shipped him off to Wilmington, North Carolina, though, to oversee the important defense of Cape Fear, particularly the strategic Fort Fisher. The *Richmond Examiner* editorialized, "Bragg has been sent to Wilmington. Goodbye Wilmington!" How true those words were, for Bragg moved with compasslike accuracy toward disaster. He had been sent to replace a good fighter, General William Henry Chase Whiting, but perhaps sensing that Whiting was someone he might find useful to torture, he kept him on as district commander.

Bragg removed half of Fort Fisher's garrison when he left briefly to try to stop William Tecumseh Sherman in Georgia and left them there when he returned to Wilmington. When Federal forces landed near Fort Fisher, Bragg did nothing. Whiting had been so concerned for Fort Fisher's safety, though, that he had taken up station there, deferring to someone he outranked, Colonel William Lamb, commander of the Fort Fisher garrison. From Fort Fisher, Whiting wired Bragg incessantly to launch a saving attack against the invading Yankees. Cut them off at the pass. Bragg did the opposite—in effect, removing Major General Robert F. Hoke's veteran Virginian division of 6,500 from the lines. He seemed to accept defeat before the battle had even begun. Then Bragg got what perhaps he had been hoping for—a personality conflict. He began mixing it up with Whiting, convincing himself that Whiting was drunk. (He had accused John C. Breckinridge of being drunk at Chattanooga.) The defense of Fort Fisher was forgotten. Instead, he dispatched Brigadier General Alfred H. Colquitt by rowboat to relieve Whiting at the now-besieged Fort Fisher. Colquitt found both Lamb and Whiting badly wounded, the Federals right outside the door. He beat a fast retreat, and Fort Fisher fell. Bragg immediately blamed everyone and everything save himself: Whiting was drunk; the troops in the garrison there were amateurs; the cavalry had let the Yankees slip through; and, finally, really reaching, he blamed the hedonistic atmosphere of blockade running that he said permeated Fort Fisher. Wilmington was lost, and Bragg had then done his job. He briefly joined General Joseph E. Johnston in trying to lasso Sherman in North Carolina and then returned to Richmond and his protector.

Bragg fled with Davis on the heels of the South's final surrender and took part in the flight of the Confederate government from Virginia to Georgia. With Davis's capture and arrest, Bragg's career as a Confederate general came to an end. He spiraled down from there, hounded by poverty and bereft of friends during Reconstruction. No one wanted to be around him. No one wanted to hear his stories. He did manage to become superintendent of the New Orleans waterworks, the grandest-sounding of the positions he held in the postwar years, but he got booted from it almost immediately. He tried, he kept trying—railroading, life insurance, and lesser jobs for which he showed absolutely no competence. Walking down a street in Galveston, Texas, in 1887, he simply fell over dead with no fuss. He hadn't entered a hospital or a sickbed; he hadn't been shot or hit over the head or given medication. He left this life all by himself, and it was no one else's fault but his own.

Fort Bragg is named in his memory. No fort in the United States bears the name of the man who stood against him at Chickamauga when others had fled and whose Army of the Cumberland bested him in the pivotal Battle of Missionary Ridge. Only a small circular park in Washington, D.C., called Thomas Circle, is dedicated to the memory of General George H. Thomas. It is not very distinguished; vehicular traffic whizzes around and beneath it, and pedestrians who pass through its small space inhale a good share of the world's pollution. George H. Thomas, the Virginian who fought for the Union, has not become a household word. After Chattanooga Grant wanted to relieve him before the important battle of Nashville. Thomas held firm, as he had at Chickamauga, not allowing himself to be replaced, not moving against Confederate General John Bell Hood until the freezing weather lifted. While his replacement was on the way, he soundly defeated Hood's Army of Tennessee on December 16, 1864, and saved Nashville. The Confederate Army of Tennessee was never an army after that.

Thomas was never the life of a party. He neither rose from poverty nor went off the deep end through drink or craziness. He kept his life private and did not write his memoirs. Could it be that although Thomas is one of the great heroes of the Civil War, he is not as remembered as Lee and Jackson or as Grant and Sherman because he was not colorful? Could Thomas be a little too boring to fit comfortably into the American mythology? We want our heroes flawed and humbled at times, so they can be made into good copy. Thomas seems to have always, maddingly, done the right thing. When asked, after the Battle of Missionary Ridge, if the dead should be buried by the states they represented, he said, "No, no, no. Mix them up. I am tired of states rights."

On September 20, 1889, 12,000 veterans, blue and gray, attended a barbecue to celebrate the twenty-sixth anniversary of the Battle of Chickamauga. Fifteen thousand pounds of beef and 12,000 loaves of bread were consumed, and 14,000 peace pipes, carved from Chickamauga wood, were handed out as souvenirs. William Starke Rosecrans came, riding a fine horse. Old Rosey was lifted affectionately from his mount (as, ironically, he had been lifted out of the saddle in Chattanooga after the defeat at Chickamauga) and, while standing on a picnic table and shedding a few tears, made a short speech to wild cheers. The band played "Dixie."

Now, of course, every Civil War soldier has been laid to rest. Gone, too, is the culture of horse travel and the prevalence of the locomotive and telegraph in daily life. Men rarely rose in height to six feet back then (Grant was five feet eight inches), and the passions that made that bloody war come to pass are harder and harder to comprehend. We do not fully appreciate why they fought so hard and died in such numbers.

Here is a description of one dead Confederate, in Patrick R. Cleburne's corps at Chickamauga, as described by a Federal soldier who ran across him the day after the Battle of Missionary Ridge. It says more than reams of official reports. "He was not over fifteen years of age, and very slender in size. He was clothed in a cotton suit, and was barefooted; barefooted [in] that cold and wet . . . November. I examined his haversack. For a day's ration there was a handful of black beans, a few pieces of sorghum, and a half dozen roasted acorns. That was an infinitely poor outfit for marching and fighting, but that Tennessee Confederate had made it answer his purpose."

The Confederate cause would go on—down finally to the Sons and Daughters of the Confederacy and Rebel flags being waved at ball games. But after Chickamauga and Chattanooga, it was a dead issue, and its sun had set forever.

Acknowledgments

A book doesn't just spring full blown between covers, and there are many people who have helped make this one possible. I wish to express my gratitude to a few of them. First, to Buz Wyeth for his complete graciousness and fine touch as an editor; to James McPherson, who over a lunch at Princeton impressed upon me the need always to walk over where the fighting took place, to try to see it as it really was; to Jim Ogden, tour guide extraordinaire and historian at Chickamauga, who gave me a walking tour of the battlefield and left no doubt, contrary to the motel owner's opinion, that here was where the battle was fought.

I am grateful to the highly competent staff at Butler Library, Columbia University, where the incomparable tomes of the Official Records of the Union and Confederate Armies were always at hand, all 129 volumes. At Carlisle Barracks in Pennsylvania, where a large repository of Civil War material is stored, I ran across some unpublished letters of Daniel Harvey Hill and gained access to official regimental histories of the battle. Dr. Dick Summers, archivist, and Louise Arnold, librarian, were especially helpful in making this material available to me. My thanks go, too, to Dr. Jay Luvas, for providing me with insights on Chickamauga, and to Lieutenant Colonel Rick Eiserman, for letting me have an unpublished copy of his graduate thesis on James Longstreet's monumental troop movement to Chickamauga from Virginia. I cannot leave Carlyle Barracks without expressing my thanks to Colonel Rod Paschall, USA (Ret.), who is not only a friend but a military buff of the first water. Thanks, too, to Georges Borchardt, my agent and good friend, for his support in this project. He is someone who remains affectionate toward Tennesseans despite having served closely with them in the U.S. Army. All of us with an interest in preserving Civil War material and places owe thanks to the inestimable George Craig, a Civil War scholar, who has been instrumental in helping to set up the Longstreet/Thomas Memorial Library at Chickamauga. Thanks to Grace Brading Spurrell, an old friend from Johnson City, Tennessee, for sharing her great-grandfather's memoirs on Chickamauga. I wish to thank Lis for her help and suggestions and for using her gifted editorial eye on this book in manuscript, which made it much better than it would have been otherwise.

Finally, my gratitude goes to the Civil War Round Tables throughout the country that keep alive the components of this watershed event in American history. I am indebted to the New York City branch, which meets in a tradition-laden, yellow-lit banquet room in the Seventh Regiment Armory on Park Avenue. I am appreciative of the arguments that break out there, especially during a question-and-answer period following an after-dinner speech. Those moments always seem to me to bring back some of the unresolved issues of the war itself. Not long ago, a lauded historian from Virginia came to speak. He was received with quite a bit of fanfare by all, including those whose rightful sympathies might be thought to favor the old Northern cause. The speaker, long accustomed, it was evident, to receiving the perks of a traveling Civil War "expert" (free eats, a bed, and an honorarium), confidently nailed down his territory and did not brook any interference. The war had happened *this* way; the heroes were *these*. One who places a toe in the waters of Civil War lore soon learns, often to his sorrow, that it is a crowded field of this type of "expert" who guards his specialty and stage bits like a mother hen or denizen of Hollywood. The Virginia gentleman went on and on the evening in question, beating the drum for Ambrose P. Hill; Stonewall Jackson; and, of course, the one who allows some Southerners to believe they come out of the womb gentlemen and ladies—General Robert E. Lee. Of course, Lee was a fine man and often a great general, but like any mortal, he does bear some scrutiny. The speaker's eyes misted over, his voice almost trembled, at the speaking of Lee's name. The Northerners in the audience nearly swooned—a real live honest-to-God *Southerner*! But not all present felt that way. A question was shot at the speaker from the audience: "You have left out, I believe, General George H. Thomas in your roll call of great Virginians. What is your opinion of him—as a soldier and a man and as someone who had a great deal to say about how the conflict ended?"

The speaker had undoubtedly faced this question before. He endured it. He uttered a few words in Thomas's behalf, head ducked, mumbling to near inaudibility. It was unpleasant for him, but it was part of the job. He shouldered it, and then he gladly moved off to Stonewall, allowing his smile to return. The thought then was obvious: Why the short shrift for Thomas, the man who practically saved the Union? If it was not for Thomas, I thought, you wouldn't be up here tonight except through courtesy of a visa. Yet, paradoxically enough, the Virginia speaker let me understand, viscerally, why a lot of western Confederate soldiers held certain eastern Confederate soldiers in contempt—as airheads and mock aristocrats. The fact is that when one Southerner meets another, there is not instant harmony and an immediate rendition of "The Bonny Blue Flag." There was dissension in the Confederate ranks, and it lives today. I thank the Virginia speaker for reminding me of that fact. Rather than shoulder arms in some common cause with him and his ilk, I'd rather go to a Federal penitentiary like my grandfather.

Bibliography

Abbazia, Patrick. *Chickamauga Campaign, December 1862–November 1863*. Gallery Books, 1988.

Abbott, John S. C. *The History of the Civil War in America: Origin and Progress of the Rebellion*. Henry Bill, 1863.

Alexander, E. P. *Military Memoirs of a Confederate*. Charles Scribner's Sons, 1907.

Autumn of Glory: The Army of Tennessee, 1862–1865. Louisiana State University Press, 1971.

"Battle of Chickamauga." *Civil War Times* (September 1990).

The Battle of Chickamauga. Eastern Acorn Press, 1969.

The Battles for Chattanooga. Eastern Acorn Press, 1989.

Beatty, John. *Memoirs of a Volunteer, 1861–63*. W. W. Norton & Co., 1946.

Bierce, Ambrose. *Ambrose Bierce's Civil War*. Gateway Editions, 1956.

Black, Robert C., III. *The Railroads of the Confederacy*. University of North Carolina Press, 1952.

"Bombing Braxton Bragg." *Civil War Times* (July 1988).

Brother Against Brother. Time-Life Books History of the Civil War. Time-Life Books, 1990.

Catton, Bruce. *The American Heritage Picture History of the Civil War*. American Heritage Publishing Co., 1960.

———. *Grant Takes Command*. Little Brown, 1968.

———. *This Hallowed Ground*. Doubleday, 1956.

Cist, Henry M. *The Army of the Cumberland*. Charles Scribner's Sons, 1882.

Civil War Almanac. Gallery Books, 1983.

Cleaves, Freeman. *Rock of Chickamauga: The Life of General George H. Thomas*. University of Oklahoma Press, 1948.

Commager, Henry Steele, ed. *The Blue and the Gray: The Story of the Civil War as Told by Participants*. Bobbs-Merrill Co., 1950.

Connelly, Thomas L. *Civil War Tennessee*. University of Tennessee Press, 1979.

Coppee, Henry. *General Thomas*. D. Appleton & Co., 1901.

Davis, William C. *Jefferson Davis: The Man and His Hour*. HarperCollins, 1991.

Downey, Fairfax. *Storming of the Gateway Chattanooga, 1863*. David McKay Co., 1960.

Eiserman, Frederick A. *Longstreet's Corps at Chickamauga: Lessons in Inter-Theater Deployment*. Unpublished thesis, U.S. Army Command and General Staff College, Fort Leavenworth, Kans., 1985.

The Fight for Chickamauga: Chickamauga to Missionary Ridge. Time-Life Books History of the Civil War. Time-Life Books.

Foote, Shelby. *The Civil War: A Narrative* (3 vols). Random House, 1958–75.

Freeman, Douglas Southall. *Lee's Lieutenants, a Study in Command*, 3 vols. Charles Scribner's Sons, 1942–44.

Gracie, Archibald. *The Truth about Chickamauga*. Houghton Mifflin Co., 1911.

"Grant—Genius or Fortune's Child?" *Civil War Times* (June 1965).

Grant, U. S. *Personal Memoirs*. Charles L. Webster & Co., 1885.

"Lee and Jackson." *Civil War Times* (November 1991).

Leech, Margaret. *Reveille in Washington*. Harper & Bros., 1941.

Longstreet, James. *From Manassas to Appomattox*. Philadelphia, 1866.

Luvas, Jay. *Chickamauga*. South Mountain Press, 1991.

Lyle, W. W. *Lights and Shadows of Army Life*. Cincinnati, 1865.

Lytle, Andrew. *Bedford Forrest & His Critter Co*.

Mary Chesnut's Civil War. C. Vann Woodward, ed. Yale University Press, 1981.

McDonough, James. *Chattanooga—A Death Grip on the Confederacy*. University of Tennessee Press, 1984.

McFeely, William S. *Grant: A Biography*. Norton, 1982.

McMasters. *On the United States, 1863*.

McPherson, James M. *Battle Cry of Freedom*. Oxford University Press, 1988.

McWhiney, Grady. *Braxton Bragg and Confederate Defeat*. Columbia University Press, 1969.

National Historical Society. *The South Besieged*, vol. 5. Doubleday & Co., 1983.

Nevins, Allan. *The Ordeal of the Union*. Macmillan, 1960.

Norwood, C. W. *Chickamauga Campaigns and Chattanooga Battlefields*. Chattanooga, Tenn.: Office of the Librarian of Congress in Washington, 1898.

O'Connor, Richard. *Thomas: Rock of Chickamauga*. Prentice-Hall, 1948.

Personal Memoirs of P. H. Sheridan. Charles L. Webster & Co., 1888.

Porter, Horace. *Campaigning with Grant*. New York, 1897.

Price, William H. *Civil War Handbook*. L. B. Prince Co., 1961.

Regimental Histories (from the U.S. Army War College, Carlisle, Pennsylvania):

Sixth Regiment Indiana Volunteer Infantry

Eighty-Sixth Regiment Indiana Volunteer Infantry

Twenty-First Regiment Ohio Volunteer Infantry

Opdycke Tigers: One Hundred and Twenty-Fifth Ohio Volunteer
    Infantry

The Fifteenth Ohio Volunteers

Twentieth Tennessee Regiment Volunteer Infantry

Nineteenth Tennessee

Fifteenth Alabama Regiment

"Rock of Chickamauga." *Civil War Times* (September 1988).

Seitz, Don C. *Braxton Bragg General of the Confederacy*. State Co., 1924.

Shaara, Michael. *The Killer Angels*. Random House, 1974.

Sherman, General W. T. *Memoirs*. D. Appleton & Co., 1875.

Sorrel, G. Moxley. *Recollections of a Confederate Staff Officer*. Neale Publishing Co., 1917.

Stivers, Charles Edwin. "Memoir of Charles Edwin Stivers, First Lieutenant, Eighteenth Ohio Volunteer Infantry," unpublished, privately owned manuscript.

"That Devil Forrest." *Civil War Times* (September 1990).

Thomas, Wilbur. *General George H. Thomas: The Indomitable Warrior*. Exposition Press, 1964.

Tucker, Glenn. *Chickamauga Bloody Battle in the West*. Bobbs-Merrill, Inc., 1961.

War of the Rebellion: A Compilation of the Official Records of the Union and Confederate Armies (129 vols.). Washington, D.C., 1880–1901. Butler Library, Columbia University.

Ward, Geoffrey C. *The Civil War*. Alfred A. Knopf, 1990.

Watkins, Sam. *Company Aich: A Side Show of the Big Show*. Broadfoot Publishing Co., 1990.

Wiley, Bell I. *The Life of Billy Yank*. Louisiana State University Press, 1971.

———. *The Life of Johnny Reb*. Louisiana State University Press, 1971.

Wills, Brian Steel. *A Battle from the Start: The Life of Nathan Bedford Forrest*. HarperCollins, 1992.

Wolfe, Thomas. "Chickamauga." In *The Portable Thomas Wolfe*. Viking Press, 1948.

Wyeth, John A. *Life of Lt. General Nathan Bedford Forrest*. Harper & Bros., 1899.

———. *With Sabre and Scalpel*. Harper & Bros., 1917.

Index

Adams, Daniel W., 106

Adams, William, 106

Alexander's Bridge, 64

American psyche
  Chickamauga as expression of, 160
  Grant's appeal to, 180, 181

Amphibious assaults at Chattanooga, 191–92, 200–203

Anaconda Plan, 141–42

Anderson, J. Patton, 227

Anderson's Gap, 177, 178

Andersonville prison, xvi

Antidraft riots, 2

"Antony and Cleopatra" (Lytle), 126, 127

Arms technology, North's use of, 38–39, 57, 65, 128

Army of Northern Virginia, 45, 50–57.

See also Longstreet, James

Army of Tennessee, 2. See also Bragg, Braxton
  dissatisfaction of, 17
  growth of, 43

Army of the Ohio, Grant's command of, 183

Avery, William, 229

Baird, Absalom
  at Chickamauga, 67, 73, 87, 97, 117
  retreat, 154
  at Missionary Ridge, 219, 233

Banks, Nathaniel P., 182–83, 198

Bate, William B., 227

Battle Above the Clouds (battle of Lookout Mountain), 206–13

Beatty, John, 28–29, 103

Beauregard, Pierre G. T., 3, 21, 166
Bee, Barnard E., 73
Bierce, Ambrose, 101, 156
  at Chickamauga, 146–47
Blacks, Union soldier's attitude toward,
  8–9, 205
Bond, Frank S., 115
Bowers, T. R., xiii–xv
Bowers, William A., xi, xiii, xv
Bradley, Luther P., 9–10
Bragg, Braxton, xiii, xv
  background of, 19–21
  bad luck of, 10–11, 33, 34, 37, 109,
    194
  baptism of, 35
  at Chattanooga
    defense of Missionary Ridge, 212
    ineffectiveness of orders, 193–94,
      195–96
    starvation plan, 171, 177
    strategy, 159–60, 164, 171, 177
  at Chickamauga, 132–33
    attempts to locate battle, 84, 85
    Federal retreat and, 118, 157–60,
      165–66, 173
    goals, 48
    ineffectiveness of orders, 98–100,
      118, 131, 133
    Longstreet's arrival, 92–94
    plan for first strike, 50, 59–60
    replacement sought for, 50
    strategy, 93–94, 106–7, 109–11,
      118, 133
    troops sent to support, 50–57
  controversy following, 10
  Davis' relationship with, 4–5, 17–19,
    34, 43, 167, 237, 238
  death of, 238

Forrest and, 159–60, 167–69
  at Fort Fisher, 237
  health problems of, 12, 17, 19, 21,
    38, 39, 41
  Hill and, 171
  Hindman and, 166
  ineffectiveness of command, 98–100,
    118, 131, 133, 193–96
  jailing of mother and, xv, 21
  lack of confidence in, 3–4, 17–19,
    34, 38, 41, 165–71
  Longstreet and, 196–97
  love of writing, 3
  in Mexican War, 4–5, 27, 167
  at Missionary Ridge, 215, 220,
    223–24
    aftermath of, 235–38
    blame for defeat, 236–37
    escape, 233
    ineffectiveness of orders, 231–32
    strategy, 225–26
  mother of, 186
  at Murfreesboro
    blame for defeat, 3, 10–15, 16
    retreat, 16–17, 34
    strategy, 14–16
  at Perryville, 5, 7, 18
  personality of, 2–3, 17, 18, 20–21,
    41–43, 118, 173
  physical appearance of, 2, 17, 20
  Polk and, 166, 169–70
  postwar life, 238
  replacement sought for, 50, 166–71
  Rosecrans' approach to Chattanooga
    and, 40–45
  Rosecrans' attempt to trap, 37–39
  at Shiloh, 5, 7
  similarities between Grant and, 186

staged retreat from Chattanooga, 41
strategy of, 6–7, 14–16
tactics of, 7
  bayonet charges, 65
  swinging-door maneuver, 94, 50,
    133
Thomas' relationship with, 204
at Tullahoma, 38
unpopularity of, 38, 165, 173, 193–96,
  204
unpredictability of, 30
on view from Missionary Ridge,
  172–73
Wheeler and, 196–97
wife of, 35, 38, 43
Bragg, John, 20
Bragg, Margaret Crossland, 21
Bragg, Thomas, Jr., 20
Bragg, William, 20
Brannan, John Milton, at Chickamauga, 67, 71, 73, 82, 88, 115,
  117, 142, 150
Bread riot, 141
Breckinridge, John Cabell, 4
  at Chattanooga, 237
  at Chickamauga, 57, 94, 100, 101,
    110, 154
  at Missionary Ridge, 225–27, 233
  at Murfreesboro, 12–15, 33–34
Brotherton, Adaline, 122
Brotherton family, 118–19, 122–23,
  209
Brown's Ferry, Federal assault on,
  189–96
Buckner, Simon Bolivar
  at Chickamauga, 85, 94
    arrival, 44, 45
  lack of confidence in Bragg, 170, 171

Bull Run, 76, 160, 205–6. *See also*
  Manassas
Burnside, Ambrose E., 169
  Knoxville taken by, 53, 56
  Longstreet transferred to fight, 196
  replaced by Grant, 183
  Rosecrans' approach to Chattanooga
    and, 40

Cairnes, William, 107
Carson, William J., 89
Chalmer, James Ronald, 11
Chancellorsville, Virginia, 50, 57, 110,
  189
Chase, Salmon P., 77
Chattanooga. *See also* Missionary Ridge
  amphibious assaults at, 191–92,
    200–201, 203
  Bragg's plan for, 171
  Confederate siege of, 171, 185
  Cracker Line, 190, 195–96, 197
  Federal retreat to, 153–54
  Federal supply lines to, 175, 177–79,
    185, 188
  frontier roots of, 175–76
  Grant's arrival in, 185–86
  Lookout Mountain, 39, 41, 175, 193,
    206–13
  map, 202
  origin of name, 175
  pause before battle, 197–98
  proximity of Confederate and Federal
    troops, 197–99
  Rosecrans' approach to, 39–42
  Rosecrans' retreat to, 137–38
  starvation of forces at, 171, 176–77,
    184, 185, 187
  terrain surrounding, 199

Chattanooga (*cont.*)
  Wheeler's raid and, 177–79
Cheatham, Benjamin Franklin
  at Chickamauga, 94, 107, 108
  lack of confidence in Bragg and, 18,
    170, 171
  at Murfreesboro, 8, 10–11, 15, 16
Cherokee Indians, 45, 49, 91, 175
Chesnut, Mary Boykin, 4, 55
Chickamauga
  aftermath of, 160, 172
  Alexander's Bridge, 64
  anniversary of battle, 239
  arms captured at, 156
  arrival at, 43–45
  burials at, 156, 160, 162
  casualties, 92, 105, 106, 108, 110–11,
    126–27, 130, 151, 154, 156–57,
    160–62
  chaos at, 73–74, 78, 82, 84, 88–89,
    104–5, 122, 124, 129, 131, 152
  Crawfish Springs, 67
  as decisive battle of Civil War, xi–xii,
    xvi, 74, 91, 111, 160–61
  difficulty of locating battles, 75–78,
    84, 85
  as expression of American psyche,
    160
  Federal retreat at, 124, 134–35,
    153–55, 157–58
  Federal stand at Snodgrass Hill and,
    140, 142–43, 145–53, 163–64
  fires at, 156
  as frontier, 70
  gap in Federal line, 114–17, 121, 129
  Jay's Mill, 72
  lack of command at, 73–74, 84, 85,
    154

La Fayette road, 43–45, 65, 67, 81
last stand of Federal army, 155
literary descriptions of, 101–3,
    152–53
location of, xiv
Longstreet's presence at, 50–57,
    78–80
map, 66
nights at, 92
Northern artillery at, 128
rations, 120, 144–45
Reed's Bridge, 59, 63–64
return of veterans to, 163–64
Snodgrass Hill, 131–32, 142
in Southern psyche, xi–xiv
spies at, 76–78
terrain surrounding, 48, 49, 91,
    102–3, 119, 152
transfer of troops via train to,
    50–58
Union command post at, 77–82, 84,
    128–29
Chickamauga: Bloody Battle of the West
    (Tucker), 161
"Chickamauga" (Bierce), 101–2
Cist, Henry M., 25
Clark, Will, 224
Cleburne, Patrick R., 3–4
  background of, 86–87
  at Chickamauga, 86, 89–90, 94, 97,
    100, 101, 108, 110
    arrival, 43–45
    Federal retreat, 154
  holding of Tunnel Hill and, 216–21,
    225, 228
  at Murfreesboro, 8
  personality of, 86–87
  tactics of, 86, 87

Clem, John Lincoln, 163
Coburn, John, 35–36
Cockfighting, 48
Cold Harbor, 186, 219
Colors, morale and, 211, 230
Colquitt, Alfred H., 237
Colquitt, Peyton H., 110
Confederate army. *See also specific topics*
    arms of, 38
    attacks on railroads by, 30
    Federal stand at Snodgrass Hill and, 142–43
    losses at Chickamauga, 151, 161
    names of regiments in, 93
    popular support for, 55
    rations, 120
    retreat from Missionary Ridge, 232–34
    shortages and, 36
    siege of Chattanooga, 171, 185
    tactics of, 87
    transfer by train of, 50–57
Corinth, Battle of, 24
Cowan, J. B., 168, 169
Cox, Jacob, 29
Cracker Line, 190, 195–96, 197
Crane, Stephen, 101
Craven farmhouse, 209–11
Crawfish Springs, 67
Crittenden, Thomas Leonidas
    at Chickamauga, 48, 67, 95
        arrival, 43–45
    at Murfreesboro, 30, 33
    personality of, 95
    Rosecrans' approach to Chattanooga and, 39–41
Cruft, Charles
    at Chattanooga, 207, 220
    at Chickamauga, 104

Dana, Charles
    at Chickamauga, 76, 78
        retreat, 134, 138
    field reports from, 174–75, 179
Davis, Jefferson
    attempts to replace Bragg and, 17–19, 34, 166–71
    Bragg's relationship with, 4–5, 43–45, 167, 237, 238
    bread riot and, 141
    Helm and, 104
    Johnston and, 171
    in Mexican War, 167
    personality of, 166
    Rosecrans and, 26
    transfer of Longstreet and, 196
Davis, Brig. Gen. Jefferson C. (Union army)
    at Chickamauga, 83, 84, 125
        retreat, 134, 135
    personality of, 83–84
Deas, Zachariah C., 227
Deshler, James, 108
Devil's Den, 56
Draft riots, 2
Drinking
    Grant's, 181, 183, 185, 189
    by officers, 10–11, 16, 29
    by soldiers, 56

Early, Jubal A., 20
East, Federal soldiers from the, 204–6, 208
    Yankees, xiv–xv, 9, 38, 83
East Tennessee. *See also specific topics*

East Tennessee (*cont.*)
  strategic importance of, 5, 174
  terrain of, 37
Ector, General, 74–75
Eighteenth Ohio regiment, 163
Emerson, Ralph Waldo, 73
Ewing, Hugh B., 218
Experts, importance of, 52

Farm boys, as soldiers, 8–9, 76
Federal army. *See also* Union soldiers;
    and specific topics
  arms of, 38
  at Chickamauga
    last stand, 155
    losses, 157, 161
    retreat, 124, 134–35, 153–55,
    stand at Snodgrass Hill, 140,
      142–43, 145–53, 163–64
  manpower of, 36
  names of regiments in, 93
  popular support for, 58
  supplies of, 36, 144–45
    siege of Chattanooga and, 175,
      177–79, 185, 188–96
  transfer of troops by train and, 57–58
  westerners vs. easterners in, 204–6,
    208
Federal Army of the Cumberland, 3.
    See also Rosecrans, William Starke
  arrival at Chickamauga Creek, 43–45
  attempt to surround Chattanooga,
    39–42
  at Murfreesboro, 30–34
  placed under Grant's command, 183
  spying on, 76–78
  supply base of, 29
"Field Artillery Song," 208

Fifteenth Kentucky Federal regiment,
    104–5
First Manassas, 73, 160, 235
Foot soldiering, 87
Forrest, Nathan Bedford, xiii, 36
  background of, 60–61
  Bragg's conflict with, 159–60, 167–69
  at Chickamauga, 60, 63–65, 71–75,
    94
    arrival, 43
    Federal stand at Snodgrass Hill,
      146–47
    tactics, 109
  Lee and, 61
  legend of, 159
  personality of, 60–62, 72, 109
  physical appearance of, 60–61
    as embodiment of Southern charac-
      ter, 61–63
  tactics of, 61–62, 109
Fort Bragg, 238
Fort Donelson, 23, 181
Fort Fisher, 237–38
Fort Sumter, 21
Fourth Kentucky Confederate regiment,
    104
Fredericksburg, Virginia, 69, 157
Frontier, Tennessee as, 175–76
Frontier life, 60

Garesche, Julius P., 24, 25, 31, 76, 114
Garfield, James A., 29
  background of, 76–77
  at Chickamauga, 95, 98
    gap in Federal line, 115–16
    retreat, 134, 136–38, 153
  personality of, 77
  as undercover agent, 76, 77

Garland, Hamlin, 9
Geary, John W., at Chattanooga, 193–95, 207
Generals. See also specific generals
  decisiveness of, 139–40
  disciplinarian, 143
Gettysburg, battle of, 51, 52, 69, 117, 141, 142
  Pickett's Charge, 51, 62, 69–70, 118, 150, 221, 236
Gist, States Rights, 72–73, 94
Glenn, Widow, 77–78, 128–29
Gould, Lieutenant, 62–63
Gracie, Archibald, Jr., at Chickamauga, 150–51
Granger, Gordon, 37
  at Chickamauga, 48, 96
    protection of Rossville Gap, 143–47
    stand at Snodgrass Hill, 146–48
  at Missionary Ridge, 223–24, 229
  personality of, 143–45
Grant, Jesse, 199
Grant, Ulysses S., xiii
  at Chattanooga
    arrival, 184–86
    liberation of supply lines, 188–96
    strategy, 188, 191–92, 203–4
  Clem and, 163
  at Cold Harbor, 186
  drinking of, 181, 183, 185, 189
  health problems of, 189
  love for horses of, 182–83
  in Mexican War, 27, 51–52
  at Missionary Ridge
    order to charge, 220–22
    storming of ridge, 229–30
    strategy, 215–17, 219, 224, 228–29

  mother of, 186
  need for intimates, 199
  personality of, 26, 30, 77, 179–80, 181, 182, 184, 186, 187–89, 215
  physical appearance of, 184, 188–89
  popularity of, 180, 182
  riding accident of, 183
  Rosecrans replaced by, 179–80, 183–84
  similarities between Bragg and, 186
  Thomas and, 187
  "unconditional surrender" coined by, 23
  at Vicksburg, 37
  victories of, 181–82
  war experience of, 181
  West Point and, 179–81
  writing of, 179, 181
Greeley, Horace, 76

Halleck, Henry W., 25, 182, 196
  as general in chief, 37
  transfer of troops by train and, 56–57
Hardee, William J., 10, 171
  at Missionary Ridge, 225, 234
  at Murfreesboro, 6, 8, 12–14, 16
Harker, Charles G.
  at Chickamauga, 129, 140–41
    stand at Snodgrass Hill, 142
  at Missionary Ridge, 232–33
Harris, John W., 173
Harrison, William Henry, 26
Harvard University, 73, 76
Hatred, between South and North, 72, 74, 83
Hayes, Rutherford B., 28

Hazen, William Babcock, 142, 229
"Hebrew Maiden's Lament, The"
    (song), 96–97
Helm, Benjamin Hardin, 103–5
Helm, Emily Todd, 104, 105
Henry, Patrick, 18
Hill, Daniel Harvey
    Bragg's conflict with, 171
    at Chickamauga, 86, 94, 99–101, 106,
        109, 110, 157
        arrival, 42–44
    personality of, 42
Hindman, Thomas C.
    at Chickamauga, 85, 94, 119, 123–25,
        130
        arrival, 43–44
        Federal stand at Snodgrass Hill, 143,
            149
        retreat, 154
    personality of, 124–25
    physical appearance of, 124
    suspension of, 166
Hoke, Robert F., 237
Hood, John Bell
    at Chattanooga, 194
        Missionary Ridge, 228, 234
    at Chickamauga, 82–85, 94, 118, 122
        transfer of troops by train and, 50–56
        wound, 130
    death of, 130
    personality of, 118, 128, 129, 130
    physical appearance of, 129
Hooker, Joe, 20
    at Chancellorsville, 189
    at Chattanooga, 192–94, 204
        Lookout Mountain, 206–8, 211, 212
        Missionary Ridge, 215, 216, 219, 220,
            222
    dispatched to Chickamauga, 57
    personality of, 189, 193
    physical appearance of, 205
Hopkins, Stephen, 26
Horses
    Grant's love of, 182–83
    starvation of, 197
Hospitals, 8
Hotchkiss, Jedediah, 52
Howard, Oliver Otis, 184–85, 193, 218
    dispatched to Chickamauga, 58
Humphreys, George, at Chickamauga,
    103

Infantry, 109
Ingraham, John, 162
Intestinal parasites, 19

Jackson, John K. (Mudwall), 209–11
Jackson, Thomas J. (Stonewall), 2, 3,
    42, 110, 174
    background of, 21, 60
    at Chancellorsville, 189
    death of, 50
    Lee and, 50
    mapmaker employed by, 52
    in Mexican War, 19, 27
    nickname of, 73
    personality of, 20, 26, 77, 112,
        139–40
    Shenandoah Valley Campaign and,
        139–40
    Sunday school taught by, 26
    tactics of, 61
Jenkins, Micah, 194
Johnson, Andrew, xiv
Johnson, Bushrod
    background of, 123

Johnson, Bushrod (*cont.*)
  at Chickamauga, 57, 59, 64, 82, 94, 119, 121–24, 129, 130
    Federal retreat, 154
    Federal stand at Snodgrass Hill, 143, 149
  personality of, 123
  physical appearance of, 123
Johnson, Richard A., at Chickamauga, 88
Johnson, Richard W.
  at Chickamauga, 140
  at Missionary Ridge, 221, 233
Johnston, Joseph Eggleston, 34–35
  Davis and, 171
  investigation of Bragg by, 17–19, 34
  personality of, 17–18, 112
  transfer by train of troops by, 51
  at Vicksburg, 37
Josselyn, Simeon T., 230

Kellogg, Sanford C., 114–15
Kelly, John Herbert, 151
Kentucky, 103. *See also* Perryville
  allegiances in, 104–5
Kershaw, Joseph Brevard, at Chickamauga, 94, 119, 129, 130, 131
  Federal retreat and, 154
  Federal stand at Snodgrass Hill, 142–43, 148, 149
Kilgore, C. B., at Chickamauga, 75
Knoxville, Union victory at, 53, 56

La Fayette road, 43–45, 65, 67, 81
Lamb, William, 237
Langdon, Bassett, 232
Law, E. MacIver, 50, at Chickamauga, 82, 94, 119, 129, 130–31

Lee, Light Horse Harry, 21
Lee, Robert E., 3, 18
  background of, 21
  Davis' plan to replace Bragg with, 50
  Forrest and, 61
  at Fredericksburg, 69
  at Gettysburg, 51, 52, 69, 236
  Helm and, 104
  Jackson and, 50
  love of Virginia, 50
  in Mexican War, 27
  personality of, 42, 112, 180, 236
  popular opinion of, 180
  suggested as replacement for Bragg, 166
  on war, 69, 211–12
Lee & Gordon's Mills, 43, 44, 49
Liberty Gap, 38
Liddell, St. John Richardson
  at Chattanooga, 193–94
  at Chickamauga, 73, 94
    Federal retreat and, 154
  conflict between Bragg and Forrest and, 167
  at Murfreesboro, 14, 16
Lieutenant Gould, 62–63
Lights and Shadows of Army Life (Lyle), 160–61
Lilly, Eli, at Chickamauga, 63, 64
Lincoln, Abraham
  background of, 60
  brother–in–law, 103–5
  on Davis (Union general), 84
  fixation with East Tennessee, 174
  McClellan and, 36
  personality of, 26, 60
  prescience of, 5
  reaction to field reports, 173

Lincoln, Abraham (*cont.*)
  Rosecrans and, 23
  strategy of, 141–42
Lincoln, Mary Todd, 104
Little Round Top, 56
Longstreet, James, xiii, 26, 45
  Bragg's transfer of, 196–97
  at Chattanooga, Bragg's orders and,
    193–94, 195–96
  at Chickamauga, 100, 140
    arrival, 92–94
    Bragg's orders and, 131–32
    confidence of victory, 120, 130–32,
      133
    fears concerning outcome, 52
    Federal stand at Snodgrass Hill, 145,
      149–50
    Rosecrans and, 78–80
    strategy, 118, 119, 128, 131–32
  at Fredericksburg, 69
  at Gettysburg, 51
  Lee and, 50, 51
  personality of, 51–52, 93, 94, 117–18,
    128, 132
  physical appearance of, 120
  suggested as replacement for Bragg,
    166–67, 171
  transfer of troops by train and, 50–57
Look Homeward, Angel (Wolfe), 111
Lookout Mountain, 39, 41, 175, 193
  battle of (Battle Above the Clouds),
    206–13
    casualties, 212
Louisiana, 3
Lyle, W. W., 160
Lyman Bridge, 223
Lytle, William H., 125–28, 134

MacArthur, Arthur, 230

MacArthur, Douglas, 230
McClellan, George B., 36, 180
McCook, Alexander McDowell, 7–8
  at Chickamauga, 48, 95, 96, 114
    arrival, 43
    retreat, 124
  at Murfreesboro, 30–31
  personality of, 95, 97
  Rosecrans' approach to Chattanooga
    and, 39, 40
  at Tullahoma, 38
McCook, Dan, 201
McKinley, William, 28
McLemore's Cove, 43, 44
Manassas, 209. *See also* Bull Run
  First, 73, 160, 235
Manigault, Arthur Middleton, 172
Mathes, Harvey, 168
Meade, George Gordon, transfer of
    troops by train and, 57
Medical care, 8, 160–62
  infections, 162
Mendehall, John, at Murfreesboro, 34
Mexican War, 127
  Civil War generals in, 4–5, 16, 18,
    19, 26, 42, 43, 51–52, 167, 179
  parasites and, 19
Midwest, soldiers from, 8–9, 204–6, 208
Mills, Robert Q., at Chickamauga,
    108
Minty, Robert H. G., at Chickamauga,
    59, 63–65
Missionary Ridge, 44, 45, 121, 154,
    215–34
  aftermath of battle, 235–40
  assault on Tunnel Hill, 216–21, 225,
    228, 234
  casualties, 219, 235, 240
  Confederates at

Missionary Ridge (*cont.*)
  Bragg's defense, 212
  confusion at, 226–28, 231–33
  prisoners, 232
  retreat, 232–34
  Federal army at
    assault on Tunnel Hill, 203, 204,
      215–19
    attack, 220–22, 224
  origin of name, 175
  view from, 172–73
Mississippi regiments
  arms of, 11
  at Murfreesboro, 11
  Warren Light Artillery of, 217
Moore, John C., 209, 210
Morale, colors and, 211, 230
Morton, John Watson, at Chicka-
      mauga, 64
Murfreesboro, battle of, 3–16, 30–34, 163
  aftermath of, 34–35
  Army of Tennessee at, 3, 11
  blame for Southern defeat at, 3,
      10–15, 16
  casualties, 8, 10, 11, 13, 31–34
  Mississippi regiments at, 11
  retreat, 3, 16–17, 34
  Round Forest, 13, 14, 32–34

Nashville–Atlanta corridor, 5
Nassau bacon, 132
National Cemetery, 162
Negley, James S., at Chickamauga, 82,
      96–98
  Federal stand at Snodgrass Hill, 147
  gap in Federal line, 116
Nelson, William, 83–84
New Englanders, 9
Newt, Clark, 224

New York, 9
New York Tribune, 76
North, the. *See also* Federal army; *and*
      specific topics
  manpower of, 57
  prisons and, xvi
  strategy of, 5
  technology employed by, 38–39, 57,
      58, 65, 128
North Carolina, 2–3
  antebellum, 19–20
Northerners. *See* Union soldiers; Yankees
Northern Virginia, Army of, 42
Nuckols, Joseph P., at Chickamauga,
      104–5

Offensive army, supply base of, 29
Officers
  drinking by, 10–11, 16, 29
  posturing of, 14
  Southerners as, 10, 19–21
115th Illinois Volunteers, 144
Opdycke, Emerson, 141
Osterhaus, Peter J., 206, 207, 220

Palmer, John McCauley, at Chicka-
      mauga, 88, 111
  stand at Snodgrass Hill, 142
Payne, Edwin W., 221
Pegram, John, xiii
  at Murfreesboro, 12, 15
Pemberton, John Clifford, 20, 170
  at Vicksburg, 38
Perryville, 5, 7
  Bragg's retreat from, 5, 7, 18, 34
Pettus, Edmund W., 209, 210
Pickett, George E., 69, 118
Pickett's Charge, 51, 62, 69–70, 118,
      150, 221, 236

Pigeon Mountain, 43

Polk, Leonidas Lafayette
  advises Davis to replace Bragg, 166
  Bragg's conflict with, 98–100, 118,
    133, 166, 169–70
  at Chickamauga, 93, 94
    arrival, 43–45
    Bragg's orders ignored by, 98–100,
      118, 133
    Federal retreat, 157–58
    Federal stand at Snodgrass Hill, 145,
      151
    plan for first strike, 49–50
  at Murfreesboro, 6, 11, 13, 14–16
  nephew of, 107
  personality of, 107
  suspension of, 166
  at Tullahoma, 38

Polk, Lucius E., at Chickamauga, 106–8

Porter, Horace, 187–88

Preston, William, at Chickamauga, 94,
    119, 127, 128, 131
  Federal retreat and, 154–55
  Federal stand at Snodgrass Hill,
    149–50

Prisons and prisoners, xv–xvi

Racism, 61
  of Union soldiers, 7–8, 205

Railroads
  private ownership of, 53
  rebel attacks on, 30
  transfer of troops via, 50–57

Rations, 19, 120. *See also* Starvation

Rawlins, John A., 182

Rebel army. *See* Confederate army

Rebel yell, 30, 32, 81, 147

Red Badge of Courage, The (Crane), 101

Reed's Bridge, 59, 63–64

Regiments, names of, 93

Reid, Whitelaw, 25

Religious revival, 35, 56, 172

Reynolds, Joseph J.
  at Chickamauga, 82, 88, 115, 117
    retreat, 154
  at Missionary Ridge, 225

Rice, Captain, 79–80

Rifle and Light Infantry Tactics
    (Hardee), 6

Rifles, rapid fire, 38–39, 65, 128

Riots
  bread, 141
  draft, 2

Roller skating, 2

Romanticism, Southern, 6, 111–12

Rosecrans, Crandell, 26

Rosecrans, William Starke, 23–33
  accident and, 27–28
  aftermath of Murfreesboro and,
    35–37
  approach to Chattanooga, 39–42
  attempt to trap Bragg, 37–39
  background of, 26
  Bragg's staged retreat from Chat-
    tanooga and, 41
  Catholicism of, 25–27
  caution of, 35–37
  at Chickamauga
    anniversary, 239
    arrival, 45
    attempts to locate battle, 75–78
    cautious approach, 75–76
    depression following, 173–75
    gap in Federal line, 114–17
    goals, 48
    indecision, 136–38
    interrogations, 78–80
    Longstreet and, 78–80

Rosecrans, William Starke (*cont.*)
 move toward Chattanooga, 65, 67
 retreat, 134–38, 153
 spying on, 76–78
 strategy, 95–97
 at Corinth, 24
 drinking by, 29
 Garfield's reports on, 76, 77
 Grant chosen to replace, 179–80,
  183–84
 Grant's opinion of, 184
 as great strategist, 25–26
 industrial pursuits of, 27–28
 loss of confidence in, 174–75, 179
 at Murfreesboro, 30–33
 personality of, 24–26, 28–29, 30, 95,
  96, 113–14, 116
 physical appearance of, 24, 28, 76, 113
 Thomas chosen to succeed,
  183–84
 trust in Thomas of, 67
Rossville Gap, 143
Round Forest, 13, 14, 32–34

Schurz, Carl, 193, 194
Scott, Winfield, in Mexican War, 18,
  19, 27, 141
Sentimentality, as Southern characteristic, 62–63
Sequatchie Valley, Wheeler's raid
  through, 177
Shanks, W. F. G., 29
Shenandoah, 134
Sheridan, Philip (Little Phil)
 at Chickamauga, 85, 114
  retreat, 125, 134, 135
 at Missionary Ridge, 221
  charge, 229–34
 at Murfreesboro, 31–32

personality of, 32
 scouting by, 35, 36
Sherman, William Tecumseh, xiii
 background of, 198
 at Chattanooga
  arrival, 198–99
  assault on Tunnel Hill, 216–21, 225,
   228, 234
  Grant's strategy and, 199–200
  Missionary Ridge, 201, 203, 204,
   215–22
 dispatched to Chickamauga, 57
 Grant and, 182
 personality of, 26, 198
 physical appearance of, 198, 205
Shiloh, battle of, 4, 5, 7, 124, 129, 165
 Forrest at, 62
 Grant at, 181, 198
 Sherman at, 198
Sims, Frederick W., transfer of troops
  by train and, 52–53, 56
Sixth Kentucky Confederate regiment,
  104
Sixth Wisconsin regiment, 218
Slave trade, 60
Smallpox, 153
Smith, Edmund Kirby, 103
Smith, Preston, 89
Smith, William F., 188
 at Chattanooga, 191–92, 200, 203
Snodgrass Hill, Federal stand at, xiv,
  89, 135–37, 139–40, 142–43,
  145–53, 163–64
 literary description of, 152–53
 Rosecrans' order to withdraw, 153–54
Society, during Civil War, 1–2
Soldiers
 backgrounds of, 8–9
 daily life of, 18, 143

Soldiers, (*cont.*)
diet of, 19, 132
drinking by, 56
farm boys as, 8–9, 76
health problems of, 19
intelligent, 91
Southerners as, 9–10
thirst of, 92
transfer by train of, 50–58
Union
hatred of, 72, 74
racism of, 8–9, 205
reasons for enlisting, 9–10
Son of the Middle Border, A (Garland), 9
Sorrel, Gilbert Moxley, 55
South, the. *See also* Confederate army;
and other specific topics
medical care in, 162
railroads of, 53, 57–58
use of technology in, 38–39, 128
Southern character, 71, 126, 149
Forrest as embodiment of, 61–63
romanticism and, 6, 111–12
technology and, 65
violence and, 61, 63
Southerners. *See also* Confederate
army
attitude toward Yankees, 9, 83
fighting Southerners, 104–5
hatred of, 72, 74
as officers, 10
prisoners, xiv
on Rosecrans, 25–26
as soldiers, 9–10
Spencer carbines, 38–39, 65, 128
Spies. *See* Undercover agents
Stanley, Davis S., at Murfreesboro, 8,
10

Stanton, Edwin McMasters
dispatch of troops to Chickamauga
and, 57
field reports to, 76–78, 138, 174–75
Grant chosen to replace Rosecrans
by, 179–80, 183–84
Rosecrans and, 23
Starvation, 171, 172, 187
at Chattanooga, 176–77, 184, 185,
187
Steedman, James Blair, at Chickamauga,
144, 145, 148–49, 154
Steinwehr, Adolph von, 193
Stevens Gap, 39, 41
Stewart, Alexander P. (Old Straight),
234
at Chickamauga, 80–82, 94, 118, 123,
131
Stone's River. *See* Murfreesboro,
battle of
Stout, Bob, 89
Strivers, Charles Edwin, 163–64
Supply base of offensive army, 29. *See
also* Federal army, supplies of
Surrender, unconditional, 23
Swinging gate maneuver, 50, 94

Taylor, Marion C., 105
Technology, North's use of, 38–39, 57,
65, 128
Tennesseans, character of, 82
Tennessee. *See also* East Tennessee;
West Tennessee
as frontier, 175–76
Texans, 83
character of, 129
at Chickamauga, 129–30
Thirst, 92

Thomas, George H., xiii
  background of, 70–71
  Bragg's relationship with, 204
  at Chattanooga, 184, 187, 192, 204
    Grant's strategy and, 199–200
    Missionary Ridge, 216, 219–20, 224, 229
  at Chickamauga, 48, 70, 86–88, 90, 95–97, 111, 129
    arrival, 43–45
    Bragg's plan to attack, 109
    burials, 162
    gap in Federal line, 114–17
    last stand, 155
    move toward Chattanooga, 65, 67
    retreat, 153–55, 155
    stand at Snodgrass Hill, 89, 135–37, 139–40, 142–43, 145–53, 163–64
    strategy, 140
  chosen to succeed Rosecrans, 183–84
  Grant and, 187
  health problems of, 140
  memorial to, 238–39
  at Murfreesboro, 30
  personality of, 67, 71, 95, 139–40, 140, 239
  physical appearance of, 71, 140
  reason for fighting for North, 70–71
  Rosecrans' approach to Chattanooga and, 39, 40
  Rosecrans' trust in, 67
  Turner's rebellion and, 71
Thomas Circle, 238–39
Thomasson, E. W., 127
Trains. See Railroads
Tucker, Glenn, 161
Tullahoma, 34, 35
  attempt to trap Bragg at, 37–39

Tunnel Hill, 203, 204
  Federal assault on, 203, 204, 215–19, 216–21, 225, 228, 234
Turner, Nat, 71
Twenty-fourth South Carolina regiment, 111
Twenty-fourth Wisconsin regiment, 230
Twenty-second Michigan regiment, 163

Unconditional surrender, 23
Undercover agents, 76–78, 174–75
Union soldiers. See also Federal army
  hatred of, 72, 74
  racism of, 8–9, 205
  reasons for enlisting, 9–10

Van Cleve, Horatio P., at Chickamauga, 81, 129
Van Dorn, Earl (Buck), 35
Vicksburg, 37, 38
  Grant at, 181–82, 199
Violence, as Southern characteristic, 61, 63
Virginia, 3
  battles of, 9
  Lee's love of, 50
Virginian, as pejorative term, 205

Walden's Ridge, 177
Walker, William Henry Talbot
  at Chattanooga, 210–11
  at Chickamauga, 64, 72, 73, 94
    arrival at Chickamauga Creek, 44, 45
Walthall, Edward C., 209
War, Lee on, 69, 211–12

Ware, John, 227
Warren Light Artillery of Mississippi, 217
Watkins, Sam, 4, 11, 101, 105–6, 156–57
Watson, Robert, 227
Wauhatchie, 193, 194
West, Douglas, 127
West, Federal soldiers from the, 204-6, 208
West Point, Civil War generals from, 16, 20, 24, 26, 32, 35, 70, 80, 81, 95, 123, 143, 150, 179, 188, 198
  Grant and, 179–81
West Tennessee, 60. *See also* Shiloh, battle of
Wharton, John Austin, 15
Wheeler, Joe, xiii
  Bragg's transfer of, 196–97
  at Chickamauga, 43, 94, 131
  Forrest's corps turned over to, 167–68, 177, 178
  at Murfreesboro, 6, 14, 16
  raid on federal supply lines, 177

Whitaker, Walter C., 207
Whiting, William Henry Chase, 237–38
Wilder, John T., 38–39
  background of, 65
  at Chickamauga, 63–65, 74, 85, 128
  personality of, 65
  at Tullahoma, 38
Winston Gap, 39
Withers, Jones Mitchell, at Murfreesboro, 15–16
With Sabre and Scalpel (Wyeth), 161
Wolfe, Thomas, 102–3, 152–53
Wood, Mary, 18
Wood, Thomas J.
  at Chickamauga, 85, 115–17, 121
  at Missionary Ridge, 221, 231–33
Wounds, treatment of, 161–62
Wyeth, John A., xiii, xv–xvi, 161, 168

Yankees, xiv–xv
  characteristics of, 38
  Southern attitude toward, 9, 83

Brilliant Strategies, Stunning Maneuvers—
and the High Cost of Victory

WAR HISTORIES FROM
AVON BOOKS TRADE PAPERBACKS

CHICKAMAUGA AND CHATTANOOGA:
The Battles That Doomed the Confederacy
by John Bowers
72509-6/$12.50 US/$16.00 Can

FATAL VICTORIES
by William Weir
72359-X/$12.50 US/$16.00 Can

CHILDREN OF GRACE:
The Nez Perce War of 1877
by Bruce Hampton
72487-1/$12.50 US/$16.00 Can

BLUE ON BLUE:
A History of Friendly Fire
by Geoffrey Regan
77655-3/$12.50 US/$16.00 Can

THE BOER WAR
by Thomas Pakenham
72001-9/$15.00 US

REDCOATS AND REBELS
by Christopher Hibbert
71544-9/$10.95 US